COLLI..
DICTIONARY
OF
BUSINESS
QUOTATIONS

COLLINS
DICTIONARY
OF
BUSINESS
QUOTATIONS

COMPILED BY
SIMON JAMES & ROBERT PARKER

HarperCollins*Publishers*

HarperCollins Publishers
P.O. Box, Glasgow G4 0NB

First published in this edition 1991
First published in hardback by Routledge as *A Dictionary of Business Quotations*

© Simon James and Robert Parker 1990

Reprint 10 9 8 7 6 5 4 3 2 1 0

ISBN 0 00 434379 4

A catalogue record for this book is available from the British Library.

Printed in Great Britain by HarperCollins Manufacturing, Glasgow

CONTENTS

CONTENTS

PREFACE

The quotations in this book are broadly of two kinds: what businessmen have said about themselves and their activities and what others have said about them. Tracking the quotations down has not always been easy for, as Thornton Wilder said, 'Businessmen aren't writers' [Topic 27, Quotation 35] and, in the words of Oscar Wilde, 'it is very vulgar to talk about one's business' [25.85]. Few have believed with Daniel Defoe that 'a true-bred merchant is a universal scholar' [27.11]. We have enjoyed our task, despite all its difficulties, and hope that our readers will find both pleasure and profit in browsing through this collection. For ourselves we expect, as Margaret Thatcher has put it, to find 'profit in other people's pleasure' [150.25].

We have compiled this dictionary both systematically (ploughing our way through, for example, many books on business both serious and humorous) and also by picking up quotations from our professional and general reading. Fortunately we have different tastes in fiction.

This book is in the same series as *A Dictionary of Economic Quotations* and *A Dictionary of Legal Quotations*. There is clearly a considerable overlap between Economics, Law and Business and it did not seem sensible to exclude a quotation simply because it had already appeared in one of the earlier books. However we were also concerned to avoid too much duplication and, as a result, for some topics further quotations will be found in the other volumes. We have also had to exclude some quotations for copyright reasons.

Like the earlier books, the quotations here are organized under topics (from Accounts to Workers). The list of headings (215 in all) precedes this preface. Not all quotations fit neatly into only one topic. If the reader is in any difficulty he or she is invited to consult the detailed Index of Key Words at the end of the volume. If the key word sought is the same as a topic title, the topic should be consulted first as the Index of Key Words does not usually repeat words appearing under the same topic. We have also provided an Index of Authors and Sources.

The key word index gives a two-figure reference for each quotation in which the key word plays an important part, the first figure referring to the topic and the second to the quotation itself. Part or all of the quotation is given to indicate the context. For example, an entry under 'witch doctors' reads: 'Accountants are the w. 4.6'. This refers to the sixth quotation appearing under the fourth topic, Accountants. The numbers and the titles of the topics appear at the top of the pages, and within each topic the quotations are arranged alphabetically by author or source.

We have wherever possible given the dates of birth and death for deceased persons but have made no attempt to provide the dates of birth for living persons.

Those books of quotations (and there are many) which identify an author without giving a source can be more annoying than useful and may, furthermore, be misleading or even plain wrong. We have tried to avoid this fault. Wherever possible we have checked the original source. Quotations in foreign languages have been translated into English.

Words change their meanings over time. 'Business' for example did not acquire its trading and commercial connotation until the eighteenth century. However, we have not excluded an appropriate quotation simply because the earlier meanings were intended.

'A man', wrote Samuel Johnson 'will turn over half a library to make one book' (Boswell's *Life of Johnson*, 6 April 1775). The libraries turned over to write this one are mostly in the UK and Australia. We have also made good use of newspapers and magazines, one of which, the *Australian Listener*, ceased publication almost as soon as we quarried it for quotations (David Williamson's 'There is no-one quite as angry as someone who has just lost a lot of money' [124.101]. We are very grateful for the assistance of staff in a number of libraries, in particular those at the University of Exeter Library.

No dictionary is ever complete or without fault. Suggestions for additions and improvements for later editions would be very welcome and should be sent to the authors at the Department of Economics, University of Exeter, Amory Building, Rennes Drive, Exeter EX4 4RJ, UK.

Simon James
Robert Parker
University of Exeter

1 ACCOUNTS

See also 3 ACCOUNTANCY, 4 ACCOUNTANTS, 13 AUDITORS

1 It sounds extraordinary but it's a fact that balance sheets can make fascinating reading.
Mary Archer, *Independent*, 'Quote Unquote', 7 January 1989

2 A Tradesman's Books, like a Christian's Conscience, should always be kept clean and clear; and he that is not careful of both will give but a sad account of himself either to God or Man.
Daniel Defoe (*c*.1660–1731), *The Complete English Tradesman*, 2nd ed., 1727, vol. I, letter XX

3 A Tradesman's books [of account] are his repeating clock, which upon all occasions are to tell him how he goes on, and how things stand with him in the world; there he will know when 'tis time to go on, or when 'tis time to give over . . . His books being so essential to his trade, he that comes out of his time without a perfect knowledge of the method of book-keeping, *like a bride undrest*, is not ready to be married; he knows not what to do, or what step to take.
Daniel Defoe (*c*.1660–1731), *ibid.*

4 Next to being prepar'd for death, with respect to Heaven and his soul, a Tradesman should be always in state of preparation for Death, with respect to his books.
Daniel Defoe (*c*.1660–1731), *ibid.*

5 A death-bed is no place, and a sick languishing body no condition, and the last breath no time for repentance; so I may add, neither are these the place, the condition, or the time to make up our accounts; there's no posting the books on a death-bed, or balancing the Cash-book in a high fever.
Daniel Defoe (*c*.1660–1731), *ibid.*

6 The system of book-keeping by double entry is, perhaps, the most beautiful one in the wide domain of literature or science. Were it less common, it would be the admiration of the learned world.
Edwin T. Freedley (1827–1904), *Practical Treatise on Business*, 1853, ch. VI

7 What advantages a merchant derives from double entry bookkeeping! It is among the finest inventions of the human mind; and every good householder should introduce it into his economy.
Johann Wolfgang von Goethe (1749–1832), *Wilhelm Meister's Apprenticeship*, 1795–6, I, x

8 We like to feel that, not only do the figures in the balance sheet show you the true position, but that the real position is a little better still.
W.E. Hubbard, speech to shareholders at the annual meeting, London and County Bank, 7 February 1901, *The Economist*, 1901, p. 204

9 Keeping accounts, Sir, is of no use when a man is spending his own money, and has nobody to whom he is to account. You won't eat less beef to-day, because you have written down what it cost yesterday.
Samuel Johnson (1709–1784), Boswell's *Life of Johnson*, 30 March 1783

10 Did you ever fit [adjust] accounts with him?
James Kelly, *Scottish Proverbs*, 1721, D, no. 13

11 He's an articled clerk. He seems to know his job. He can't get over the way our accounts are kept. He told me he never expected a theatre to be run on such business-like lines. He says the way some of those firms in the City keep their accounts is enough to turn your hair grey.
W. Somerset Maugham (1874–1965), *Theatre*, 1937, ch. 1

12 The accounts are a snapshot of a business at a moment in time. Take a picture the following day and the scene may look very different. As with many of us, companies like to look their best when they are photographed and sometimes dress for the occasion.
M.A. Pitcher, *Management Accounting for the Lending Banker*, 1979, pp. 13–14

13   O my good lord
At many times I have brought in my accounts,
Laid them before you; you would throw them off,
And say you found them in mine honesty.
William Shakespeare (1564–1616), *Timon of Athens*, 1607–8, act II, sc. II

14 Sir Anthony, I would send her, at nine years old, to a boarding-school, in order to learn a

little ingenuity and artifice. Then, sir, she should have a supercilious knowledge in accounts.
Richard Brinsley Sheridan (1751–1816), *The Rivals*, 1775, act I, sc. II

15 Learning to read a balance sheet does not take a great deal more intelligence than learning to read racing form, and is more consistently rewarding.
T. Sykes, *Two Centuries of Panic*, 1988, ch. 23

2 ACCOUNTABILITY

1 The sovereign press for the most part acknowledges accountability to no one except its owners and publishers.
Zechariah Chafee (1885–1957), *The Press Under Pressure*, 1948

2 Good men prefer to be accountable.
Sir Michael Edwardes in Ray Wild, *How to Manage*, 1982, p. 164

3 ACCOUNTANCY
See also 1 ACCOUNTS, 4 ACCOUNTANTS, 5 ACTUARIES, 13 AUDITORS

1 If you make the mistake of adding the date to the right side of an accounting statement, you must add it to the left side as well.
Anonymous

2 An accountant's is a sensible yet glamorous occupation.
John Braine, *Room at the Top*, 1957, ch. 2

3 Justice is not capable of being measured out by an accountant's computer.
Sir Nicolas Browne-Wilkinson, *Observer*, 'Sayings of the Week', 22 November 1987

4 We have no desire to say anything that might tend to encourage women to embark on accountancy, for although women might make excellent book-keepers, there is much in accountancy proper that is, we think, unsuitable for them.
Council of the Institute of Chartered Accountants in England and Wales, *The Accountant*, 14 September 1912, p. 341

5 Modern accountancy has developed into an elaborate art.
Irving Fisher (1867–1947), 'Income in Theory and Practice', *Econometrica*, vol. 5, 1937

6 Accounting: A respectable, conscious or unconscious way of disclosing, hiding or misrepresenting financial information to give a skillfully adapted economic picture of a company or its components.
Paulsson Frenckner, address to the 7th Annual Congress of the European Accounting Association, Saint-Gall, Switzerland, 1984

7 Accounting is conventionalized written statistical history.
Stephen Gilman, *Accounting Concepts of Profit*, 1939, p. 604

8 The significance of periodic accounting profit is . . . the algebraic sum of the separate significances of the various conventions, doctrines, rules, and practices which at any particular time constitute the common law of accounting.
Stephen Gilman, *ibid.*, p. 605

9 Accounting does not require an apologist even though it often requires an interpreter.
Stephen Gilman, *ibid.*, p. 610

10 It may be said that in commercial or investment banking or any business extending credit success depends on knowing what not to believe in accounting.
Robert H. Jackson, *Federal Power Commission* v. *Hope Natural Gas Company*, 1944, 320 US 591, 644 (fn)

11 The counting-house of an accomplished merchant is a school of method wherein the great science may be learned of ranging particulars under generals, of bringing the different parts of a transaction together, and of showing at one view a long series of dealing and exchange.
Samuel Johnson (1709–1784), preface to Richard Rolt, *A New Dictionary of Trade and Commerce*, 1756

12 Accounting and control — that is *mainly* what is needed for the 'smooth working', for the proper functioning, of the *first phase* of communist society.
V.I. Lenin (1870–1924), *The State and Revolution*, 1917, ch. 5.4

13 The current fashion for vigorous

quantitative analysis has thrown out the baby of relevance in the search for an unimpeachably hygienic variety of methodological bathwater.
A. McCosh and S. Howell in D. Cooper, R. Scapens and J. Arnold (eds.), *Management Accountancy Research and Practice*, 1983

14 There are few subjects, other than economics, that have succeeded in being simultaneously denounced by both academics and practitioners. Accounting has attained that pinnacle.
Colin Mayer, 'The Real Value of Company Accounts', *Fiscal Studies*, vol. 9, no. 1, February 1988

15 As the proverb says: 'Frequent accounting makes for lasting friendship'.
Luca Pacioli (*c*.1445–*c*.1517), *Particularis de Computis et Scripturis*, 1494, ch. 29

16 Accountancy is fun.
E.E. Ray, speech to the West Yorkshire Society of Chartered Accountants, 28 October 1982

17 With 'creative accountancy', who needs cheating?
Katharine Whitehorn, *Observer*, 25 January 1987

4 ACCOUNTANTS
See also 1 ACCOUNTS, 3 ACCOUNTANCY, 5 ACTUARIES, 13 AUDITORS

1 An accountant is a man hired to explain that you didn't make the money you did.
Anonymous

2 What is an inaccurate accountant good for? 'Silly man, that dost not know thy own silly trade!' was once well said; but the trade here is not silly.
Edmund Burke (1729–1797), *Impeachment of Warren Hastings*, 7 May 1789

3 He was a CPA [certified public accountant] and looked it every inch. He even had ink on his fingers and there were four pencils in the pocket of his open vest.
Raymond Chandler (1888–1959), *The Lady in the Lake*, 1943

4 Of course I'm doing something about my

overdraft: I'm seeing my accountant.
Barry Fantoni, *The Times*, 22 June 1985

5 Nowadays it isn't sufficient to be a good innkeeper; you must become a cost accountant too.
Arthur Hailey, *Hotel*, 1965, ch. 10

6 Accountants are the witch doctors of the modern world.
Mr Justice Harman (1894–1970), *Miles* v. *Clarke*, 1953

7 The accountant transcends the conservatism of the proverb, 'Do not count your chickens before they are hatched', saying 'Here are a lot of chickens already safely hatched, but for the love of Mike, use discretion and don't count them all for perhaps some will die.'
H.R. Hatfield (1866–1945), *Accounting*, 1927, p. 256, n. 13

8 As an accountant I am by nature a pessimist.
Hammond Innes, *The Strode Venturer*, 1965, pt. I, III

9 Everyone knew that as regards doing anything useful, accountants were much like eunuchs; they knew how it was done, but they couldn't do it themselves.
James Leasor, *The Sea Wolves*, 1978, ch. 8

10 All in all, he looked the typical youngish chartered accountant of ability whose intelligence was so absorbed by his work that there was none left over for anything else.
Bruce Marshall, *The Bank Audit*, 1958, ch. 1

11 Chartered accountants in Edinburgh . . . must be like pretty prostitutes in Paris: a good one waiting under every other lamp-post.
Bruce Marshall, *ibid.*

12 And what have I achieved? Three women in my life and one of *them* turned out to be a chartered accountant over thirty!
John Mortimer, *Two Stars for Comfort*, act I, sc. II

13 The whole affairs in bankruptcy have been handed over to an ignorant set of men called accountants, which is one of the greatest abuses ever introduced into law.
Mr Justice Quain in A.H. Woolf, *A Short History of Accountants and Accountancy*, 1912, p. 177

14 A very gifted boy, very, very gifted. He should have been a mathematician, but he became a chartered accountant.
Nevil Shute (1899–1960), *Beyond the Black Stump*, 1956, ch. 4

15 Accountants are a little like pollsters; they produce variable results from the same data. Predictive accounting is especially difficult because it depends on prior assumptions made by those who hire the accountants.
The Times Higher Education Supplement, 13 March 1987

16 Yes, Virginia, accountants *are* people.
Robert Townsend, *Up the Organization*, 1971

17 Men with accountancy training occupy positions in business from book-keeper to chairman. All of them will be referred to, often in a derogatory sense, as accountants.
R. Ian Tricker, *The Accountant in Management*, 1967, pt. I, ch. 1

5 ACTUARIES
See also 4 ACCOUNTANTS

1 An actuary is someone who moved out of accountancy because he couldn't stand the excitement.
Anonymous

2 Actuaries have the reputation of being about as interesting as the footnotes to a pension plan.
George Pitcher, *Observer*, 10 July 1988

3 Actuaries are to market research what brain surgeons are to foot massage.
George Pitcher, *ibid.*

6 ADVERTISING
See also 119 MARKETING, 172 SALES, 179 SELLING

1 The essence of good advertising is not to inspire hope, but to create greed.
Charles Adams, *Common Sense in Advertising*, 1966

2 The great art in writing advertisements is the finding out a proper method to catch the reader's eye; without which a good thing may pass over unobserved, or be lost among commissions of bankrupt.
Joseph Addison (1672–1719), *The Tatler*, no. 224, 1710

3 The codfish lays ten thousand eggs,
    The homely hen lays one.
The codfish never cackles
    To tell you what she's done.

And so we scorn the codfish,
    While the humble hen we prize,
Which only goes to show you
    That it pays to advertise.
Anonymous

4 If you call a spade a spade, you won't last long in the advertising business.
Anonymous

5 If you've got nothing to say, sing it.
Anonymous, Ken Hornsby, *The Padded Sell*, 1980

6 Nothing works faster than Anadin . . . So get nothing!
Anonymous, *ibid.*

7 Remember, the client's indecision is final.
Anonymous, *ibid.*

8 When business is good it pays to advertise; When business is bad you've got to advertise.
Anonymous

9 Women come in two types: young and not so young.
Anonymous advertising maxim

10 Advertising is of the very essence of democracy.
Bruce Barton in James Beasley Simpson, *Best Quotes of '54, '55, '56*, 1957

11 The major part of *informative* advertising is, and always has been, a campaign of exaggeration, half-truths, intended ambiguities, direct lies, and general deception . . . Advertisements of the *non*-informative kind present a psychological museum of rare interest, but with some depressing exhibits.
A.S.J. Baster, *Advertising Reconsidered*, 1935, ch. II, pp. 50, 70

12 *Some* sort of advertising — of information service to customers — is clearly absolutely essential in any exchange economy. But in

practice, the truth alone is not commonly selected as a medium for advertising.
A.S.J. Baster, *ibid.*, ch. III, p. 114

13 In advertising there is a saying that if you can keep your head while all those around you are losing theirs — then you just don't understand the problem.
Hugh M. Beville in James Beasley Simpson, *Best Quotes of '54, '55, '56*, 1957

14 My idea of heaven is where all advertisements are true.
Sir Chatres Biron in Gilbert Russell, *Nuntius: Advertising and Its Future*, III

15 The business that considers itself immune to the necessity for advertising sooner or later finds itself immune to business.
Derby Brown in Tryon Edwards, *The New Dictionary of Thoughts*

16 The basic purpose of every advertisement is to induce a required response from the person to whom it is addressed.
Robert Caplin, *Advertising — A General Introduction*, 1967

17 Advertising is the life of trade.
Calvin Coolidge (1872–1933) in Tryon Edwards, *The New Dictionary of Thoughts*

18 We predict that advertising expenditures will be a function of sales in the previous time period at least as much as the reverse will be true.
R.M. Cyert and J.C. March, 'A Behavioural Theory of Organizational Objectives', in M. Haire (ed.), *Modern Organization Theory*, 1959

19 You can tell the ideals of a nation by its advertisements.
Norman Douglas (1868–1952), *South Wind*, 1917, ch. 7

20 Blessings on the man . . . who first invented the loud trumpet of advertisements.
Edward Gibbon (1737–1794), letter to J.B. Holroyd, 25 September 1772

21 Socialists have never liked the advertising industry.
Philip Hanson, *Advertising and Socialism*, 1974, ch. 1

22 Advertisements of commodities are addressed quite as much to the shopkeepers as to the consumers.
R.G. Hawtrey (1879–1971), *The Economic Problem*, 1926, ch. XVIII

23 One of the chief aims of advertising is to produce the impression that the thing advertised is of a kind that everybody buys.
R.G. Hawtrey (1879–1971), *ibid.*

24 Children have always been the focus of the advertising — but that is just because it was the easiest way of showing what the product was about.
Len Heath (Advertising Manager, Birds Eye), *The Times*, 2 September 1985, p. 9

25 The science of advertising is the science of psychology.
Elbert Hubbard (1856–1915), *Notebook*, 1927, p. 64

26 We are living so fast, and inventing so fast, and changing so fast, and there are so many of us, that he who does not advertise is left to the spiders, the cockroaches and the microbes.
Elbert Hubbard (1856–1915), *ibid.*

27 All literature is advertising. And all genuine advertisements are literature.
Elbert Hubbard (1856–1915), *ibid.*

28 It used to be that a fellow went on the police force after everything else failed, but today he goes into the advertising game.
Elbert Hubbard (1856–1915), attributed

29 Advertising: The education of the public as to who you are, where you are, and what you have to offer in way of skill, talent or commodity. The only man who should not advertise is the man who has nothing to offer the world in way of commodity or service.
Frank McKinney Hubbard (1868–1930), *The Roycroft Dictionary*, 1923

30 It is far easier to write ten passably effective Sonnets, good enough to take in the not too enquiring critic, than one effective advertisement that will take in a few thousand of the uncritical buying public.
Aldous Huxley (1894–1963), 'Advertisement', *On the Margin*, 1923

31 No one should be allowed to talk about the *mot juste* or the polishing of style who has not tried his hand out at writing an advertisement of something which the public does not want, but which it must be persuaded into buying.
Aldous Huxley (1894–1963), *ibid.*

32 Advertisements are now so numerous that

they are very negligently perused, and it is therefore becoming necessary to gain attention by magnificence of promises and by eloquence sometimes sublime and sometimes pathetick. Promise, large promise, is the soul of an advertisement . . . The trade of Advertising is now so near to perfection that it is not easy to propose any improvement.
Samuel Johnson (1709–1784), *The Idler*, 20 January 1759

33 Advertising may be described as the science of arresting the human intelligence long enough to get money from it.
Stephen Leacock (1869–1944), attributed

34 You can fool all the people all of the time if the advertising is right and the budget is big enough.
Joseph E. Levine, attributed

35 Undoubtedly some advertisements lead to fantasies. Life would be pretty intolerable without fantasies.
Lord McGregor (Chairman, Advertising Standards Authority). *Observer*, 'Sayings of the Week', 31 August 1986

36 Ads are the cave art of the twentieth century.
Marshall McLuhan (1911–1980) in Robert I. Fitzhenry, *The David & Charles Book of Quotations*

37 Of course no amount of expenditure on advertising will enable any thing, which the customers can fairly test for themselves by experience (this condition excludes medicines which claim to be appropriate to subtle diseases, etc.), to get a permanent hold on the people, unless it is fairly good relatively to its price.
Alfred Marshall (1842–1924), *Industry and Trade*, 1919, bk. II, ch. VII, 7

38 The best ad. is a good product.
Alan H. Meyer in J. Green, *A Dictionary of Contemporary Quotations*

39 Advertising lives in the kingdom of cliché and has been trying to improve its brand image since it first began.
Keith Miles, *The Finest Swordsman in all France: A Celebration of the Cliché*, 1984

40 Advertising is both its own worst enemy and best advertisement.
Keith Miles, *ibid.*

41 The advertising industry is an incestuous little business.
Russell Miller, 'My Goodness We Need Genius', *Sunday Times Magazine*, 1 September 1985, p. 18

42 I may be old fashioned, but . . . I look with the utmost distaste at the advancement of permission for advertisement by chartered accountants and solicitors on television, in newspapers and so on.
Lord Mishcon, House of Lords, 14 January 1985

43 Advertising is an incredibly powerful agent of male supremacy.
Jill Nicholls and Pat Moan, *Spare Rib*, 72, July 1978

44 Advertising is the rattling of a stick inside a swill bucket.
George Orwell (1903–1950) in Fred Metcalf, *The Penguin Dictionary of Modern Humorous Quotations*

45 Living in an age of advertisement, we are perpetually disillusioned.
J.B. Priestley (1894–1984), attributed

46 It is no accident that countries with the highest levels of advertising per capita are also the wealthiest in terms of GNP per head.
W. Duncan Reekie, *The Economics of Advertising*, 1981, ch. 8, sec. 6.

47 The Robbing Hoods of America [advertising men].
Will Rogers (1879–1935) in Donald Day, *Will Rogers: A Biography*, 1962, ch. 13

48 Advertising is the manufacturer's shop window.
Gilbert Russell, *Nuntius: Advertising and Its Future*, 1926, I

49 Advertising is the foot on the accelerator, the hand on the throttle, the spur on the flank that keeps our [American] economy surging forward.
Robert W. Sarnoff in James Beasley Simpson, *Best Quotes of '54, '55, '56*, 1957

50 This advertisement is five days old.
William Shakespeare (1564–1616), *Henry IV, Pt. I*, 1597–8, act III, sc. II

51 Yet doth he give us bold advertisement.
William Shakespeare (1564–1616), *ibid.*, act IV, sc. I

52 We are advertis'd by our loving friends.
William Shakespeare (1564–1616), *Henry VI, Pt III*, 1590–1, act V, sc. III

53 I by my friends am well advertised.
William Shakespeare (1564–1616), *Richard III*, 1592–3, act IV, sc. IV

54 Advertising is capitalism's soft sell.
Sue Sharpe, *Just Like a Girl*, 1976, ch. 3

55 Puffing [advertising] is of various sorts; the principal are, the puff direct, the puff preliminary, the puff collateral, the puff collusive, and the puff oblique, or puff by implication.
Richard Brinsley Sheridan (1715–1816), *The Critic*, 1779, act I

56 Two ads a day keep the sack away.
Jeremy Sinclair, *Sunday Times*, 21 August 1988

57 Advertising is selling in print.
Daniel Starch, *Principles of Advertising*, 1926, pt. I, ch. I

58 Many a small thing has been made large by the right kind of advertising.
Mark Twain (1835–1910), *A Connecticut Yankee in King Arthur's Court*, 1889, ch. 22

59 I know half the money I spend on advertising is wasted, but I can never find out which half.
John Wanamaker (1838–1922), attributed

60 The only truly bad publicity is no publicity.
E.M. Wellings, *Village Cricketers*, 1983, ch. 11

61 It is the glory and the boast of the skilful advertiser that he can make people buy things that they do not want.
Hartley Withers (1867–1950), *Poverty and Waste*, 1914

---

7 AGRICULTURE

---

1 Farmers are very good at turning grass into milk, but they are not so good at turning milk into money.
John Cochrane, *Financial Review*, 11 April 1986

2 Will the Government take steps to have the horse recognised as an agricultural animal?
Harry Greenway, *Observer*, 'Sayings of the Week', 12 June 1988

3 The farmers' . . . main concern is to plant seeds and grow rich.
Peter Hillmore, *Observer*, 1 February 1987

4 A farmer is never satisfied; don't expect it.
E.W. Howe (1853–1937), *Country Town Sayings*, 1911

5 The farmer of today is a businessman — he is no longer a serf. Of all men he is an economist. You can get along without lawyers, but the farmer is a necessity.
Elbert Hubbard (1856–1915), *Notebook*, 1927, p. 116

6 Farmers did not trust the bankers as a rule, and certainly, as a rule, bankers did not trust the farmers.
Elbert Hubbard (1856–1915), *ibid.*, p. 131

7 Farmer . . . A man who makes his money in the country and blows it in when he comes to town. (Farms were first devised as an excuse for the Agricultural Department at Washington.)
Frank McKinney Hubbard (1868–1930), *The Roycroft Dictionary*, 1923

8 American farm leaders are correct in arguing that our agriculture still must look forward to a definite 'surplus' problem. What they tend to overlook, however, is of what our 'surplus' consists. Fundamentally America's long-term agricultural problem is not one of 'surplus' cotton, wheat or grapefruit. Rather it is one of 'surplus' farmers.
William H. Nicolls in P.A. Samuelson, *Economics*, 8th ed. 1970

9 To the average British farmer, organic farming is about as relevant as caviar and a flight on Concorde.
Oliver Walston, *Observer*, 'Sayings of the Week', 15 January 1989

10 When tillage begins, other arts follow. The farmers therefore are the founders of human civilization.
Daniel Webster (1782–1852), *On Agriculture*, 1840

8 AMBITION
See also 32 CAREERS, 193 SUCCESS

1 Ambition, *n.* An overmastering desire to be vilified by enemies while living and made ridiculous by friends when dead.
Ambrose Bierce (1842–1914?), *The Devil's Dictionary*, 1911

2 What seems to be generosity is often only disguised ambition — which despises small interests to gain great ones.
François, Duc de La Rochefoucauld (1630–1680), *Maxims*, 1678

3 Ambition often puts men upon doing the meanest offices; so climbing is performed in the same posture with creeping.
Jonathan Swift (1667–1745), *Thoughts on Various Subjects*, 1706

4   'Tis a common proof
That lowliness is young ambition's ladder,
Whereto the climber-upward turns his face;
But when he once attains the utmost round,
He then unto the ladder turns his back,
Looks in the clouds, scorning the base
      degrees
By which he did ascend.
William Shakespeare (1564–1616), *Julius Caesar*, 1599–1600, act II, sc. I

5 There is always room at the top.
Daniel Webster (1782–1852), attributed

9 APPRENTICESHIPS

1 There needs a long apprenticeship, to understand the mystery of the world's trade.
Thomas Fuller (1654–1734), *Gnomologia*, 1732, no. 4943

10 ARTS

1 The works of art, by being publicly exhibited and offered for sale, are becoming articles of trade, following as such the unreasoning laws of markets and fashion; and even public and private patronage is swayed by their tyrannical influence.
Albert, Prince Consort (1819–1861), speech, May 1851

2 Blessed are the pure in art.
Anonymous

3 When I hear artists or authors making fun of business men I think of a regiment in which the band makes fun of the cooks.
Anonymous

4 I never thought that I would earn enough money from my pictures to make a living.
Francis Bacon, *Observer*, 'Sayings of the Week', 26 May 1985

5 An artist cannot speak about his art any more than a plant can discuss horticulture.
Jean Cocteau (1891–1963) in James Beasley Simpson, *Best Quotes of '54, '55, '56*, 1957

6 Efficiency is the enemy of originality and it can smother talent.
Sir Denis Foreman, *Observer*, 'Sayings of the Week', 2 September 1984

7 I always suspect an artist who is successful before he is dead.
John Murray Gibbon in Robert I. Fitzhenry, *The David & Charles Book of Quotations*

8 Theatres have to be run on obsessions.
Sir Peter Hall, *Observer*, 'Sayings of the Week', 10 August 1986

9 Art has to move you and design does not, unless it's a good design for a bus.
David Hockney, *Observer*, 'Sayings of the Week', 30 October 1988

10 Above all, in art work to please yourself . . . Michelangelo would not paint a picture to order.
Elbert Hubbard (1856–1915), *Notebook*, 1927, p. 21

11 Art is only the best way of doing things.
Elbert Hubbard (1856–1915), *ibid.*, p. 198

12 There are still too many in the arts world who have yet to be weaned away from the welfare state mentality, the attitude that the taxpayer owes them a living.
Richard Luce, *Observer*, 'Sayings of the Week', 12 July 1987

13 No artist retires: he can't.
Henry Moore (1898–1986), *Observer*, 'Sayings of the Week'

14 Conversations between artist and sitter are private affairs — like those that take place when you go to a doctor or a solicitor.
Bryan Organ, *Observer*, 'Sayings of the Week', 11 December 1983

15 The task of the artist at any time is
uncompromisingly simple — to discover
what has not yet been done, and to do it.
Craig Raine, *Observer*, 'Sayings of the
Week', 21 August 1988

16 I am sorry somebody referred to Movies as
an art . . . For since then everybody
connected with them stopped doing
something to make them better and they
commenced getting worse.
Will Rogers (1879–1935) in Donald Day,
Will Rogers: A Biography, 1962, ch. 21

17 The manager of a theatre is a man of
business.
George Bernard Shaw (1856–1950), *The
Shewing-Up of Blanco Posnet*, 1909, preface

18 The notion of making money by popular
work, and then retiring on the proceeds, is
the most familiar of all the devil's traps for
artists.
Logan Pearsall Smith (1865–1946) in
Rudolf Flesch, *The Book of Unusual
Quotations*, 1959

19 Art is a human activity having for its
purpose the transmission to others of the
highest and best feelings to which men have
risen.
Count Leo Tolstoy (1828–1910), *What is
Art?*, 1898, ch. 8

20 All art is quite useless.
Oscar Wilde (1854–1900), *The Picture of
Dorian Gray*, 1891

11 ASSETS

1 No one has a greater asset for his business
than a man's pride in his work.
Mary Parker Follett (1868–1933), *Freedom
and Co-ordination*, 1949, ch. II

2 Cultivate courtesy as a business asset.
Elbert Hubbard (1856–1915), *Notebooks*,
1917, p. 19

12 AUCTIONS

1 Auctioneer, *n*. The man who proclaims with
a hammer that he has picked a pocket with
his tongue.
Ambrose Bierce (1842–1914?), *The Devil's
Dictionary*, 1911

2 If they could forget, for a moment, the
correggiosity of Correggio, and the learned
babble of the saleroom and varnishing
auctioneer.
Thomas Carlyle (1795–1881), *Frederick
the Great*, bk. I, ch. 6

13 AUDITORS

See also 1 ACCOUNTS, 3 ACCOUNTANCY,
4 ACCOUNTANTS

1 Auditors are the troops who watch a battle
from the safety of a hillside and when the
battle is over come down to count the dead
and bayonet the wounded.
Anonymous

2 An auditor is not to be confined to the
mechanics of checking vouchers and making
arithmetical computations. He is not to be
written off as a professional 'adder-upper
and subtractor'.
Lord Denning, *Fomento (Sterling Area) Ltd.
v. Selsdon Fountain Pen Co. Ltd.*, 1958

3 Who says auditors are human?
Arthur Hailey, *The Money Changers*, 1975,
ch. 13

4 I don't want to know that I'm losing money
three months after it has happened, so I've
an auditor here almost full time.
Sir Freddie Laker in Roger Eglin and Berry
Ritchie, *Fly me I'm Freddie!*, 1980, ch. 15

5 An auditor is not bound to be a detective
. . . He is a watch-dog, but not a
bloodhound.
Lord Justice Lopes (1828–1899), In re
Kingston Cotton Mill Co. (no. 2), 1896

6 It is the duty of the auditor to see that the
authority to charge is not made a pretext for
extravagance or favouritism.
Mr Justice Lush (1807–1881), *R. v.
Cumberlege*, 1877

7 Any auditor, we know, is a watchdog and
not a bloodhound, but a chartered
accountant who fails to find a fraud when
he has been tipped off about it is like a
soldier who neglects to destroy his enemy on
the field of battle.
Bruce Marshall, *The Bank Audit*, 1958,
ch. 1

8 Auditors are like St Thomas; they require to see before they believe.
Bruce Marshall, *The Divided Lady*, 1960

9 A kind of auditor; one that hath abundance of charge too.
William Shakespeare (1564–1616), *Henry IV, Pt. I*, 1597–8, act II, sc. I

10 If you suspect my husbandry of falsehood, Call me before the exactest auditors And set me on the proof.
William Shakespeare (1564–1616), *Timon of Athens*, 1607–8, act II, sc. II

---

14 AVIATION
See also 127 MOTOR VEHICLES, 164 RAILWAYS, 182 SHIPPING, 207 TRANSPORT

---

1 Aviation, to an even greater extent than the sea, is unforgiving of any incapacity, carelessness or neglect.
Air Safety Slogan

2 If you've time to spare, go by air.
Anonymous, Nevil Shute, *Requiem for a Wren*, 1955, ch. 7

3 Airlines have to market something. Nowadays any fool can hurl people around the globe in an aluminium tube.
Bryan Appleyard, *The Times*, 24 July 1986

4 Nobody has ever built an airplane capable of airlifting its own blueprints.
Charles Carpentier, *Flight One*, 1972, pt. III

5 The chopper has changed my life as conclusively as it did for Anne Boleyn.
Queen Elizabeth, the Queen Mother (following a period of travel by helicopter), *Sydney Morning Herald*, 'Sayings of the Week', 3 August 1985.

6 Legislated safety regulations do not mean less accidents per hour flown. It means less total accidents due to less hours flown.
Robert Kaiser in Dan Poynter, *Hang Gliding*, 1977

7 The airline [British Airways] has been conducted in the past as though money grows on trees.
Sir John King, *Observer*, 'Sayings of the Week', 24 October 1982

8 If I give Laker three tickets on Concorde every time he gets married, I should go broke — the way he did.
Lord King, *Sunday Telegraph*, 1 September 1985, p. 2

9 Science, freedom, beauty, adventure. What more could you ask of life? Aviation combined all the elements I loved.
Charles Lindbergh (1902–1974) in Thomas Block, *Skyfall*, 1987

10 In developing aviation, in making it a form of commerce, in replacing the wild freedom of danger with the civilized bonds of safety, must we give up this miracle of the air? Will men fly through the sky in the future without seeing what I have seen, without feeling what I have felt? Is that true of all things we call human progress — Do the gods retire as commerce and science advance?
Charles Lindbergh (1902–1974) in Dan Poynter, *Hang Gliding*, 1977

11 Never before in history would so many have been disturbed so much by so few.
Bo Lundburg (reference to supersonic flight) in Charles Carpentier, *Flight One*, 1972, pt. II

---

15 BANKERS
See also 16 BANKING

---

1 Every banker knows that if he has to *prove* that he is worthy of credit, however good may be his arguments, in fact his credit is gone.
Walter Bagehot (1826–1877), *Lombard Street*, 1873, ch. 2

2 But those who keep immense sums with a banker gain a convenience at the expense of a danger.
Walter Bagehot (1826–1877), *ibid.*

3 Any careful person who is experienced in figures, and has real sound sense, may easily make himself a good banker.
Walter Bagehot (1826–1877), *ibid.*, ch. 9

4 But when times are bad and the breath of fear has already chilled the markets, the banker must be cautious, conservative, and severe. His business has been aptly compared to that of a man who stands ready

to lend umbrellas when it is fine and demand them back when it starts to rain.
Sir Geoffrey Crowther (1907–1972), *An Outline of Money*, 1940, ch. 2

5 What good is a banker who cannot see at first sight from the face of his client whether or not he has got money in his pocket?
A. Dumas, *fils* (1824–1895), *La Question d'Argent*, 1857, act 2, sc. 10

6 Bankers have no right to establish a customary law among themselves, at the expense of other men.
Mr Justice Foster (1689–1763), *Hankey* v. *Trotman*, 1746

7 As a general proposition, the community believes in the banker who believes in the community.
Elbert Hubbard (1856–1915), *Notebook*, 1927, p. 173

8 Banking establishments are more dangerous than standing armies.
Thomas Jefferson (1743–1826), letter to Elbridge Gerry, 26 January 1799

9 A 'sound' banker, alas! is not one who foresees danger and avoids it, but one who, when he is ruined, is ruined in a conventional and orthodox way along with his fellows, so that no one can really blame him.
John Maynard Keynes (1883–1946), 'The Consequences to the Banks of the Collapse of Money Values', *Essays in Persuasion*, 1933, pt. II

10 Bankers sometimes look on politicians as people who, when they see light at the end of the tunnel, order more tunnel.
John Quinton, *Independent*, 'Quote Unquote', 15 April 1989

11 The distinctive function of the banker begins as soon as he uses the money of *others*.
David Ricardo (1772–1823) in W. Bagehot, *Lombard Street*, 1873, ch. 2

16 BANKING
See also 15 BANKERS

1 A solvent bank is an institution which is able to meet its liabilities as long as nobody desires that it should do so, and which can't meet them at any other time. It is built on the principle that everybody can have his money if he doesn't want it, and not otherwise.
Anonymous, *The Bulletin*, Sydney, *c.*1893, in T. Sykes, *Two Centuries of Panic*, 1988, ch. 9

2 A large bank always tends to become larger and a small bank to become smaller.
Walter Bagehot (1826–1877) in J.A. Hobson, *The Evolution of Modern Capitalism*

3 The cardinal maxim is, that any aid to a present bad bank is the surest mode of preventing the establishment of a future good bank.
Walter Bagehot (1826–1877), *ibid.*, ch. 4

4 Adventure is the life of commerce, but caution, I had almost said timidity, is the life of banking.
Walter Bagehot (1826–1877), *ibid.*, ch. 8.

5 In First Mercantile American, as in any banking system, an acknowledged status symbol was the size of a loan which a bank official had power to sanction.
Arthur Hailey, *The Money Changers*, 1976, pt. 1, ch. 4

6 Banking is a very peculiar business, and it depends so much upon credit that the least blast of suspicion is sufficient to sweep away, as it were, the harvest of a whole year.
L. Holland, Meeting of the Proprietors of the Bank of England, 13 September 1866. (See W. Bagehot, *Lombard Street*, 1873, note D)

7 I once wondered how the banks made their money, but when I procured a loan, I found out.
E.W. Howe (1853–1937), *Country Town Sayings*, 1911

8 If you owe your bank a hundred pounds, you have a problem, but if you owe it a million it has.
John Maynard Keynes (1883–1946) in *The Economist*, 13 February 1982, p. 11

9 Banking is an occupational hazard . . . Whatever your walk of life, banking is on hand with a long leg to trip you up.
Keith Miles, *The Finest Swordsman in all France: A Celebration of the Cliché*, 1984

10 Cashpoint — the sharp end of banking.
Keith Miles, *ibid.*

11 Bank statement — No!
Keith Miles, *ibid.*

12 What is a bank? . . . an institution which issues twice-yearly a misleading statement of its position.
The Times, 16 November 1920

17 BANKRUPTCY

1 Bankruptcy is the process where you put your money in your trouser pocket and give your coat to your creditors.
Anonymous

2 Capitalism without bankruptcy is like Christianity without hell.
Frank Borman, *Observer*, 'Sayings of the Week', 9 March 1986

3 How often have I been able to trace bankruptcies and insolvencies to some lawsuit about ten or fifteen pounds, the costs of which have mounted up to large sums.
Henry Peter Brougham (1778–1868), House of Commons, 7 February 1828

4 Beggars can never be bankrupts.
Thomas Fuller (1654–1734), *Gnomologia*, 1732, no. 963

5 Trash and Trumpery
Is the way to beggary.
Thomas Fuller (1654–1734), *ibid.*, no. 6091

6 A cynic has observed that if you go 'bust' for £700 you are probably a fool, if you go 'bust' for £7,000 you are probably in the dock, and if you go bust for £7 million you are probably rescued by the Bank of England.
Lord Meston, House of Lords, 15 January 1985

7 There are three roads to ruin: women, gambling and technology. The most pleasant is with women, the quickest is with gambling, but the surest is with technology.
Georges Pompidou (1911–1974), *Straits Times*, Singapore, 11 April 1987

8 I am ashamed to owe debts I cannot pay but I am not ashamed of being classed with those to whose rank I belong. The disgrace is in being an actual bankrupt not in being made a legal one.
Sir Walter Scott (1771–1832), *Journal*, 16 February 1826

9 Poor bankrupt.
William Shakespeare (1564–1616), *Romeo and Juliet*, 1595–6, act II, sc. II

10 You don't go broke making a profit.
Sir Nicholas Shehadie, *Sydney Morning Herald*, 'Sayings of the Week', 26 March 1987

11 There are few faster ways of going broke than by buying goods and then passing them on to customers who cannot pay for them.
T. Sykes, *Two Centuries of Panic*, 1988, ch. 23

18 BARGAINS

1 Remember, there are no bargains.
Anonymous, Bernard Levin, *The Times*, 4 September 1986

2 What is ordinarily termed a good bargain is, morally, a bad bargain.
John Bates Clark (1847–1938), *Philosophy of Wealth*, 1887, ch. IX, p. 162

3 Some bargain's dear bought.
John Davies (1565?–1618), *The Scourge of Folly*, 1611

4 Here's the rule for bargains: 'Do other men, for they would do you'. That's the true business precept.
Charles Dickens (1812–1870), *Martin Chuzzlewit*, 1843–4, ch. 11

5 A bargain is something you have to find a use for once you have bought it.
Benjamin Franklin (1706–1790), attributed

6 Bargaining has neither friends nor relations.
Benjamin Franklin (1706–1790), *Poor Richard's Almanac*, 1736

7 Good bargains are pick-pockets.
Thomas Fuller (1654–1734), *Gnomologia*, 1732, no. 1701

8 It is a bad bargain, where both are losers.
Thomas Fuller (1654–1734), *ibid.*, no. 2839

9 Make the best of a bad bargain.
Thomas Fuller (1654–1734), *ibid.*, no. 3325

10 More words than one to a bargain.
Thomas Fuller (1654–1734), *ibid.*, no. 3465

11 On a good bargain think twice.
    George Herbert (1593–1633), *Jacula Prudentum*, 1651

12 One of the difficult tasks in this world is to convince a woman that even a bargain costs money.
    E.W. Howe (1853–1937) in Rudolf Flesch, *The Book of Unusual Quotations*, 1959

13 It is an ill bargain, where no man wins.
    James Kelly, *Scottish Proverbs*, 1721, I, no. 42

14 My old father used to have a saying: If you make a bad bargain, hug it all the tighter.
    Abraham Lincoln (1809–1865), letter to Joshua Speed, 25 February 1842

15 The best of a bad bargain.
    Samuel Pepys (1633–1703), *Diary*, 14 August 1663

16 Bargains made in speed are commonly repented at leisure.
    George Pettie (1548–1589), *Petite Palace of Pettie His Pleasure*, 1576

17 Make every bargain clear and plain,
    That none may afterward complain.
    John Ray (1628–1705), *English Proverbs*, 1670

18 To sell a bargain well is as cunning as fast and loose.
    William Shakespeare (1564–1616), *Love's Labour's Lost*, 1594–5, act III, sc. I

19 To make a world-without-end bargain.
    William Shakespeare (1564–1616), *ibid.*, act V, sc. II

---

19 BOARDROOM

1 You ask what constitutes a crisis here. Well, if we ran out of white wine in the boardroom.
   Patrick Cobbold, *Observer*, 'Quotes of the Year', 19 December 1982

2 When an academic decries business for being so boring, you know he's never seen the thrills and spills of a boardroom.
   Katharine Whitehorn, *Observer*, 29 March 1987

20 BORROWING
See also 57 CREDIT, 58 CREDITORS, 61 DEBT, 104 INTEREST

1 An acquaintance is someone we know well enough to borrow from, but not well enough to lend to.
   Anonymous

2 A new man, with a small capital of his own and a large borrowed capital, can undersell a rich man who depends on his own capital only.
   Walter Bagehot (1826–1877), *Lombard Street*, 1873, ch. 1.

3 Owe no man anything.
   Bible, Authorized Version, Romans 13:8

4 It is no use borrowing if you mean to pay.
   Marcus Clarke, 'On Borrowing Money', *A Marcus Clarke Reader*, ed. Bill Wannan, 1963

5 If you would know the value of money, go and try to borrow some; for he that goes a-borrowing goes a-sorrowing.
   Benjamin Franklin (1706–1790), *Poor Richard's Almanac*, 1754

6 Borrow not too much on time to come.
   Thomas Fuller (1654–1734), *Gnomologia*, 1732, no. 1007

7 He that trusts to borrowed ploughs, will have his land lie fallow.
   Thomas Fuller (1654–1734), *ibid.*, no. 2337

8 He that goes a borrowing,
   Goes a sorrowing.
   Thomas Fuller (1654–1734), *ibid.*, no. 6334

9 There can be no doubt that it is a rule of borrowing and lending that *to him that hath shall be lent*.
   J.R. Hicks, *The Social Framework*, 1942, pt. III, ch. IX

10 The habit of borrowing small sums of money — anticipating pay-day — is a pernicious practice and breaks many a friendship. It is no kindness to loan money to a professional borrower.
    Elbert Hubbard (1856–1915), *Notebook*, 1927, p. 184

11 Neither a borrower nor a lender be:
For loan oft loses both itself and friend;
And borrowing dulls the edge of husbandry.
William Shakespeare (1564–1616),
Hamlet, 1599–1600, act I, sc. III

12 I can get no remedy against this
consumption of the purse: borrowing only
lingers and lingers it out, but the disease is
incurable.
William Shakespeare (1564–1616), *Henry
IV, Pt. II*, 1597–8, act I, sc. II

13 How can you have production unless you
borrow the money to produce? I do not
believe in the theory that you must first
produce and then borrow the money. That
is not what my grandfather did. He
borrowed the money and then produced.
Earl of Stockton (Harold Macmillan)
(1894–1986), House of Lords, 23 January
1985

14 You may be assured that there is no practice
more dangerous than that of borrowing
money. For when the money can be had in
this way, repayment is seldom thought of in
time; the interest becomes a moth; exertions
to raise it by dint of industry cease — it
becomes easy and is spent freely . . . In the
meantime the debt is accumulating like a
snowball rolling.
George Washington (1732–1799), letter to
Samuel Washington, 12 July 1797

21 BOSSES
See also 117 MANAGEMENT,
118 MANAGEMENT CONSULTANCY,
138 PERSONNEL MANAGEMENT

1 A final word to bosses. Keep the staff so
busy that they have no time to think about
anything except getting their daily work
completed.
Albert Allen, *Are Your Books Being
Cooked?*, 1968, finale

2 Factory Rules: Rule 1. The foreman is
always right. Rule 2. If the foreman is
wrong, Rule 1 applies.
Anonymous

3 [Regarding the supply of office chairs] the
boss's bum is more important than anyone
else's bum.
Bill Aris. *Observer*. 9 November 1986

4 The boss is the one who makes good.
Elbert Hubbard (1856–1915), *Notebook*,
1927, p. 28

5 Real Bosses Don't Say 'Thank You'.
Ellen Nevins, title of book, 1983

6 In economic matters . . . bosses tend to get
the workers they deserve.
Martin J. Wiener, *English Culture and the
Decline of the Industrial Spirit 1850–1950*,
1981, ch. 1

22 BROKERS

1 He's called a 'broker' because after you deal
with him you are.
Anonymous

2 An honest broker.
Prince von Bismarck (of himself), speech,
19 February 1878

3 Two cunning knaves need no broker.
Thomas Fuller (1654–1734), *Gnomologia*,
1732, no. 5322

23 BUDGETS

1 A budget is a numerical check of your worst
suspicions.
Anonymous

2 A budget is the way to go broke
methodically.
Anonymous

3 What is the essence of this new budgetary
policy? It is that the budget is made with
reference to available man-power, not to
money; that it becomes, in Mr Bevin's
phrase, a 'human budget'.
Sir William Beveridge (1879–1963), *Full
Employment in a Free Society*, 1945, p. 136

We didn't actually overspend our budget.
The Health Commission allocation simply
fell short of our expenditure.
Keith Davis (Chairman, Wollongong
Hospital), *Sydney Morning Herald*, 'Sayings
of the Week', 14 November 1981

5 Annual income twenty pounds, annual
expenditure nineteen, nineteen and six,

result happiness. Annual income twenty pounds, annual expenditure twenty pounds ought and six, result misery. [Mr Micawber]
Charles Dickens (1812–1870), *David Copperfield*, 1849–50, ch. 12

6 The largest determining factor of the size and content of this year's budget is last year's budget.
Aaron Wildavsky, *The Politics of the Budgetary Process*, 1964

24 BUREAUCRACY
See also 38 CIVIL SERVICE, 42 COMMITTEES, 92 GOVERNMENT, 132 ORGANIZATION(S)

1 It is harder to change a decision than to make one.
Anonymous

2 Do remember that the speed of the bureaucratic machine makes British Rail look like Concorde.
Jeffrey Archer, *First Among Equals*, 1984, ch. 23

3 [Bureaucracy] . . . the giant power wielded by pygmies.
Honoré de Balzac, *Les Employés*, 1836

4 Large business bureaucracies never die — they just borrow money from the government.
Thomas L. Martin Jr., *Malice in Blunderland*, 1973, p. 52

5 Governors by profession, which is the essence and meaning of bureaucracy.
John Stuart Mill (1806–1873), *Representative Government*, 1860

6 Big bureaucracies are run largely on inertia.
Thomas J. Peters, 'Symbols, Patterns, and Settings: An Optimistic Case for Getting Things Done', *Organizational Dynamics*, Autumn 1978

7 Bureaucracy is not an obstacle to democracy but an inevitable complement to it.
Joseph Schumpeter (1883–1950), *Capitalism, Socialism and Democracy*, 1942, ch. XVIII

8 The purely bureaucratic type of administrative organization . . . is, from a purely technical point of view, capable of attaining the highest degree of efficiency and is in this sense formally the most rational

known means of carrying out imperative control over human beings. It is superior to any other form in precision, in stability, in the stringency of its discipline, and in its reliability.
Max Weber (1864–1920), *The Theory of Social and Economic Organization*, 1947, III, II, 5

25 BUSINESS
See also 27 BUSINESSMEN, 204 TRADE

1 Prosperity is what business creates for politicians to take the credit.
Anonymous

2 Pull off a coup and you're a national hero, fail and you're an evil criminal; in business it's the same difference between bankruptcy and making a fortune.
Jeffrey Archer, *A Quiver Full of Arrows*, 1980, 'The Coup'

3 The 'theory of business' leads to a life of obstruction, because theorists do not see the business, and the men of business will not reason out the theories.
Walter Bagehot (1826–1877), *Economic Studies*, ed. Hutton, 1880, I, pp. 9–10

4 Business is really a profession often requiring for its practice quite as much knowledge, and quite as much skill, as law and medicine; and requiring also the possession of money.
Walter Bagehot (1826–1877), *Lombard Street*, 1873, ch. 9

5 Business is really more agreeable than pleasure; it interests the whole mind, the aggregate nature of man more continuously, and more deeply. But it does not look as if it did.
Walter Bagehot (1826–1877), *The English Constitution*, 1867

6 Business patterns are perhaps the most volatile, the most voluntary, and the most abstract, of all groupings of mankind.
Miriam Beard, *A History of Business*, 1938, vol. II, p. 141

7 Business is more exciting than any game.
Lord Beaverbrook (1879–1964), attributed

8 The nature of business is swindling.
August Bebel (1814–1913), speech, 1892

9 More influences forming the opinions,
habits, and characters of men spring out of
business than out of almost all other
relations which men sustain.
Henry Ward Beecher (1813–1887),
Proverbs from Plymouth Pulpit, 1887

10 Good judgment is to business what good
steering is to navigation. Moral elements
enter largely into good judgment.
Henry Ward Beecher (1813–1887), *ibid.*

11 No man ever manages a legitimate business
in this life without doing indirectly far more
for other men than he is trying to do for
himself.
Henry Ward Beecher (1813–1887), *ibid.*

12 Be . . . not slothful in business.
Bible, Authorized Version, Romans, 12:11

13 The big unions and the big companies, like
easter eggs, are attractively packaged in
their respective mythologies.
Geoffrey Blainey, *The Politics of Big
Business: A History*, The Academy of the
Social Sciences in Australia Annual Lecture,
Canberra, 1976

14 The best class of scientific mind is the same
as the best class of business mind. The great
desideratum in either case is to know how
much evidence is enough to warrant action.
It is as unbusiness-like to want too much
evidence before buying and selling as to be
content with too little.
Samuel Butler (1835–1902), *Note Books*,
ed. Festing Jones, 1912, ch. XIV

15 Few people do business well who do
nothing else.
Lord Chesterfield (1694–1773), letter to his
son, 7 August 1749

16 The maxim of the British people is 'Business
as usual'.
Winston Churchill (1874–1965), speech,
1914

17 To those who are engaged in commercial
dealings, justice is indispensable for the
conduct of business.
Cicero (106–43 BC), *De Officiis*, bk. II, ch.
XI

18 The fact that a business is large, efficient
and profitable does not mean that it takes
advantage of the public.
Charles Clore in Hearn Stephenson,
Contradictory Quotations

19 I always make it a point of business ethics
never to tell a lie unless I think I can get
away with it.
Kenneth Cook and Kerry Cook, *The
Film-Makers*, 1983, ch. 4

20 The business of America is business.
Calvin Coolidge (1872–1933), address
before the Society of American Newspaper
Editors, Washington DC, 17 January 1925

21 Business neglected is business lost.
Daniel Defoe (*c*.1660–1731), *The Complete
English Tradesman*, 2nd ed., 1727, vol. 1,
letter IX

22 He that makes his pleasure be his business,
will never make his business be a pleasure.
Daniel Defoe (*c*.1660–1731), *ibid.*

23 It's enough for a man to understand his own
business, and not to interfere with other
people's.
Charles Dickens (1812–1870), *A Christmas
Carol*, 1843, stave 1

24 Business has only two basic functions —
marketing and innovation.
Peter F. Drucker, attributed

25 Business is very simple; it's other people's
money.
A. Dumas, *fils* (1824–1895), *La Question
d'Argent*, 1857, act 2, sc. 7

26 That peculiarly spiteful envy which the
British reserve for those who succeed in
business.
Kenneth Fleet, *The Times*, 11 December
1986

27 The chief weakness in business organisation
is lack of co-ordination.
Mary Parker Follett (1868–1933), lecture,
New York, 10 December 1926

28 Some day the ethics of business will be
universally recognized, and in that day
Business will be seen to be the oldest and
most useful of all the professions.
Henry Ford (1863–1947) in Tryon
Edwards, *The New Dictionary of Thoughts*

29 A business that makes nothing but money is
a poor kind of business.
Henry Ford (1863–1947), attributed

30 Boldness in business is the first. second and
third thing.
Thomas Fuller (1654–1734), *Gnomologia*,
1732, no. 1006

31 Business is the salt of life.
Thomas Fuller (1654–1734), *ibid.*, no. 1026

32 Do business, but be not a slave to it.
Thomas Fuller (1654–1734), *ibid.*, no. 1304

33 He that thinks his business below him, will always be above his business.
Thomas Fuller (1654–1734), *ibid.*, no. 2333

34 With an honest and a good man, business is soon ended.
Thomas Fuller (1654–1734), *ibid.*, no. 5793

35 If drawn by Bus'ness to a Street unknown,
Let the sworn Porter point thee through the Town;
Be sure observe the Signs, for Signs remain,
Like faithful Land-marks to the walking Train.
Seek not from Prentices to learn the Way,
Those fabling Boys will turn thy steps astray;
Ask the grave Tradesman to direct thee right,
He ne'er deceives, but when he profits by't.
John Gay (1685–1732), *Trivia*, 1716, bk. II

36 Business is so much lower a thing than learning that a man used to the last cannot easily bring his stomach down to the first.
Lord Halifax (1633–1695) in Rudolf Flesch, *The Book of Unusual Quotations*, 1959

37 Business is fun. You can't take it too seriously.
Gerry Harvey, *Sydney Morning Herald*, 3 June 1982

38 A climate in which business can be reliably assumed to tell the truth is not only morally superior to the alternative, it is economically more efficient.
Rupert Haupt, 'Beckoning a Day of Reckoning', *Sydney Morning Herald*, 31 December 1988

39 Who likes not his business, his business likes not him.
William Hazlitt (1778–1830), *English Proverbs*, 1869

40 Great businesses turn on a little pin.
George Herbert (1593–1632), *Outlandish Proverbs*, 1640

41 Big business is only small business with an extra nought on the end.
Robin Holmes à Court, *Sydney Morning Herald*, 'Sayings of the Week', 24 August 1985

42 In thousands of years there has been no advance in public morals, in philosophy, in religion or in politics, but the advance in business has been the greatest miracle the world has ever known.
E.W. Howe (1853–1937), *The Blessings of Business*, 1918

43 Business is usually good in a good store.
E.W. Howe (1853–1937), *Country Town Sayings*, 1911

44 There is always plenty of business, if you are smart enough to get it.
E.W. Howe (1853–1937), *ibid.*

45 The word business was first used in the time of Chaucer to express contempt for people who were useful. The word was then spelled busyness.
Elbert Hubbard (1856–1915), *Notebook*, 1927, p. 16

46 Business is a fight — a continual struggle — just as life is.
Elbert Hubbard (1856–1915), *ibid.*, p. 50

47 The business that begins small and grows is a safe business. The business that begins big is the one that goes by the board.
Elbert Hubbard (1856–1915), *ibid.*, p. 184

48 Some girls idea o' business is resignin' a twelve-dollar job t' marry a seven-dollar husband.
Frank McKinney Hubbard (1868–1930), *New Sayings by Abe Martin*, 1917

49 Many a man has busted in business because his necktie did not match his socks.
Frank McKinney Hubbard (1868–1930), *Epigrams*, 1923

50 Business: 1. Looking a payroll in the eye and kiting checks. 2. A method of reducing a landlady to her lowest terms.
Frank McKinney Hubbard (1868–1930), *The Roycroft Dictionary*, 1923

51 I think business the best remedy for grief.
Samuel Johnson (1709–1784), letter to Mrs Thrale, 11 April 1781

52 Fix on some business where much money may be got and little virtue risqued.
Samuel Johnson (1709–1784), *Johnsonian Miscellanies*, 1897, vol. I, p. 314

53 Love your neighbour is not merely sound Christianity; it is good business.
David Lloyd George (1863–1945), *Observer*, 'Sayings of the Week', 20 February 1921

54 Small businesses . . . are all different. The more you generalise, the more you distort.
Hamish MacRae, *Guardian*, 5 October 1985

55 The world of business is an avenue in which parasites cling to the trees; a garden where weeds spring up among the flowers; an orchard in which bees carry the pollen of managerial science from one plant to another; a wood in which the branches of economic theory are strictly for the birds.
C. Northcote Parkinson, *In-Laws and Outlaws*, 1959, ch. 11

56 As the proverb says; 'He who does business without knowing all about it, sees his money go like flies'.
Luca Pacioli (*c.*1445–*c.*1517), *Particularis de Computis et Scripturis*, 1494

57 Mind your own business.
Proverb

58 Business is business.
Proverb, 18th century

59 Business before pleasure.
Proverb, 19th century

60 An excellent monument might be erected to the Unknown Stock-holder. It might take the form of a solid stone ark of faith apparently floating in a pool of water.
Felix Reisenberg (1879–1939) in Tryon Edwards, *The New Dictionary of Thoughts*

61 A friendship founded on business is better than a business founded on friendship.
John D. Rockefeller (1839–1937), attributed

62 We demand that big business give the people a square deal; in return we must insist that when any one engaged in big business honestly endeavors to do right he shall himself be given a square deal.
Theodore Roosevelt (1858–1919), *Autobiography*, 1913

63 I am so full of businesses I cannot answer thee acutely.
William Shakespeare (1564–1616), *All's Well that Ends Well*, 1602–4, act I, sc. I

64 I know my business.
William Shakespeare (1564–1616), *ibid.*, act II, sc. II

65   I find thee
Most fit for business.
William Shakespeare (1564–1616), *Antony and Cleopatra*, 1606–7, act III, sc. III

66 To business that we love we rise betime,
And go to 't with delight.
William Shakespeare (1564–1616), *ibid.*, act IV, sc. IV

67 The business of this man looks out of him.
William Shakespeare (1564–1616), *ibid.*, act V, sc. I

68 My business cannot brook this dalliance.
William Shakespeare (1564–1616), *The Comedy of Errors*, 1592–3, act IV, sc. I

69 There's business in these faces.
William Shakespeare (1564–1616), *Cymbeline*, 1609–10, act V, sc. V

70 Now, my masters, happy man be his dole, say I: every man to his business.
William Shakespeare (1564–1616), *Henry IV, Pt. I*, 1597–8, act II, sc. II

71 To groan and sweat under the business, Either led or driven as we point the way.
William Shakespeare (1564–1616), *Julius Caesar*, 1599–1600, act IV, sc. I

72 On serious business, craving quick despatch.
William Shakespeare (1564–1616), *Love's Labour's Lost*, 1594–5, act II, sc. I

73   When you have
A business for yourself, pray Heaven you then
Be perfect.
William Shakespeare (1564–1616), *Measure for Measure*, 1604–5, act V, sc. I

74 One business does command us all; for mine Is money.
William Shakespeare (1564–1616), *Timon of Athens*, 1607–8, act III, sc. IV

75 Business only contributes fully to society if it is efficient, profitable and socially responsible.
Lord Sieff, attributed

76 A good business novel or business biography is not about business. It is about love, hate, pride, craftmanship, comradeship, ambition, pleasure.
H.A. Simon, *The New Science of Management Decision*, 1960, p. 50

77 I'm still convinced that successful business is devastatingly uninteresting.
C.P. Snow (1905–1980), *Strangers and Brothers*, 1951

78 It is not by any means certain that a man's business is the most important thing he has to do.
Robert Louis Stevenson (1850–1894) in Rudolf Flesch, *The Book of Unusual Quotations*, 1959

79 Militarism, as Englishmen see plainly enough, is fetish worship. It is the prostration of men's souls and the laceration of their bodies to appease an idol. What they do not see is that their reverence for economic activity and industry and what is called business is also fetish worship, and that, in their devotion to their idol, they torture themselves as needlessly and indulge in the same meaningless antics as the Prussians did in their worship of militarism.
R.H. Tawney (1880–1962), *The Acquisitive Society*, 1921, ch. 4

80 'No business before breakfast, Glum!' says the King. 'Breakfast first, business next.'
William Makepeace Thackeray (1811–1863), *The Rose and the Ring*, 1855, ch. 11

81 Business is business, and must not be made a pleasure of.
Anthony Trollope (1815–1882), *The Last Chronicle of Barset*, 1867, vol. II, ch. XIV

82 The first rule of business: Find out what the man you are dealing with wants, and give it him.
Warren Tute, *The Golden Greek*, 1960, ch. 6

83 Wise business management, and more particularly what is spoken of as safe and sane business management . . . reduces itself in the main to a sagacious use of sabotage.
Thorstein Veblen (1857–1929), *The Nature of the Peace*, 1919, ch. VII

84 Business is a game, the greatest game in the world if you know how to play it.
Thomas J. Watson Sr., attributed

85 It is very vulgar to talk about one's business. Only people like stockbrokers do that, and then merely at dinner parties.
Oscar Wilde (1856–1900), *The Importance of Being Earnest*, 1895, act II

86 Big business is not dangerous because it is big, but because its bigness is an unwholesome inflation created by privileges and exemptions which it ought not to enjoy.
Woodrow Wilson (1856–1924), speech, 1912

87 Business underlies everything in our national life, including our spiritual life. Witness the fact that in the Lord's Prayer, the first petition is for daily bread. No one can worship God or love his neighbour on an empty stomach.
Woodrow Wilson (1856–1924), speech, 1912

88 Business is like riding a bicycle. Either you keep moving or you fall down.
John David Wright, in James Beasley Simpson, *Best Quotes of '54, '55, '56*, 1957

26 BUSINESS CYCLE

1 The answer to the problem of the trade cycle is government intervention to stop the laws of economics working.
Anonymous (student essay)

2 The modern world regards business cycles as the ancient Egyptians regarded the overflowings of the Nile. The phenomenon recurs at intervals; it is of great importance to everyone, and the natural causes of it are not in sight.
John Bates Clark (1847–1938), 'Introduction' to K. Rodbertus, *Overproduction and Crises*, 1898

3 I am perfectly convinced that these decennial crises do depend upon meteorological variations of like period, which again depend, in all probability, upon cosmic variations of which we have evidence in the frequency of sun-spots, auroras, and magnetic perturbations.
W. Stanley Jevons (1835–1882), *Investigations in Currency and Finance*, 1884, VIII, pp. 235–6

4 The frequent recurrence of economic crises
and depressions, is evidence that the
automatic functioning of our business
system is defective.
Wesley Clair Mitchell (1874–1948), *The
Backward Art of Spending Money*, 1937,
p. 91

27 BUSINESSMEN

See also 25 BUSINESS, 76 ENTREPRENEURS,
205 TRADERS

1 A businessman is someone who talks golf all
morning in the office and business all
afternoon on the golf course.
Anonymous

2 The man who attends strictly to his own
business usually has plenty of business to
attend to.
Anonymous

3 The outlook for the businessman is usually
brighter than the outlook of the
businessman.
Anonymous

4 Why do businessmen complain about bad
business over the most expensive dinners?
Anonymous

5 Men of business have a solid judgement — a
wonderful guessing power of what is going
to happen — each in his own trade; but they
have never practised themselves in reasoning
out their judgements and in supporting their
guesses by argument: probably if they did so
some of the finer and correcter parts of their
anticipations would vanish.
Walter Bagehot (1826–1877), *Economic
Studies*, ed. Hutton, 1880, I, p. 9

6 Most men of business love a sort of twilight.
They have lived all their lives in an
atmosphere of probabilities and of doubt,
where nothing is very clear, where there are
some chances for many events, where there
is much to be said for several courses, where
nevertheless one course must be determindly
chosen and fixedly adhered to. They like to
hear arguments suited to this intellectual
haze. So far from caution or hesitation in the
statement of the argument striking them as
an indication of imbecility, it seems to them
a sign of practicality. They got rich
themselves by transactions of which they
could not have stated the argumentative
ground — and all they ask for is a distinct
though moderate conclusion, that they can
repeat when asked; something which they
feel *not* to be abstract argument, but
abstract argument diluted and dissolved in
real life.
Walter Bagehot (1826–1877), *The English
Constitution*, 1867, ch. IV

7 [The businessman] still struggles on
unfathered and unhallowed, lacking annals
and allegories, a mellowed lineage, a shell of
myths in which to creep. He is his own
ancestor, and, usually, his memory does not
reach back even to the last business crisis.
Miriam Beard, *A History of the Business
Man*, 1938

8 There cannot be a situation where a
businessman says, 'I base all my business on
moral considerations.' Equally, you can't
say you can run a business without morality.
Sir Timothy Bevan (Chairman of Barclays
Bank, on its withdrawal from South Africa),
Observer, 30 November 1986

9 The businessman and the artist are like
matter and mind. We can never get either
pure and without some alloy of the other.
Samuel Butler (1835–1902), *Note Books*,
ed. Festing Jones, 1912, ch. XI

10 The businessman has not simply been one of
the more unloved figures of English history;
worse than that, he has never quite been
taken seriously.
D.C. Coleman, *What Has Happened to
Economic History?*, 1972, p. 10

11 A true-bred merchant is a universal scholar,
his learning excels the mere scholar in Greek
and Latin as much as that does the illiterate
person that cannot write or read. He
understands languages without books,
geography without maps; his journals and
trading voyages delineate the world; his
foreign exchanges, protests, and
procurations speak all tongues. He sits in his
counting house and converses with all
nations, and keeps up the most exquisite
and extensive part of human society in a
universal correspondence.
Daniel Defoe (*c.*1660–1731), *The Best of
Defoe's Review*, 3 January 1706, pp. 124–5

12 He must be a perfect *complete hypocrite*, if
    he will be a *complete tradesman*.
    Daniel Defoe (*c*.1660–1731), *The Complete
    English Tradesman*, 2nd ed., 1727, vol. I,
    letter VIII

13 The tradesman that does not love his
    business, will never give it due attendance.
    Daniel Defoe (*c*.1660–1731), *ibid*., letter IX

14 Whenever you see a successful business,
    someone once made a courageous decision.
    Peter F. Drucker, attributed

15 A man can never leave his business. He
    ought to think of it by day and dream of it
    by night.
    Henry Ford (1863–1947), attributed

16 Business is never so healthy as when, like a
    chicken, it must do a certain amount of
    scratching for what it gets.
    Henry Ford (1863–1947), attributed

17 I am impatient with the slavish and
    stereotyped thinking which has led some
    businessmen to consider security a bad word
    and to brand all concern for human and
    social progress as Communism or creeping
    socialism.
    Henry Ford II in James Beasley Simpson,
    Best Quotes of '54, '55, '56, 1957

18 Men of business must not break their word
    twice.
    Thomas Fuller (1654–1734), *Gnomologia*,
    1732, no. 3401

19 Each [of my wives] was jealous and resentful
    of my preoccupation with business. Yet
    none showed any visible aversion to sharing
    in the proceeds.
    J. Paul Getty (1892–1976), *As I See It*, 1976

20 Rent-seekers are [Australian] businessmen
    who are eternally blaming the Government
    for their problems and forever demanding
    that the Government help them out.
    Ross Gittins, *Sydney Morning Herald*,
    'Sayings of the Week', 26 April 1986

21 The most sensible people to be met with in
    society are men of business and of the
    world, who argue from what they see and
    know, instead of spinning cobweb
    distinctions of what things ought to be.
    William Hazlitt (1778–1830), *The
    Ignorance of the Learned*, 1821

22 He was a self-made man who owed his lack
    of success to nobody.
    Joseph Heller, *Catch-22*, 1955, ch. 3

23 It is said that Americans are businessmen.
    This is not so. They are idealists, with a
    slightly naïve realism.
    Edouard Herriot in C. Bingham, *Wit and
    Wisdom*, 1982

24 If you can forgive the magnificence and
    vanity of a successful politician, why are you
    unable to forgive a successful business man?
    Every time I strike a match, or turn an
    electric button, or use the telephone, I am
    indebted to a business man, but if in debt to
    any politician, I do not know it.
    E.W. Howe (1853–1937), attributed

25 Have you ever as a businessman had a
    certain scheme presented and did you reject
    it as foolish and fanciful, and later behold it
    make a million dollars for the enemy?
    Elbert Hubbard (1856–1915), *Notebook*,
    1927, p. 49

26 No business remains greater than the man
    who runs it.
    Elbert Hubbard (1856–1915), *ibid*., p. 83

27 Businessman: One who gets the business
    and completes the transaction — all the rest
    are clerks and labourers.
    Frank McKinney Hubbard (1868–1930),
    The Roycroft Dictionary, 1923

28 Every man to his own business.
    J.S. Knowles (1784–1862), *The
    Love-Chase*, 1837, act V

29 Every businessman should have one day in
    his life to see what it is like coming down.
    Sir Freddie Laker, *Observer*, 'Sayings of the
    Week', 11 September 1983

30 He [the businessman] is the only man who is
    forever apologizing for his occupation.
    H.L. Mencken (1880–1956), attributed

31 Men, some to bus'ness, some to pleasure
    take.
    Alexander Pope (1688–1744), *Moral
    Essays, Epistle II*, 1735

32 I am a first rate business man, and make
    splendid arrangements, which nobody ever
    keeps.
    George Bernard Shaw (1856–1950), letter
    to Frederick H. Evans, 27 August 1895

33 To be relieved of all responsibility except to oneself, means of course an enormous simplification of business. We can recognise that it is practical and need not be surprised that it is highly popular among businessmen.
E.F. Schumacher (1911–1977), *Small is Beautiful*, 1973, pt. I, ch. 3

34 Finding your way round an obstruction without breaking the law seems to me what enterprising businessmen have done since the beginning of time.
Warren Tute, *The Golden Greek*, 1960, ch. 5

35 Businessmen aren't writers, your honour. There's only one businessman in a thousand that can write a good letter of recommendation.
Thornton Wilder (1897–1975), *The Matchmaker*, 1954, act I

28 BUYING

1 *It is* naught, *it is* naught, saith the buyer: but when he is gone his way, then he boasteth.
Bible, Authorized Version, Proverbs 20:14

2 Better buy than borrow.
Thomas Fuller (1654–1734), *Gnomologia*, 1732, no. 884

3 I will not buy a pig in a poke.
Thomas Fuller (1654–1734), *ibid.*, no. 2642

4 The buyer needs a hundred eyes, the seller not one.
George Herbert (1593–1633), *Jacula Prudentum*, 1651

5 He that blames would buy.
George Herbert (1593–1633), *ibid.*

6 To buy the pig in the poke.
John Heywood (1506–1565), *Proverbs*, 1546, pt. II, ch. IX

7 Salesmen are decent, but buyers don't have to be. Buyers are inhuman, without bowels, passions or a sense of humour. Happily they never reproduce . . . all buyers go to hell.
Elbert Hubbard (1856–1915), *Selected Writings of Elbert Hubbard*, 1922, vol. VIII

8 Don't a fellow feel good after he gets out of a store where he nearly bought something?
Frank McKinney Hubbard (1868–1930) in Rudolf Flesch, *The Book of Unusual Quotations*, 1959

9 Better buy than borrow.
James Kelly, *Scottish Proverbs*, 1721, B, no. 25

10 Let the buyer beware (*caveat emptor*).
Legal maxim

11 When you go to buy use your eyes, not your ears.
Proverb

29 CAPITAL
See also 30 CAPITALISM, 31 CAPITALISTS

1 Capital is simply a book-keeping term.
Anonymous

2 Many a firm has been known to pay its debts with cash, but not one has drawn a cheque on working capital.
Anonymous

3 Capital, in the sense of capital *value*, is simply future income discounted or, in other words, *capitalised*.
Irving Fisher (1867–1947), *The Theory of Interest*, 1930, ch. I, p. 12

4 Capital is a result of labour, and is used by labour to assist it in further production. Labour is the active and initial force, and labour is therefore the employer of capital.
Henry George (1839–1897), *Progress and Poverty*, 1879, bk. III, ch. I

5 What is capital? It is what is left over when the primary needs of society have been satisfied.
Aldous Huxley (1894–1963) in Rudolph Flesch, *The Book of Unusual Quotations*, 1959

6 Capital . . . is nothing but maintenance of labourers.
W. Stanley Jevons (1835–1882), *Theory of Political Economy*, 4th ed., 1911, Appendix III

7 The demand for capital goods . . . is merely the demand for future income.
Frank H. Knight (1885–1972), *Risk, Uncertainty and Profit*, 1921, p. 163

8   Capital consists in a great part of knowledge and organization: and of this some part is private property and other part is not.
    Alfred Marshall (1842–1924), *Principles of Economics*, 8th ed., 1920, bk. IV, ch. I, 1, p. 138

9   The value of the capital already invested in improving land or erecting a building; in making a railway or a machine is the aggregate discounted value of its estimated future net income.
    Alfred Marshall (1842–1924), *ibid.*, bk. VI, ch. VI, 6, p. 593

10 In bourgeois society capital is independent and has individuality, while the living person is dependent and has no individuality.
    Karl Marx (1818–1883) **and Friedrich Engels** (1820–1895), *The Communist Manifesto*, 1848

11 Capital is dead labour that, vampire-like, lives only by sucking living labour, and lives the more, the more labour it sucks.
    Karl Marx (1818–1883), *Das Kapital*, 1867, I

12 Capital is that part of the wealth of a country which is employed in production, and consists of food, clothing, tools, raw materials, machinery, etc., necessary to give effect to labour.
    David Ricardo (1772–1823), *Principles of Political Economy*, 1817

13 Capital is saved from profits.
    David Ricardo (1772–1823), *Notes on Malthus*, in *Works*, ed. Sraffa, vol. II, p. 19

14 *Owning* capital is not a productive activity.
    Joan Robinson (1903–1983), *An Essay on Marxian Economics*, 1947, ch. III, p. 18

15 Capital is simply spare subsistence.
    George Bernard Shaw (1856–1950), 'The Economic Basis of Socialism', in *Fabian Essays*, 1889

16 Risk capital is gambling money such as might be staked upon a horse race.
    Nevil Shute (1899–1960), *Slide Rule*, 1954, ch. 7

17 Capitals are increased by parsimony, and diminished by prodigality and misconduct.
    Adam Smith (1723–1790), *Wealth of Nations*, 1776, bk. II, ch. III

18 Parsimony, and not industry, is the immediate cause of the increase of capital. Industry, indeed, provides the subject which parsimony accumulates. But whatever industry might acquire, if parsimony did not save and store up, the capital would never be greater.
    Adam Smith (1723–1790), *ibid.*

19 Some of the nicest fellows I have known in my life have experienced this confusion between capital and income, but they usually ended up in rather dreary lodging houses.
    Earl of Stockton (Harold Macmillan) (1894–1986), House of Lords, 23 January 1985

---

30 CAPITALISM
See also 29 CAPITAL, 31 CAPITALISTS

---

1   Capitalism still possesses quite substantial and far from exhausted resources.
    President Chernenko (1911–1985), *Observer*, 'Sayings of the Week', 29 April 1984

2   The inherent vice of capitalism is the unequal sharing of blessings. The inherent virtue of socialism is the equal sharing of miseries.
    Sir Winston Churchill (1874–1965), House of Commons, 22 October 1945

3   Since human nature has been trained to be contrary to any system other than individualism, any other system appears to be 'contrary to human nature', whereas it may be merely contrary to human nurture.
    John Maurice Clark (1884–1963), *Social Control of Business*, 1926, p. 82

4   Any capitalist . . . who had made sixty thousand pounds out of sixpence, always professed to wonder why the sixty thousand nearest Hands didn't each make sixty thousand pounds out of sixpence, and more or less reproached them every one for not accomplishing the little feat. What I did you can do. Why don't you go and do it?
    Charles Dickens (1812–1870), *Hard Times*, 1854, bk. II, ch. 1

5 History suggests only that capitalism is a necessary condition for political freedom. Clearly it is not a sufficient condition.
Milton Friedman, *Capitalism and Freedom*, 1962, ch. 1

6 If I had to give a definition of capitalism I would say: the process whereby American girls turn into American women.
Christopher Hampton, *Savages*, 1973, sc. 16

7 The unpleasant and unacceptable face of capitalism.
Edward Heath, House of Commons, 15 May 1973

8 The defence of capitalism consists mainly in ignoring positive attacks and in concentrating upon the errors, follies, and divided counsels of its assailants.
J.A. Hobson (1858–1940), *Confessions of an Economic Heretic*, 1938, ch. XIV

9 [Capitalism] . . . an ungodly and rapacious scramble for ill-gotten gains, in the cause of which the rich appeared to get richer and the poor poorer.
Quintin Hogg (Lord Hailsham), *The Case for Conservatism*, 1947, pp. 51–2

10 To believe that there is no way out of the present crisis for capitalism is an error. No situation is ever absolutely hopeless.
V.I. Lenin (1870–1924), Speech, March 1919, William C. White, *Lenin*, 1936, p. 45

11 There is a serious tendency towards capitalism among the well-to-do peasants.
Mao Tse-Tung (1893–1976), *Quotations from Chairman Mao Tse-Tung*, 1976, p. 32

12 Capitalist production is not merely the production of commodities; it is essentially the production of surplus value.
Karl Marx (1818–1883), *Das Kapital*, 1867, I

13 Capitalist society, is the realisation of what we should call economic democracy . . . the power which belongs to the entrepreneurs and capitalists can only be acquired by means of the consumers' ballot, held daily in the market place.
Ludwig von Mises (1881–1973), *Socialism*, English ed., 1936, p. 21

14 As we see nowadays in South-East Asia or the Caribbean, the misery of being exploited by capitalists is nothing compared to the misery of not being exploited at all.
Joan Robinson (1903–1983), *Economic Philosophy*, 1962, ch. 2

15 Capitalism with near-full employment was an impressive spectacle.
Joan Robinson (1903–1983), 'The Second Crisis of Economic Theory', *American Economic Review*, May 1972, p. 7

16 The capitalist achievement does not typically consist in providing more silk stockings for queens but in bringing them within the reach of factory girls in return for steadily decreasing amounts of effort.
Joseph A. Schumpeter (1883–1950), *Capitalism, Socialism and Democracy*, 1942, ch. V, p. 67

17 Capitalism . . . is by nature a form or method of economic change and not only never is but never can be stationary.
Joseph A. Schumpeter (1883–1950), *ibid.*, ch. VII, p. 82

18 Capitalism is too serious a subject to be left to the economic historian alone.
Fritz Stern, 'Capitalism and the Cultural Historian' in D.B. Weiner and W.R. Keylor, *From Parnassus: Essays in Honor of Jacques Barsan*, 1976

19 Religion and the Rise of Capitalism.
R.H. Tawney (1880–1962), title of book, 1926. See also Weber below.

20 Popular capitalism is a crusade: a crusade to enfranchise the many in the economic life of Britain.
Margaret Thatcher, *Observer*, 'Sayings of the Week', 16 November 1986

21 The Protestant Ethic and the Spirit of Capitalism.
Max Weber (1864–1920), title of book, 1920. See also Tawney above.

31 CAPITALISTS
See also 29 CAPITAL, 30 CAPITALISM

1 What is the benefit done by a good King Alfred, or by a Howard, or Pestalozzi, or Elizabeth Fry, or Florence Nightingale, or any lover, less or larger, compared with the involuntary blessing wrought on nations by the selfish capitalists, who built the Illinois, Michigan and the network of the

Mississippi valley roads which have evoked not only the wealth of the soil, but the energy of millions of men.
Ralph Waldo Emerson (1803–1882), *The Conduct of Life*, 1860, 'Considerations along the Way'

2   By bourgeoisie is meant the class of modern capitalists, owners of the means of social production and employers of wage labour.
Friedrich Engels (1820–1895), *Notes to The Communist Manifesto*, 1888 edition

3   While the miser is merely a capitalist gone mad, the capitalist is a rational miser.
Karl Marx (1818–1883), *Das Kapital*, 1867, vol. I, pt. II, ch. IV

4   You can't be a feminist and a capitalist.
Ruth Wallsgrove, *Observer*, 'Sayings of the Week', 25 July 1982

32 CAREERS
See also 77 EQUAL OPPORTUNITIES,
153 PROMOTION, 193 SUCCESS

1   You've forgotten the grandest moral attribute of a Scotsman, Maggie, that he'll do nothing which might damage his career.
Sir James Barrie (1860–1937), *What Every Woman Knows*, 1908, act II

2   Being a wife is the best career in the world. It's a woman's job to love her husband and children, protecting him from being unhappy, badly fed or bored.
Barbara Cartland, *Sunday Today*, 'Quotes of the Week', 15 February 1987

3   A woman's career, particularly if it is successful, is often blamed for the break-up of a marriage, but never a man's.
Eva Figes, *Patriarchal Attitudes*, 1970, ch. 8

4   For a career in the City one needs to be honourable and trustworthy, but for a career in industry one needs a more determined will to win.
Sir James Goldsmith in Geoffrey Wansell, *Sir James Goldsmith*, 1982, ch. 8

33 CARTELS
See also 125 MONOPOLY

1   Cartels are a producer's best friend.
Economist, 23 July 1988

2   When th' manufacturers o' some article meet an' decide t' charge more fer it they give out the prediction that th' price'll go up.
Frank McKinney Hubbard (1868–1930), *New Sayings by Abe Martin*, 1917

3   Cartels are like babies: we tend to be against them until we have one of our own.
Lord Mancroft, attributed

4   People of the same trade seldom meet together, even for merriment and diversion, but the conversation ends in a conspiracy against the public, or in some contrivance to raise prices.
Adam Smith, (1723–1790), *Wealth of Nations*, 1776, vol. I, bk. I, ch. X

5   In a free trade an effectual combination cannot be established but by the unanimous consent of every single trader, and it cannot last longer than every single trader continues of the same mind.
Adam Smith (1723–1790), *ibid.*

6   That group of manufacturers which adopts as a permanent principle restriction of output, in order to hold up prices, is robbing the world.
F.W. Taylor (1856–1915), 'The Principles of Scientific Management', *Bulletin of the Taylor Society*, December 1916

34 CATERING

1   The aim of fast food marketing is to minimise the time and distance between a man and his meal.
Anonymous

2   In the past Naval cooking at sea involved a choice between the lesser of two weevils.
Anonymous

3   British fish and chip shops deserve a battering.
Anonymous

4   Cookery is become an art, a noble science; cooks are gentlemen.
Robert Burton (1577–1640), *The Anatomy of Melancholy*, Democritus to the Reader, pt. I, sec. 2

5 With few, honorable exceptions, good restaurants outside London have a hard time making a living.
Alan Crompton-Batt, *Independent*, 23 July 1988

6 Any cook should be able to run the country.
V.I. Lenin (1870–1924), attributed

7 Woman accepted cooking as a chore but man has made of it a recreation.
Emily Post (1873–1960), *Etiquette*, 1922, ch. 34

8 Behind the scenes of the food business lurk the tastemakers.
Jeremy Round, *Independent*, 23 July 1988

9 The cook was a good cook, as cooks go; and as cooks go she went.
Saki (1870–1916), *Reginald*, 1904, 'Reginald on Besetting Sins'

10 'Tis an ill cook that cannot lick his own fingers.
William Shakespeare (1564–1616), *Romeo and Juliet*, 1595–6, act IV, sc. II

35 CHAIRMEN
See also 42 COMMITTEES

1 A tired chairman is a bad chairman. A dead one is usually worse.
Sir Nicholas Goodison in Ray Wild, *How to Manage*, 1982, p. 233

2 I can't bear being called Chair. Whatever I am, I am not a piece of furniture.
Baroness Seear, *Observer*, 'Sayings of the Week', 23 October 1988

3 I can imagine no worse chairman for a company in its difficult early days than a banker.
Nevil Shute (1899–1960), *Slide Rule*, 1954, ch. 7

36 CHARITY

1 Blessed is he that considereth the poor.
Bible, Authorized Version, Psalms 41:1

2 But when thou doest alms, let not thy left hand know what thy right hand does: that thine alms may be in secret.
Bible, Authorized Version, Matthew 6:3

3 The care of the aged poor and the like is a charity . . . whether the persons who devote their lives to it are actuated by the love of God, a desire for their own salvation, or mere pique, or disgust with the world.
Mr Justice Farwell (1845–1915), Re *Delany*, 1902

4 He that feeds upon charity, has a cold dinner and no supper.
Thomas Fuller (1654–1734), *Gnomologia*, 1732, no. 2, 103

5 Our charity begins at home,
And mostly ends where it begins.
Horace Smith (1779–1849), *Horace in London*, 1815, bk. II, ode 15

6 In all the ages, three-fourths of the support of the great charities has been conscience money.
Mark Twain (1835–1910), *A Humane Word from Satan*, 1905

37 THE CITY
See also 186 SPECULATION, 191 STOCK MARKETS

1 Provided that the City of London remains as it is at present, the clearing-house of the world.
Joseph Chamberlain (1836–1914), speech, 1904

2   Unreal City
Under the brown fog of a winter dawn,
A crowd flowed over London Bridge, so many,
I had not thought death had undone so many.
T.S. Eliot (1888–1965), *The Waste Land*, 1922

3 The 30,000 people who come to work [in the City] are reaping the benefits of the reputation for honesty, integrity and fair dealing which has been created by generations of their predecessors. That sort of reputation is beyond price . . . Free and open markets may be the key to financial success, but if they are to operate fairly and honestly, someone has to write the rules and to see that they are rigidly enforced . . . Rules and structures may be important, but much more important are the unwritten

rules and the will to abide by them.
Queen Elizabeth II, speech, 8 February 1989, *Independent*, 14 February 1989

4 'Think the unthinkable but wear a dark suit' is a handy maxim for the city.
Katharine Whitehorn, *Observer*, 25 January 1987

5 When the City of London starts volunteering earnest homilies about 'social responsibility in investment', then something terrible must surely be afoot.
J.T. Winkler, 'The Coming Corporatism' in Robert Skidelsky (ed.), *The End of the Keynesian Era*, 1977, p. 78

---

38 CIVIL SERVICE
See also 24 BUREAUCRACY, 132 ORGANIZATION(S)

---

1 Civil servants have many good qualities but when it comes to running businesses they tend, albeit for reasons largely outside their control, to be disastrous failures.
Leslie Chapman, *Your Disobedient Servant*, 1978, ch. 6

2 The CSE [Civil Service Entrance] examinations are unavoidable for anyone trying to join the civil service. Based on the results, the Treasury has first choice of the cream, which enables that department to foul up the British economy with impeccable references.
Frederick Forsyth, *The Devil's Alternative*, 1979, ch. 2

3 You can cut any public expenditure except the Civil Service, those lads spent a hundred years learning to look after themselves.
Sir Richard Marsh, *Observer*, 'Sayings of the Week', 19 September 1976

4 The civil servant wants to show that he took the right decision, gave the right advice, asked the right questions and obtained the right facts before placing the right minute before the right authority. What actually *happens* is of little consequence.
C. Northcote Parkinson, *In-Laws and Outlaws*, 1959, ch. 9

5 The civil service is a sacred institution. You mustn't hope to hurry it.
John Pearson, *James Bond: The Authorised Biography of 007*, 1973, ch. 8

6 Britain has invented a new missile. It's called the civil servant — it doesn't work and it can't be fired.
General Sir Walter Walker, *Observer*, 'Sayings of the Year', 3 January 1982

7 The Treasury could not, with any marked success, run a fish and chip shop.
Lord Wilson of Rievaulx (Harold Wilson), *Observer*, 'Sayings of the Week', 30 December 1984

---

39 CLASS
See also 185 SOCIETY

---

1 The law doth punish man or woman
That steals the goose from off the common,
But lets the greater felon loose,
That steals the common from the goose.
Anonymous, 18th century

2 The law in its majestic egalitarianism, forbids the rich as well as the poor to sleep under the bridges, to beg in the streets, and to steal bread.
Anatole France (1844–1924), *Le Lys Rouge*, 1894, ch. 7

3 The poor and ignorant will continue to lie and steal as long as the rich and educated show them how.
Elbert Hubbard (1856–1915), *Notebook*, 1927, p. 146

4 Within a few years the traditional, classic working classes will be tiny.
Clive Jenkins, *Observer*, 'Sayings of the Week', 4 September 1983

5 The lower classes of men, though they do not think it worth while to record what they perceive, nevertheless perceive everything that is worth noting; the difference between them and a man of learning often consists in nothing more than the latter's facility for expression.
Georg Christoph Lichtenberg (1742–1799) in Rudolf Flesch, *The Book of Unusual Quotations*, 1959

6 As far as the intellectual class generally is concerned I think it is fair to say that most of those who belong in that class — the writers, the poets, the artists, the clergy — have a great distaste for commerce and

industry, a distaste which for some merges into outright hostility.
Hugh Morgan, *Sydney Morning Herald,* 'Sayings of the Week', 13 July 1985

40 COLLECTIVE BARGAINING
See also 21 BOSSES, 117 MANAGEMENT, 129 NEGOTIATIONS, 206 TRADE UNIONS

1 Not a penny off the pay; not a minute on the day.
A.J. Cook (1885–1931), slogan of the coal miners' strike of 1925

2 Whatever may be the advantages of 'collective bargaining', it is not bargaining at all, in any just sense, unless it is voluntary on both sides.
Mahlon Pitney, *Hitchman Coal and Coke Co.* v. *Mitchell,* 245 US 229 250, 1917

41 COMMERCE
See also 25 BUSINESS, 204 TRADE

1 Commerce is curiously conservative in its homes, unless it is imperiously obliged to migrate.
Walter Bagehot (1826–1877), *Lombard Street,* 1873, ch. 1

2 Commercial relations tend to undermine traditional social barriers. An entrepreneur who discriminates against customers or employees on the basis of religion, social origin or sex runs an inefficient enterprise, which in a competitive market is not likely to prosper.
Ken Baker, 'The Stigma Against Commerce', *IPA Review,* vol. 41, no. 3, November 1987–January 1988

3 Commerce defies every wind, outrides every tempest and invades every zone.
George Bancroft (1800–1891), attributed

4 Men who have been very stingy and very grasping are usually men who have very strong commercial instincts.
Henry Ward Beecher (1813–1887), *Proverbs from Plymouth Pulpit,* 1887

5 No man has a right to put his character for integrity and honesty upon a commercial venture.
Henry Ward Beecher (1813–1887), *ibid.*

6 The commerce of the world is conducted by the strong; and usually it operates against the weak.
Henry Ward Beecher (1813–1887), *ibid.*

7 Commerce, *n.* A kind of transaction in which A plunders from B the goods of C, and for compensation B picks the pocket of D of money belonging to E.
Ambrose Bierce (1842–1914?), *The Devil's Dictionary,* 1911

8 Merchant, *n.* One engaged in a commercial pursuit. A commercial pursuit is one in which the thing pursued is a dollar.
Ambrose Bierce (1842–1914?), *ibid.*

9 In matters of commerce the fault of the
   Dutch
Is offering too little and asking too much.
The French are with equal advantage
   content,
So we clap on Dutch bottoms just twenty
   per cent.
George Canning (1770–1827), dispatch to Sir Charles Bagot, 31 January 1826

10 Commerce is the grand panacea, which, like a beneficent medical discovery, will serve to inoculate with the healthy and saving taste for civilization all the nations of the world.
Richard Cobden (1804–1865) in David Thomson, *England in the Nineteenth Century,* 1950, p. 32

11 Instructed ships shall sail to quick
   Commerce,
By which remotest Regions are alli'd;
Which makes one City of the Universe,
Where some may gain, and all may be
   suppli'd.
John Dryden (1631–1700), *Annus Mirabilis,* 1667, 163

12 Commerce has made all winds her messengers; all climes her tributaries; all people her servants.
Tryon Edwards (1809–1894), *The New Dictionary of Thoughts*

13 Commerce links all mankind in one common brotherhood of mutual dependence and interests.
James A. Garfield (1831–1881), attributed

14 Commerce never flourishes so much, as when it is delivered from the guardianship of legislators and ministers.
William Godwin, *Enquiry Concerning Political Justice,* 1798, vol. II, bk. IV, ch. I

15 Commerce changes intirely the fate and
genius of nations, by communicating arts
and opinions, circulating money, and
introducing the materials of luxury; she first
opens and polishes the mind, then corrupts
and enervates both that and the body.
Thomas Gray (1716–1771) in H.W. Starr
and J.R. Hendrickson, *The Complete Poems
of Thomas Gray*, 1966

16 Perfect freedom is as necessary to the health
and vigour of commerce, as it is to the
health and vigour of citizenship.
Patrick Henry (1736–1799) in Tryon
Edwards, *The New Dictionary of Thoughts*

17 Whoso that knew what would be deare,
Should neede be a marchant but one yeare.
John Heywood (1506–1565), *Proverbs*,
1546, pt. I, ch. I

18 Commerce is no longer exploitation. It is
human service, and no business concern can
hope to prosper which does not meet a
human need and add to human happiness.
Elbert Hubbard (1856–1915), *Notebook*,
1927, p. 16

19 The public becomes powerful in proportion
to the opulence and extensive commerce of
private men.
David Hume (1711–1776), *Essays*,
1741–2, 'Of Commerce'

20 Commerce is the great civilizer. We
exchange ideas when we exchange fabrics.
Robert Green Ingersoll (1833–1899),
attributed

21 Peace, commerce, and honest friendship
with all nations, entangling alliances with
none.
Thomas Jefferson (1743–1826), First
Inaugural Address, 4 March 1801

22 The selfish spirit of commerce knows no
country, and feels no passion or principles
but that of gain.
Thomas Jefferson (1743–1826),
attributed

23 Labour once spent has no influence on the
future value of any article: it is gone and lost
forever. In commerce bygones are forever
bygones.
W. Stanley Jevons (1835–1882), *Theory of
Political Economy*, 4th ed., 1911, ch. IV,
p. 164

24 A toom [empty] purse makes a bleat
[bashful] merchant.
James Kelly, *Scottish Proverbs*, 1721, A, no.
122

25 He is not a merchant bare,
That hath either money, worth, or ware.
James Kelly, *ibid.*, H, no. 346

26 Wealth depends on commerce.
John Law (1671–1729), *Money and Trade
Considered*, 1705

27 Commerce is virtually a mode of cheapening
production; and in all such cases the
consumer is the person ultimately benefited.
John Stuart Mill (1806–1873), *Principles of
Political Economy*, 1848, bk. III, ch. XVII, 4

28 The spirit of commerce unites nations.
**Charles de Secondat, Baron de
Montesquieu** (1689–1755), *The Spirit of the
Laws*, 1748, bk. XX, 2

29 Commerce is the agency whereby the power
of choice is obtained.
John Ruskin (1819–1900), *Munera
Pulveris*, 1862, IV

30 As in true commerce there is no 'profit', so
in true commerce there is no 'sale'.
John Ruskin (1819–1900), *ibid.*

31 The sail of commerce, in each sky aspires;
And property assures what toil acquires.
Richard Savage (*c.*1697–1743), *Of Public
Spirit*, 1736

32 Huge rocks, high winds, strong pirates,
                    shelves and sands,
The merchant fears, ere rich at home he
                    lands.
William Shakespeare (1564–1616), *The
Rape of Lucrece*, 1593–4, ll. 335–6

33 Faith, gentlemen, now I play a merchant's
part,
And venture madly on a desperate mart.
William Shakespeare (1564–1616), *The
Taming of the Shrew*, 1593–4, act II, sc. I

34 He's a man. I know him: his principles are
thoroughly commercial.
George Bernard Shaw (1856–1950), *Man
and Superman*, 1903, act IV

35 Commerce is undoubtedly a blessing, while
restrained within its proper channels; but a
glut of wealth brings along with it a glut of
evils: it brings false taste, false appetite, false
wants, profusion, venality, contempt of

order, engendering a spirit of licentiousness, insolence, and faction, that keeps the community in continual ferment, and in time destroys all the distinctions of civil society; so that universal anarchy and uproar must ensue.
Tobias Smollett (1721–1771), _The Expedition of Humphry Clinker_, 1771, vol. II

36 Saw the heavens fill with commerce,
        argosies of magic sails,
Pilots of the purple twilight, dropping down
        with costly bales.
Alfred, Lord Tennyson (1809–1892), _Locksley Hall_, 1842

37 Trade and commerce, if they were not made of india rubber, would never manage to bounce over the obstacles which legislators are continually putting in their way.
Henry D. Thoreau (1817–1862), _Resistance to Civil Government_, 1849

38 England a commercial country! Yes; as Venice was. She may excel other nations in commerce, but yet it is not that in which she most prides herself in which she most excels. Merchants as such are not the first men among us; though it perhaps be open to a merchant to become one of them. Buying and selling is good and necessary; it is very necessary, and may, possibly, be very good; but it cannot be the noblest work of man; and let us hope that it may not in our time be esteemed the noblest work of an Englishman.
Anthony Trollope (1815–1882), _Doctor Thorne_, 1858, ch. 1

39 I am a bad Englishman, because I think the advantages of commerce are dearly bought for some by the lives of many more.
Horace Walpole (1717–1797), letter to Horace Mann, 26 May 1762

40 The good merchant . . . you will find that commerce, in its facts and laws, seem in him embodied, and that his sagacity appears identical with the objects on which it is exercised.
Edwin P. Whipple (1819–1886), _Character and Characteristic Men_, 1866, ch. III

42 COMMITTEES
See also 24 BUREAUCRACY, 35 CHAIRMEN, 132 ORGANIZATION(S)

1 A camel is a creature which looks as though it has been designed by a committee.
Anonymous

2 A committee is something that keeps minutes but wastes hours.
Anonymous

3 All committees are cautious, and a committee of careful men of business, picked from a large city, will usually err on the side of caution if it err at all.
Walter Bagehot (1826–1877), _Lombard Street_, 1873, ch. 9

4 The English way is a committee — we are born with a belief in a green cloth, clean pens and twelve men with grey hair.
Walter Bagehot (1826–1877), attributed

5 Never let the other fellow set the agenda.
James Baker, _Observer_, 'Sayings of the Week', 20 November 1988

6 Committees are pretty much the same wherever you go.
Brian Close in Peter Walker, _Cricket Conversations_, 1978

7 A committee is a cul de sac down which ideas are lured and then quietly strangled.
Sir Barnett Cocks, _New Scientist_, 8 November 1973

8 We have committees of inquiry like other people have mice.
Bill Cotton (of BBC TV), _Sporting Life_, vol. 3, no. 111, 5 September 1985, p. 4

9 If you wish to avoid making a decision, either send a memo . . . or set up a committee to conduct an 'in-depth study'.
'Epson's Compleat Office Companion', _The Times_, 12 October 1987

10 What is a committee? A group of the unwilling, picked from the unfit, to do the unnecessary.
Richard Harkness, _New York Herald Tribune_, 15 June 1960

11 Next t' listenin' t' th' minutes of a pervious meetin' ther hain't nothin' as dull as a high brow concert.
Frank McKinney Hubbard (1868–1930), *New Sayings by Abe Martin*, 1917

12 Committee: A thing which takes a week to do what one good man can do in an hour.
Frank McKinney Hubbard (1868–1930), *The Roycroft Dictionary*, 1923

13 A committee is an animal with four back legs.
John le Carré, *Tinker, Tailor, Soldier, Spy*, 1974, ch. 34

14 There's three things you can predict in life: tax, death and more meetings.
Mike Moore, *Sydney Morning Herald*, 'Sayings of the Week' 14 September 1985

15 Living movements do not come from committees.
John Henry Newman (1801–1890) in Rudolf Flesch, *The Book of Unusual Quotations*, 1959

16 A committee should consist of three men, two of whom are absent.
Sir Herbert Beerbohm Tree (1853–1917), attributed

43 COMMUNISM
See also 184 SOCIALISM

1 If only Groucho had written *Das Kapital*.
Anonymous graffito, Montevideo, 1988

2 What is a communist? One who hath yearnings
For equal division of unequal earnings,
Idler or bungler, or both, he is willing,
To fork out his copper and pocket your shilling.
Ebenezer Elliot (1781–1849), 'Epigram'

3 A spectre is haunting Europe — the spectre of Communism.
Karl Marx (1818–1883) and **Friedrich Engels** (1820–1895), *The Communist Manifesto*, 1848, opening sentence

4 The conviction of the Communist that he represents the interests of the future of humanity can only be compared with the faith and zeal of a religious enthusiast.
Jawaharlal Nehru (1889–1964) in N.B. Sen, *Wit and Wisdom of India*, 1961

5 Communism is inequality, but not as property is. Property is the exploitation of the weak by the strong. Communism is the exploitation of the strong by the weak.
Pierre-Joseph Proudhon (1809–1865), *What is Property?*, 1840, ch. V, pt. II

6 Communism is the religion of poverty.
Pierre-Joseph Proudhon (1809–1865), attributed

7 Communism is the corruption of a dream of justice.
Adlai Stevenson (1900–1965), speech, 1951

44 COMMUTERS
See also 164 RAILWAYS

1 If God had meant us to travel in the rush hour, He would have made us much smaller.
Anonymous graffito on the London Underground, *Financial Times*, 21 February 1989

2 Watch the genus commuter rush for his Dope [newspaper] when he reaches the station in the morning.
Elbert Hubbard (1856–1915), *Notebook*, 1927, p. 81

45 COMPETENCE

1 And he was competent whose purse was so.
William Cowper (1731–1800), *The Task*, 1785, bk. II

2 There are some electricians I would not allow in the toilet, and some plumbers I would not let flush it, and there are some fitters who could not fit a sausage.
Eddie Lynton, *Observer*, 'Sayings of the Week', 13 June 1982

46 COMPETITION

1 Free competition is equivalent to a reward granted to those who furnish the best goods at the lowest price.
Jeremy Bentham (1748–1832), *Principles of Penal Law*, 1838, pt. 3, ch. 1

2   Economic competition is not war, but
    rivalry in mutual service.
    Edwin Cannan (1861–1935), *A Review of
    Economic Theory*, 1929, ch. IV, sec. 5

3   Free competition tends to give to labour
    what labour creates, to capitalists what
    capital creates, and to entrepreneurs what
    the coordinating function creates.
    John Bates Clark (1847–1938), *The
    Distribution of Wealth*, 1899, p. 3

4   Competition without moral restraints is a
    monster as completely antiquated as the
    saurians of which the geologists tell us.
    John Bates Clark (1847–1938), *The
    Philosophy of Wealth*, 1886, ch. IX, p. 151

5   By competition the total amount of the
    supply is increased, and by increase of the
    supply a competition in the sale ensues, and
    this enables the consumer to buy at lower
    rates. Of all human powers operating on the
    affairs of mankind, none is greater than that
    of competition.
    Henry Clay (1777–1852), speech in the US
    Senate, 2 February 1832

6   Every child of the Saxon race is educated to
    wish to be first. It is our system; and a man
    comes to measure his greatness by the
    regrets, envies and hatreds of his
    competitors.
    Ralph Waldo Emerson (1803–1882),
    Representative Men, 1850

7   Competition is the great teacher.
    Henry Ford (1863–1947) in S. Diamond,
    *The Reputation of the American
    Businessman*, 1955

8   UNFAIR COMPETITION: selling cheaper than
    someone else.
    Ralph Harris, 'Everyman's Guide to
    Contemporary Economic Jargon', *Growth,
    Advertising and the Consumer*, 1964, p. 24

9   Every man for himselfe and God for us all.
    John Heywood (1506–1565), *Proverbs*,
    1546, pt. II, ch. IX

10 Competition: 1. The struggle for a cake of
    ice in hell. 2. The life of trade, and the death
    of the trader.
    Frank McKinney Hubbard (1868–1930),
    The Roycroft Dictionary, 1923

11 Vulgarity of industrial competition.
    William Ralph Inge (1860–1954), *All
    Saints' Sermons*, 1907, p. 51

12 Hardnosed competition is the best
    assurance of a healthy business. It has done
    more to modernize our plants, more to train
    our people and improve our systems and
    broaden our product line than any other
    force on earth including pride, ambition and
    naked greed.
    Donald M. Kendall in Ray Wild, *How to
    Manage*, 1982, p. 215

13 The system of free competition is a rather
    peculiar one. Its mechanism is one of *fooling*
    entrepreneurs. It requires the pursuit of
    maximum profit in order to function, but it
    destroys profits when they are actually
    pursued by a larger number of people.
    Oskar Lange (1904–1965), *On the
    Economic Theory of Socialism*, 1938, p. 117

14 The work I have set before me is this —
    How to get rid of the evils of competition
    while retaining its advantages.
    Alfred Marshall (1842–1924), Farewell
    address, Bristol, 29 September 1881, A.C.
    Pigou, *Memorials of Alfred Marshall*, p. 16

15 I don't meet competition. I crush it.
    Charles Revson in Jim Fisk and Robert
    Barron, *Great Business Quotations*, 1985

16 Competition brings out the best in products
    and the worst in people.
    David Sarnoff (1891–1971) in J. Green, *A
    Dictionary of Contemporary Quotations*,
    1982

17 Competition . . . makes those who are
    destined to guide the mass subordinate
    themselves to it.
    Georg Simmel (1858–1918), *Conflict and
    the Web of Group-Affiliations*, trans. Wolff,
    1955, p. 61

18 Innumerable times, it [competition] achieves
    what usually only love can do; the
    divination of the innermost wishes of the
    other, even before he himself becomes aware
    of them.
    Georg Simmel (1858–1918), *ibid.*, p. 62

19 The natural price, or the price of free
    competition . . . is the lowest which can be
    taken, not upon every occasion indeed, but
    for any considerable time together . . . [It] is
    the lowest which the sellers can commonly
    afford to take, and at the same time
    continue their business.
    Adam Smith (1723–1790), *Wealth of
    Nations*, 1776, vol. I, bk. I, ch. VII

20 Other things being equal, old
well-established concerns tend to be more
hostile to price cutting than younger
concerns are.
G. Stocking and M. Watkins, *Monopoly
and Free Enterprise*, 1951, p. 117

21 The effects of the Industrial Revolution
prove that free competition may produce
wealth without producing well-being.
Arnold Toynbee (1852–1883), *Lectures on
the Industrial Revolution of the Eighteenth
Century in England*, 1884, ch. 8

22 While competition cannot be created by
statutory enactment, it can in large measure
be revived by changing the laws and
forbidding the practices that killed it, and by
enacting laws that will give it heart and
occasion again. We can arrest and prevent
monopoly.
Woodrow Wilson (1856–1924), Speech, 7
August 1912

23 I have never heard of circumstances in
which competition did not mean lower
prices.
Lord Young, *Independent*, 'Quote
Unquote', 25 March 1989

47 COMPUTERS
See also 198 TECHNOLOGY

1 The 'gigo' principle — garbage in garbage
out.
Anonymous

2 One computer manufacturer was so
successful he had to move to smaller
premises.
Anonymous

3 Software cannot replace greyware.
Anonymous

4 Software is the part of a computer system
which has no soul to be damned and no
body to be kicked. Hardware is the bit you
can kick.
Anonymous

5 The only important thing yet to be decided
is whether or not computers are only as
good as the information fed into them by
people, and whether or not the reverse is
also true.
John Clarke, *The Fred Dagg Scripts*, 1981,
'Computer War'

6 The crème de la crème of computerists will
form a kind of praetorian guard, to whose
whims the emperors of industry will lie as
vitally exposed as were some of the more
vulnerable Caesars of ancient Rome.
Robert Hayes, *Sydney Morning Herald*,
'Sayings of the Week', 15 May 1982

7 To err is human, but to really foul things up
requires a computer.
Philip Howard, *The Times*, 25 February
1987

8 Man is still the most extraordinary
computer of all.
John F. Kennedy (1917–1963), attributed

48 CONFERENCES

1 If you carry this resolution and follow out all
its implications and do not run away from it,
you will send a Foreign Secretary, whoever
he may be, naked into the conference
chamber.
Aneurin Bevan (1897–1960), speech to the
Labour Party Conference, 2 October 1957

2 Conference: A gathering where the
members can singly do nothing, but who
together decide that nothing can be done.
Sir David Davenport-Handley, in *Pass the
Port Again*, 1981, p. 48

49 CONGRESS
See also 92 GOVERNMENT, 133 PARLIAMENT,
142 POLITICS

1 Congress is simply bingo with billions.
Anonymous

2 How'd it do fer congress t' pass a law
requirin' dealers in th' necessities o' life t'
wait till ther wus really a crisis before
holdin' up th' consumer?
Frank McKinney Hubbard (1868–1930),
New Sayings by Abe Martin, 1917

3 If the present Congress errs in too much
talking, how can it be otherwise, in a body
to which the people send one hundred and
fifty lawyers, whose trade it is to question
everything, yield nothing and talk by the

hour? That one hundred and fifty lawyers should do business together, ought not to be expected.
Thomas Jefferson (1743–1826), *Autobiography*, 6 January 1821

4 With Congress, every time they make a joke it's a law, and every time they make a law it's a joke.
Will Rogers (1879–1935), attributed

5 It could probably be shown by facts and figures that there is no distinctly native American criminal class except Congress.
Mark Twain (1835–1910), *Following the Equator*, 1897, vol. I, 'Pudd'nhead Wilson's New Calendar', ch. 8

---

50 CONSUMERS
See also 59 CUSTOMERS

---

1 Th' consumers are full o' grievances, but ther'll be no strike.
Frank McKinney Hubbard (1868–1930), *New Sayings by Abe Martin*, 1917

2 The Concept of Consumers' Sovereignty.
W.H. Hutt, title of article, *Economic Journal*, March 1940

3 The consumer is not a moron. She is your wife.
David Ogilvy in James Beasley Simpson, *Best Quotes of '54, '55, '56*, 1957

4 The consumer, so it is said, is the king . . . each is a voter who uses his money as votes to get the thing done that he wants done.
Paul A. Samuelson, *Economics*, 8th ed., p. 55

5 When there is a real scarcity, it is in the interest of the great body of consumers that the price of corn should be raised sufficiently high, to cause such a degree of economy in consumption as may enable the supply to last throughout the year.
Robert Torrens (1780–1864), *An Essay on the External Corn Trade*, 4th ed., 1827, ch. 1, p. 7

---

51 CONSUMPTION

---

1 Consumption . . . is synonymous with use; and is, in fact, the great end and object of industry.
J.R. McCulloch (1789–1864), *Principles of Political Economy*, new ed., pt. IV, p. 523

2 Consumption never needs encouragement.
John Stuart Mill (1806–1873), *Essays on Some Unsettled Questions of Political Economy*, 1844, p. 48

3 If men ceased to consume, they would cease to produce.
David Ricardo (1772–1823), *Principles of Political Economy and Taxation*, 1821, ch. XXI

4 Consumption is the sole end and purpose of all production; and the interest of the producer ought to be attended to, only so far as it may be necessary for promoting that of the consumer.
Adam Smith (1723–1790), *Wealth of Nations*, 1776, vol, II, bk. IV, ch. VIII

5 Conspicuous consumption of valuable goods is a means of reputability to the gentleman of leisure.
Thorstein Veblen (1857–1929), *The Theory of the Leisure Class*, 1899, ch. IV

6 With the exception of the instinct of self-preservation, the propensity for emulation is probably the strongest and most alert and persistent of the economic motives proper.
Thorstein Veblen (1857–1929), *ibid.*, ch. V

---

52 CONTRACTS

---

1 A verbal contract isn't worth the paper it's written on.
Samuel Goldwyn (1882–1974), attributed

2 A contract is a mutual promise.
William Paley (1743–1805), *The Principles of Moral and Political Philosophy*, 1784, bk. III, pt. I, ch. VI

3 Contract: an agreement that is binding on
   the weaker party.
   Frederick Sawyer in Fred Metcalf, *The
   Penguin Dictionary of Modern Humorous
   Quotations*, 1986

4 Men keep their agreements when it is an
   advantage to both parties not to break them.
   Solon (*c.*630–*c.*555 BC) in Plutarch, *Lives:
   Solon*

53 CORPORATIONS

1 We have much to fear from great
   corporated, moneyed institutions. We are
   today more in danger from organised money
   than ever we were from slavery.
   Henry Ward Beecher (1813–1887),
   Proverbs from Plymouth Pulpit, 1887

2 Corporation, *n*. An ingenious device for
   obtaining individual profit without
   individual responsibility.
   Ambrose Bierce (1842–1914?), *The Devil's
   Dictionary*, 1911

3 [Corporations] cannot commit treason, nor
   be outlawed, nor excommunicate, for they
   have no souls.
   Sir Edward Coke (1552–1634), *Case of
   Sutton's Hospital*, 1612

4 A corporation aggregate of many is
   invisible, immortal, and rests only in
   intendment and consideration of the law.
   Sir Edward Coke (1552–1634), *ibid.*

5 There is the veil of corporate personality
   which protects the individual from any
   personal liability at all. That is the
   fundamental principle of our company law.
   Lord Denning, House of Lords, 15 January
   1985

6 To supervise wisely the great corporations is
   well; but to look backward to the days when
   business was polite pillage and regard our
   great business concerns as piratical
   institutions carrying letters of marque and
   reprisal is a grave error born in the minds of
   little men. When these little men legislate
   they set the brakes going uphill.
   Elbert Hubbard (1856–1915), *Notebook*,
   1927, p. 16

7 The employees and the managers of the
   modern corporation, in their sprawling
   factories and towering office blocks, have
   been formed into what they are, not by three
   hundred generations down on the farm, but
   by half a million generations in the hunting
   band.
   Antony Jay, *Corporation Man*, 1972, ch. 3

8 The great modern corporations are so
   similar to independent or semi-independent
   states of the past that they can only be fully
   understood in terms of political and
   constitutional history, and management can
   only be properly studied as a branch of
   government.
   Antony Jay, *Management and Machiavelli*,
   1967, ch. 1

9 They [corporations] were invisible,
   immortall, and . . . had no soule; and
   therefore no subpoena lieth against them,
   because they have no conscience nor soule;
   a corporation, is a body aggregate, none can
   create soules but God, but the King creates
   them, and therefore they have no soules.
   Chief Baron Manwood (1525–1592),
   Tipling v. *Pexall*, attributed 1614

10 The functioning of the corporate system has
   not to date been adequately explained . . .
   The man of action may be content with a
   system that works. But one who reflects on
   the properties or characteristics of this
   system cannot help asking why it works and
   whether it will continue to work.
   E.S. Mason, *The Corporation in Modern
   Society*, 1960, p. 2

11 The biggest corporation, like the humblest
   private citizen, must be held to strict
   compliance with the will of the people.
   Theodore Roosevelt (1858–1919), speech,
   1902

12 It is truly enough said, that a corporation
   has no conscience; but a corporation of
   conscientious men is a corporation *with* a
   conscience.
   Henry D. Thoreau (1817–1862),
   Resistance to Civil Government, 1849

13 Did you ever expect a corporation to have a
   conscience, when it has no soul to be
   damned and no body to be kicked.
   Lord Thurlow (1731–1806), attributed

14 A corporation cannot blush.
   Howel Walsh (*fl.*1820), attributed

54 CORRUPTION
See also 85 FRAUD

1 Corruption is simply business without
scruples.
Anonymous

2 Nepotism is only kin deep.
Anonymous

3 There is no one act, in which tyranny,
malice, cruelty, and oppression can be
charged, that does not at the same time
carry evident marks of pecuniary corruption.
Edmund Burke (1729–1797), *Impeachment
of Warren Hastings*, 17 February 1788

4 What makes all doctrines plain and clear? —
About two hundred pounds a year.
And that which was prov'd true before,
Prove false again? — Two hundred more.
Samuel Butler (1612–1680), *Hudibras*,
1663, part III, canto I, l. 1277

5 Corruption is like a ball of snow, when once
set a rolling it must increase.
C.C. Colton (1780–1832), *Lacon*, 1820,
vol. VI

6 An open hand makes a blind eye.
Francis Quarles (1592–1644), *Enchyridion*,
1641, Third Century, LXV

7 Corruption wins not more than honesty.
William Shakespeare (1564–1616), *Henry
VIII*, 1612–13, act III, sc. II

8 When I want to buy up any politician I
always find the anti-monopolists the most
purchasable — they don't come so high.
William Vanderbilt (1821–1885),
attributed

55 COSMETICS

1 The cosmetics business is the nastiest
business in the world.
Elizabeth Arden (1884–1966), *The Times*,
12 January 1988

2 Deuce take the man who first invented
perfumes, say I.
Aristophanes (*c.*448–*c.*388 BC), *Lysistrata*,
411 BC

3 Most women are not as young as they are
painted.
Sir Max Beerbohm (1872–1956), *A
Defence of Cosmetics*, 1922

4 In the factory we make cosmetics. In the
store we sell hope.
Charles Revson (1906–1975), attributed

5 There are no ugly women, only lazy ones.
Helena Rubenstein, attributed

56 COSTS

1 For which of you, intending to build a
tower, sitteth not down first, and counteth
the cost, whether he have sufficient to finish
it?
Bible, Authorized Version, Luke 14:28

2 Cost means sacrifice, and cannot, without
risk of hopelessly confusing ideas, be
identified with anything that is not sacrifice.
J.E. Cairnes (1824–1875), *Some Leading
Principles of Political Economy*, 1874, pt. I,
ch. III

3 If cost accounting sets out, determined to
discover what the cost of everything is and
convinced in advance that there is one figure
which can be found and which will furnish
exactly the information which is desired for
every possible purpose, it will necessarily
fail, because there is no such figure. If it
finds a figure which is right for some
purposes it must necessarily be wrong for
others.
J. Maurice Clark (1884–1963), *Studies in
the Economics of Overhead Costs*, 1923,
p. 14

4 If the choice lies between the production or
purchase of two commodities, the value of
one is measured by the sacrifice of going
without the other.
H.J. Davenport (1862–1931), 'The
Formula of Sacrifice', *Journal of Political
Economy*. 1893–4, pp. 567–8

5 If any producer can continually increase his
supply at a constant or diminished cost,
there appears no general reason why he
should not, by cutting out his competitors,
supply the entire market.
F.Y. Edgeworth (1845–1926), *Papers
Relating to Political Economy*, 1925, vol. II,
p. 87

6 As soon as we look more closely upon our varied resources and the individual activities of economic life we discover that many of our good opportunities are limited in number and extent, so that before devoting the opportunity to a particular activity it behooves us to consider from what other uses we are thus withholding it. Such consideration gives rise to the conception of opportunity cost.
D.I. Green, 'Pain-Cost and Opportunity-Cost', *Quarterly Journal of Economics*, 1893–4, p. 228

7 Costs merely register competing attractions.
Frank H. Knight (1885–1972), *Risk Uncertainty and Profit*, 1921, p. 159

8 The conception of costs in modern economic theory is a conception of displaced alternatives: the cost of obtaining anything is what must be surrendered in order to get it.
Lionel Robbins (1898–1984), 'Certain Aspects of the Theory of Costs', *The Economic Journal*, March 1934

9 We first survey the plot, then draw the model;
And when we see the figure of the house,
Then we must rate the cost of the erection;
Which, if we find outweighs ability,
What do we then but draw anew the model.
William Shakespeare (1564–1616), *Henry IV, Pt. II*, 1597–8, act I, sc. III

10 The fashion of the world is to avoid cost, and you encounter it.
William Shakespeare (1564–1616), *Much Ado About Nothing*, 1598–9, act I, sc. I

11 Spare not for cost.
William Shakespeare (1564–1616), *Romeo and Juliet*, 1595–6, act IV, sc. IV

12 Cost [is] of two kinds, either (1) the endurance of pain, discomfort, or something else undesirable, or (2) the sacrifice of something desirable, either as an end or a means.
Henry Sidgwick (1838–1900), *Principles of Political Economy*, 3rd ed., 1901, bk. III, ch. 1

13 Cost of production . . . in the sense of the historical and irrevocable fact that resources have been devoted to this or that special purpose, has no influence on the value of the thing produced, and therefore does not affect its price.
Philip H. Wicksteed (1844–1927), *The Common Sense of Political Economy*, 1910, vol. I, bk. I, ch. IX

14 To say that any kind of production involves cost simply implies that the economic means of production, which could doubtlessly have been usefully employed in other directions, are either used up in it, or are suspended during it.
Friedrich von Wieser (1851–1926), *Natural Value*, 1889

---

57 CREDIT
See also 20 BORROWING, 58 CREDITORS, 61 DEBT

---

1 Credit, like a looking glass,
Broken once, is gone, alas!
Anonymous

2 Credit in business is like loyalty in Government. You must take what you can find of it, and work with it if possible.
Walter Bagehot (1826–1877), *Lombard Street*, 1873, ch. 2

3 Credit — the disposition of one man to trust another — is singularly varying. In England, after a great calamity, everybody is suspicious of everybody; as soon as that calamity is forgotten, everybody again confides in everybody.
Walter Bagehot (1826–1877), *ibid.*, ch. 6

4 Credit demands the solid rock of integrity. It will not stand upon the shifting sands of custom.
Henry Ward Beecher (1813–1887), *Proverbs from Plymouth Pulpit*, 1887

5 The whole world is carried on on the credit system; if everyone were to demand payment in hard cash, there would be universal bankruptcy. We think as we do mainly because other people think so.
Samuel Butler (1835–1902), *Note Books*, ed. Festing Jones, 1912, ch. XX

6 Of all things that have existence only in the minds of men, nothing is more fantastical and nice than credit; it is never to be forced; it hangs upon opinion; it depends upon our passions of hope and fear; it comes many

times unsought for, and often goes away without reason; and when once lost, is hardly to be quite recovered.
Charles D'Avenant (1656–1714), *Discourses on the Public Revenues and on the Trade of England*, 1698, in *Works*, ed. Whitworth, vol. I, p. 151

7 He that takes too much credit is really in as much danger, as he that gives too much credit.
Daniel Defoe (*c.*1660–1731), *The Complete English Tradesman*, 2nd ed., 1727, vol. I, letter V

8 A tradesman's credit, and a maid's virtue, ought to be equally sacred from the tongues of men; and 'tis a very unhappy truth, that as times now go, they are neither of them regarded among us as they ought to be.
Daniel Defoe (*c.*1660–1731), *ibid.*, letter XV

9 Credit is so much a tradesman's blessing, that 'tis the choicest ware he deals in, and he cannot be too chary of it when he has it, or buy it too dear when he wants it.
Daniel Defoe (*c.*1660–1731), *ibid.*

10 Credit is or ought to be the tradesman's mistress; but I must tell him too, he must not think of ever casting her off; for if once he loses her, she hardly ever returns.
Daniel Defoe (*c.*1660–1731), *ibid.*, letter XXIV

11 As credit is a coy mistress, and will not easily be courted, so she is a mighty nice touchy lady, and is soon affronted; if she is ill used she flies at once, and 'tis a very doubtful thing whether ever you gain her favour again.
Daniel Defoe (*c.*1660–1731), *ibid.*

12 Credit makes war, and makes peace; raises armies, fits out navies, fights battles, beseiges towns; and in a word, it is more justly call'd the sinews of war, than the money itself.
Daniel Defoe (*c.*1660–1731), *ibid.*

13 They that have credit can never want money.
Daniel Defoe (*c.*1660–1731), *ibid.*

14 As a good name is to another man, and which the Wiseman says, *is better than life*, the same is credit to a Tradesman; it is the life of his trade; and he that wounds a Tradesman's credit, without cause, is as much a murtherer in trade, as he that kills a man in the dark is a murtherer in matters of blood.
Daniel Defoe (*c.*1660–1731), *ibid.*

15 He that buys for credit, and sells for ready money, or very small credit, is always safe.
Daniel Defoe (*c.*1660–1731), *ibid.*, Supplement, ch. I

16 Ah, take the cash and let the credit go.
Edward FitzGerald (1809–1883), *The Rubáiyát of Omar Khayyám*, 1859, st. 13

17 Credit lost is a *Venice*-glass broken which cannot be soder'd.
Thomas Fuller (1654–1734), *Gnomologia*, 1732, no. 1203

18 He that has lost his credit, is dead to the world.
Thomas Fuller (1654–1734), *ibid.*, no. 2142

19 More credit may be thrown down in a moment, than can be built in an age.
Thomas Fuller (1654–1734), *ibid.*, no. 3452

20 No man's credit is as good as his money.
E.W. Howe (1853–1937), *Sinner Sermons*, 1926

21 Who tells a lie to save his credit wipes his nose on his sleeve to save his napkin.
James Howell (1594?–1666), *Proverbs*, 1659

22 Credit: The life blood of commerce.
Frank McKinney Hubbard (1868–1930), *The Roycroft Dictionary*, 1923

23 A credit card is an anaesthetic which simply delays the pain, and pain, after all, serves a function.
Helen Mason, *Sunday Times*, 29 March 1987

24 Lack of credit is worse than lack of money. 'The loss of money is not deadly,' says the proverb. Money can be replaced. But what can replace credit and honour?
Joseph Roux (1834–1905), *Meditations of a Parish Priest*, trans. Hopgood, 1886, ch. VI, XVIII

25 You must hold the credit of your father.
William Shakespeare (1564–1616), *All's Well That Ends Well*, 1602–4, act I, sc. I

26 You wrong me more, sir, in denying it:
Consider how it stands upon my credit.
William Shakespeare (1564–1616), *The Comedy of Errors*, 1592–3, act IV, sc. I

27 So far as my coin would stretch; and where
it would not, I have used my credit.
William Shakespeare (1564–1616), *Henry IV, Pt. I*, 1597–8, act I, sc. I

28 Try what my credit can in Venice do.
William Shakespeare (1564–1616), *The Merchant of Venice*, 1596–7, act I, sc. I

29 Kept his credit with his purse.
William Shakespeare (1564–1616), *Timon of Athens*, 1607–8, act III, sc. II

30 Take care you don't hurt your credit by
offering too much security.
Richard Brinsley Sheridan (1751–1816), *The Rivals*, 1775, act II

31 To hear some of these worthy reasoners
talking of credit; that she is so nice, so
squeamish, so capricious; you would think
they were describing a lady troubled with
vapours or the cholick.
Jonathan Swift (1667–1745), *The Examiner*, no. 37, 19 April 1711

32 Commercial credit may be defined to be that
confidence which subsists among
commercial men in respect to their
mercantile affairs.
Henry Thornton (1760–1815), *An Enquiry into the Nature and Effects of the Paper Credit of Great Britain*, 1802, ch. I, p. 13

33 Beautiful credit! The foundation of modern
society.
Mark Twain (1835–1910) **and Charles Dudley Warner** (1820–1900), *The Gilded Age*, 1873, ch. 26

34 In business one way to obtain credit is to
create the impression that one already has it.
Miguel Unamuno (1864–1937), *Perplexities and Paradoxes*, 'Civilization is Civism', trans. S. Gross, 1945

58 CREDITORS
See also 20 BORROWING, 57 CREDIT, 61 DEBT

1 Creditors have no real affection for their
debtors, but only a desire that they may be
preserved that they may repay.
Aristotle (384–322 BC), *Nicomachean Ethics*, bk. IX, ch. 7

2 It takes a *man* to make a devil; and the
fittest man for such a purpose is a snarling,
waspish, red-hot creditor.
Henry Ward Beecher (1813–1887), *Proverbs from Plymouth Pulpit*, 1887

3 Creditor, *n*. One of a tribe of savages
dwelling beyond the Financial Straits and
dreaded for their desolating incursions.
Ambrose Bierce (1842–1914?), *The Devil's Dictionary*, 1911

4 Creditors have better memories than
debtors.
James Howell (1594?–1666), *Proverbs*, 1659

5 Not everyone is a debtor who wishes to be;
not everyone who wishes becomes creditors.
François Rabelais (1494?–1553), *Pantagruel*, 1532, bk. III, ch. III

6 I break, and you, my gentle creditors, lose.
William Shakespeare (1564–1616), *Henry IV, Pt. II*, 1597–8, epilogue

7 These griefs and losses have so 'bated me
That I shall hardly spare a pound of flesh
To-morrow to my bloody creditor.
William Shakespeare (1564–1616), *The Merchant of Venice*, 1596–7, act III, sc. III

8 Creditors! — devils.
William Shakespeare (1564–1616), *Timon of Athens*, 1607–8, act III, sc. IV

9 It's a big temptation to build up stocks,
debtors, and other assets, simply by putting
off the day when you have to pay your
creditors. The trouble is that if the creditors
get tough before you can sell your stocks
and collect the cash from your debtors, the
bailiffs are in with a sheet of inventory paper
and your name at the top. And a lot of wide
boys are buying your furniture at bargain
prices.
Clark Smith, *The Deadly Reaper*, 1956, ch. 9

59 CUSTOMERS
See also 50 CONSUMERS

1 The customer is always right.
Harry Gordon Selfridge (1857–1947), attributed

2 *Passenger*: You're one of the stupidest people I've met.
Swissair employee: And you're one of the nicest gentlemen I've ever come across. But perhaps we're both wrong.
Swissair ('ideal response to a neurotic passenger'), *Sunday Times*, 21 October 1984

60 CUSTOMS

1 Customs represent the experience of mankind; and in commerce, equity, fidelity, and integrity are simply customs. Experience is the mother of custom.
Henry Ward Beecher (1813–1887), *Proverbs from Plymouth Pulpit*, 1887

2 I very much doubt the propriety as a general principle, of legalizing customs. The moment you legalize a custom you fix its particular character; but the value of a custom is its flexibility, and that it adapts itself to all the circumstances of the moment and of the locality. All these qualities are lost the moment you crystallize a custom into legislation. Customs may not be as wise as laws, but they are always more popular.
Benjamin Disraeli (1804–1881), House of Commons, 11 March 1870

61 DEBT

See also 20 BORROWING, 57 CREDIT,
58 CREDITORS

1 Debt rolls a man over and over, binding him hand and foot, and letting him hang upon the fatal mesh until the long-legged interest devours him.
Henry Ward Beecher (1813–1887), *Proverbs from Plymouth Pulpit*, 1887

2 Debt is an inexhaustible fountain of dishonesty.
Henry Ward Beecher (1813–1887), *ibid.*

3 Debt, *n.* An ingenious substitute for the chain and whip of the slave-driver.
Ambrose Bierce (1842–1914?), *The Devil's Dictionary*, 1911

4 If I had the privilege of making the Eleventh Commandment it would be this — *Owe no man.*
Josh Billings (1818–1885) in Rudolf Flesch, *The Book of Unusual Quotations*, 1959

5 He'd run in debt by disputation,
And pay with ratiocination.
Samuel Butler (1612–1680), *Hudibras*, part I, 1663, canto I, l. 77

6 Late payment is catching.
John Cope, *Independent*, 21 July 1988

7 Debt is the prolific mother of folly and of crime.
Benjamin Disraeli (1804–1881), *Henrietta Temple*, 1837, bk. II, ch. I

8 One man thinks justice consists in paying debts, and has no measure in his abhorrence of another who is very remiss in this duty, and makes the creditor wait tediously.
Ralph Waldo Emerson (1803–1882), *Essays*, First Series, 1841, 'Circles'

9 A man in debt is so far a slave.
Ralph Waldo Emerson (1803–1882) in Rudolf Flesch, *The Book of Unusual Quotations*, 1959

10 A little debt makes a debtor, but a great one an enemy.
Thomas Fuller (1654–1734), *Gnomologia*, 1732, no. 245

11 A poor man's debt makes a great noise.
Thomas Fuller (1654–1734), *ibid.*, no. 355

12 Confess debt and beg days.
Thomas Fuller (1654–1734), *ibid.*, no. 1139

13 Debt is an evil conscience.
Thomas Fuller (1654–1734), *ibid.*, no. 1257

14 Debt is the worst poverty.
Thomas Fuller (1654–1734), *ibid.*, no. 1258

15 He who oweth, is in all the wrong.
Thomas Fuller (1654–1734), *ibid.*, no. 2398

16 It is better to pay, and have but little left; than to have much, and be always in debt.
Thomas Fuller (1654–1734), *ibid.*, no. 2918

17 One had better forgive a debt, where he cannot recover so much as his charges.
Thomas Fuller (1654–1734), *ibid.*, no. 3756

18 Out of debt, out of danger.
Thomas Fuller (1654–1734), *ibid.*, no. 3832

19 Sins and debts are always more than we think them to be.
Thomas Fuller (1654–1734), *ibid.*, no. 4179

20 Don Pedro's out of debt, be bold to say it For they are said to owe, that mean to pay it.
Sir John Harington (1560–1612), *Epigrams*, 1618, no. 64

21 A hundred load of thought will not pay one of debts.
George Herbert (1593–1633), *Jacula Prudentum*, 1651

22 Debtors are liars.
George Herbert (1593–1633), *ibid.*

23 He that gets out of debt grows rich.
George Herbert (1593–1633), *ibid.*

24 Speak not of my debts, unless you mean to pay them.
George Herbert (1593–1633), *ibid.*

25 Debt: 1. A rope to your foot, cockleburs in your hair, and a clothespin on your tongue. 2. The devil in disguise.
Frank McKinney Hubbard (1868–1930), *The Roycroft Dictionary*, 1923

26 Small debts are like small shot; they are rattling on every side, and can scarcely be escaped without a wound: great debts are like cannon; of loud noise, but little danger.
Samuel Johnson (1709–1784), letter to Joseph Simpson, 1759

27 He begs of them that borrowed of him.
James Kelly, *Scottish Proverbs*, 1721, H, no. 330

28 Out of debt out of danger.
James Kelly, *ibid.*, O, no. 13

29 Oft times the cautioner [surety] pays the debt.
James Kelly, *ibid.*, no. 39

30 It is unanimously and without qualification assumed that when anyone gets into debt, the fault is entirely and always that of the lender, and not the borrower.
Bernard Levin, *The Times*, 29 December 1986

31 Insolvency is not a very thrilling or amusing subject.
Lord Mishcon, House of Lords, 15 January 1985

32 He is my prisoner: if I let him go, The debt he owes will be requir'd of me.
William Shakespeare (1564–1616), *The Comedy of Errors*, 1592–3, act IV, sc. IV

33 Knowing how the debt grows, I will pay it.
William Shakespeare (1564–1616), *ibid.*

34 He that dies pays all debts.
William Shakespeare (1564–1616), *The Tempest*, 1611, act III, sc. II

35 To contract new debts is not the way to pay old ones.
George Washington (1732–1799), letter to James Welch, 7 April 1799

36 In Debtors' Yard the stones are hard, And the dripping wall is high.
Oscar Wilde (1854–1900), *The Ballad of Reading Gaol*, 1898, III

---

62 DIPLOMACY

---

1 Diplomacy, *n.* The patriotic art of lying for one's country.
Ambrose Bierce (1842–1914?), *The Devil's Dictionary*, 1911

2 The reason for having diplomatic relations is not to confer a compliment — but to secure a convenience.
Sir Winston Churchill (1874–1965), House of Commons, 17 November 1949

3 Diplomacy is the art of letting someone else have your way.
David Frost in Fred Metcalf, *The Penguin Dictionary of Humorous Quotations*, 1986

4 Diplomacy is to do and say the nastiest things in the nicest way.
Isaac Goldberg in James Beasley Simpson, *Best Quotes of '54, '55, '56*, 1957

5 Diplomacy: lying in state.
Oliver Herford (1863–1935), attributed

63 DIVISION OF LABOUR
See also 108 LABOUR

1 The gain which is made by manufacturers, will be greater, as the manufacture it self is greater and better. For in so vast a city manufactures will beget one another, and each manufacture will be divided into as many parts as possible, whereby the work of each artisan will be simple and easie; as for example, in the making of a watch, if one man shall make the wheels, another the spring, another shall engrave the dial-plate, and another shall make the cases, then the watch will be better and cheaper, than if the whole work be put upon any one man.
Sir William Petty (1623–1687), 'Another Essay in Political Arithmetick, Concerning the Growth of the City of London', 1682, in *The Economic Writings of Sir William Petty*, ed. Hull, vol. II, p. 473

2 More things will be produced and the work be more easily and better done, when every man is set free from all other occupations to do, at the right time, the one thing for which he is naturally fitted.
Plato (*c.*428–347 BC), *Republic*, bk. II, ch. VI

3 Communion or community of labour would be a better term than division of labour.
J.K. Rodbertus (1805–1875), attributed

4 The greatest improvement in the productive powers of labour, and the greater part of the skill, dexterity and judgement with which it is any where directed, or applied, seem to have been the effects of the division of labour.
Adam Smith (1723–1790), *Wealth of Nations*, 1776, vol. I, bk. I, ch. I

64 DRINK
See also 75 ENTERTAINMENT

1 Alcohol is a good liquid for preserving almost everything except a secret.
Anonymous

2 An alcoholic is someone who drinks and who you don't like.
Anonymous

3 Bacchus drowned more than Neptune ever did.
Anonymous

4 A hangover is the wrath of grapes.
Anonymous

5 A heavy drinker is someone who drinks more than his doctor does.
Anonymous

6 When successful brewers join the aristocracy they become part of the Beerage.
Anonymous

7 I wonder often what the Vintners buy
One half so precious as the stuff they sell.
Edward FitzGerald (1809–1883), *The Rubáiyát of Omar Khayyám*, 4th ed., 1879, st. 95

8 Come landlord fill a flowing bowl until it does run over.
Tonight we will all merry be — tomorrow we'll get sober.
John Fletcher (1759–1625), *The Bloody Brother*, 1639, act II, sc. 2

9 Nothing but ruin stares a nation in the face that is prey to the drink habit.
Mahatma Gandhi (1869–1948) in N.B. Sen, *Wit and Wisdom of India*, 1961

10 To let the world wagge, and take mine ease in mine Inne.
John Heywood (1506–1565), *Proverbs*, 1546, pt. I, ch. V

11 I pray thee let me and my fellow have
A haire of the dog that bit us last night.
John Heywood (1506–1565), *ibid.*, ch. XI

12 Saloon: The poor man's club run with intent to make the poor man poorer.
Frank McKinney Hubbard (1868–1930), *The Roycroft Dictionary*, 1923

13 Wine: an infallible antidote to commonsense and seriousness.
Frank McKinney Hubbard (1868–1930), *ibid.*

14 A man could be drowned by it [claret] before it made him drunk.
Samuel Johnson (1709–1784) in Boswell's *Life of Johnson*, 7 April 1779

15 Claret is the liquor for boys, port, for men; but he who aspires to be a hero must drink brandy.
Samuel Johnson (1709–1784), *ibid.*

16 Lord Lucan tells a very good story, which, if
not precisely exact, is certainly
characteristical: that when the sale of
Thrale's brewery was going forward,
Johnson appeared bustling about, with an
ink-horn and pen in his button-hole, like an
excise man; and on being asked what he
really considered to be the value of the
property which was to be disposed of,
answered, 'We are not here to sell a parcel of
boilers and vats, but the potentiality of
growing rich beyond the dreams of avarice.'
Samuel Johnson (1709–1784), *ibid.*, 4 April
1781

17 Ale sellers should not be tale tellers.
James Kelly, *Scottish Proverbs*, 1721, A,
no. 191

18 Eat well is drink well's brother.
James Kelly, *ibid.*, E, no. 25

19 He that buys land, buys stones;
He that buys beef, buys bones;
He that buys nuts, buys shells;
He that buys good ale, buys nowt else.
James Kelly, *ibid.*, H, no. 356

20 I never lik'd a dry bargain.
James Kelly, *ibid.*, I, no. 190

21 What you do when you're drunk, you must
pay for when you are dry.
James Kelly, *ibid.*, W, no. 40

22 If ever I marry a wife,
    I'll marry a landlord's daughter,
For then I may sit in the bar,
    And drink cold brandy and water.
Charles Lamb (1775–1834), attributed

23 If all the tears and misery that are caused by
alcohol could be rained down on this earth,
I am sure that the whole of mankind would
drown in the deluge.
Justice Lee, *Sydney Morning Herald*,
'Sayings of the Week', 5 April 1986

24 A good drink makes the old young.
Proverb

25 Drink wine, and have the gout; drink no
wine, and have the gout too.
Proverb, 17th century

26 He that drinks not wine after salad is in
danger of being sick.
Proverb, 17th century

27 Shall I not take mine ease in mine inn, but I
shall have my pocket picked?
William Shakespeare (1564–1616), *Henry
IV, Pt. I*, 1597–8, act III, sc. III

28 I will see what physic the tavern affords.
William Shakespeare (1564–1616), *Henry
VI, Pt. I*, 1589–90, act III, sc. I

29 A tapster is a good trade: an old cloak
makes a new jerkin; a withered servingman
a fresh tapster.
William Shakespeare (1564–1616), *The
Merry Wives of Windsor*, 1597–1601, act. I,
sc. III

30 In England, where, indeed, they are most
potent in potting: your Dane, your German,
and your swag-bellied Hollander, — Drink,
ho! — are nothing to your English.
William Shakespeare (1564–1616),
Othello, 1604–5, act II, sc. III

31 O God, that men should put an enemy in
their mouths to steal away their brains! that
we should with joy, pleasance, revel, and
applause, transform ourselves into beasts!
William Shakespeare (1564–1616), *ibid.*

32 Uniting the business of the wine merchant
and banker, you could manage a capital
business: since for those who took your
draughts overnight you could reciprocate by
honouring their *drafts*, in the morning.
Richard Brinsley Sheridan (1751–1816) in
W. Jerrold, *Bon-Mots of Sydney Smith and
R. Brinsley Sheridan*, p. 126

33 If the thought is slow to come, a glass of
good wine encourages it, and, when it *does*
come, a glass of good wine rewards it.
Richard Brinsley Sheridan (1751–1816),
ibid., p. 147

34 Alcohol taken once has to be taken again to
drown the regret.
Rabindranath Tagore (1861–1941) in N.B.
Sen, *Wit and Wisdom of India*, 1961

35 If the hangover came the night before and
the elation the morning after, brewers would
be out of business. The principle that a lesser
but early benefit will offset a substantial but
postponed liability is one which rules
human life; indeed it is the principle on
which the human race reproduces itself.
The Times, 13 September 1977

36 Water, taken in moderation, cannot hurt anybody.
Mark Twain (1835–1910) in Rudolf Flesch, *The Book of Unusual Quotations*, 1959

37 Work is the curse of the drinking classes.
Oscar Wilde (1856–1900), attributed

65 ECONOMICS
See also 66 ECONOMISTS

1 The science of Political Economy as we have it in England may be defined as the science of business, such as business is in large productive and trading communities.
Walter Bagehot (1826–1877), *Economic Studies*, ed. Hutton, 1880, I, p. 6

2 [Economics is] the study of the general methods by which men co-operate to meet their material needs.
Sir William Beveridge (1879–1963), 'Economics as a Liberal Education', *Economica*, January 1921, p. 2

3 Of Empty Economic Boxes.
J.H. Clapham (1873–1946), Title of article, *Economic Journal*, September 1922

4 If a religion cuts at the very fundamentals of economics it is not a true religion but only a delusion.
Mahatma Gandhi (1869–1948) in N.B. Sen, *Wit and Wisdom of India*, 1961

5 Economics: The science of the production, distribution and use of wealth, best understood by college professors on half-rations.
Frank McKinney Hubbard (1868–1930), *The Roycroft Dictionary*, 1923

6 Good economics is good politics.
Paul Keating, *Sydney Morning Herald*, 'Sayings of the Week', 27 August 1988

7 The theory of economics does not furnish a body of settled conclusions immediately applicable to policy. It is a method rather than a doctrine, an apparatus of the mind, a technique for thinking, which helps its possessor draw correct conclusions.
John Maynard Keynes (1883–1946), introduction to the Cambridge Economic Handbooks series

8 Economics is a study of mankind in the ordinary business of life.
Alfred Marshall (1842–1924), *Principles of Economics*, 8th ed., bk. I, ch. I, 1, p. 1

9 Though a simple book can be written on selected topics, the central doctrines of Economics are not simple and cannot be made so.
Alfred Marshall (1842–1924) in A.C. Pigou, *Memorials of Alfred Marshall*, p. 38

10 My favourite *dictum* is: Every statement in regard to economic affairs which is short is a misleading fragment, a fallacy or a truism. I think this dictum of mine is an exception to the general rule: but I am not bold enough to say that it *certainly* is.
Alfred Marshall (1842–1924), letter to L. Fry, 7 November 1914, *ibid.*, p. 484

11 In the domain of Political Economy, free scientific inquiry meets not merely the same enemies as in all other domains. The peculiar nature of the material it deals with, summons as foes into the field of battle the most violent, mean and malignant passions of the human breast, the Furies of private interest.
Karl Marx (1818–1883), *Das Kapital*, preface to the first German edition, 25 July 1867

12 The main motive of economic study is to help social improvement.
A.C. Pigou (1877–1959), *Economics of Welfare*, 4th ed., 1932, p. ix

13 Economics is a science which studies human behaviour as a relationship between ends and scarce means which have alternative uses.
Lionel Robbins (1898–1984), *An Essay on the Nature and Significance of Economic Science*, 1935, p. 16

14 The purpose of studying economics is not to acquire a set of ready-made answers to economic questions, but to learn how to avoid being deceived by economists.
Joan Robinson (1903–1983), *Marx, Marshall and Keynes*, 1955

15 To try to understand the workings of the economy by means of macroeconomics is rather like trying to understand how a clock works by observing the movements of the hands on its face.
David Simpson, 'What Economists Need to Know', *Royal Bank of Scotland Review*, December 1988

16 Economics is what economists do.
Jacob Viner (1892–1970) in Lionel
Robbins, *American Economic Review,
Papers and Proceedings*, May 1981, p. 1

17 I have maintained from first to last that the
laws of Economics are the laws of life.
Philip H. Wicksteed (1844–1927), *The
Common Sense of Political Economy*, 1910,
vol. II, bk. II, ch. I

18 Those who have never seen the inhabitants
of a nineteenth-century London slum can
have no idea of the state to which dirt, drink
and economics can reduce human beings.
Leonard Woolf (1880–1969), *Sowing*,
1960

66 ECONOMISTS
See also 65 ECONOMICS

1 You can make even a parrot into a learned
political economist — all he must learn are
the two words 'supply' and 'demand'.
Anonymous

2 I found out where George Bush is today.
He's visiting his economists. He's at
Disneyland right now.
Lloyd Bentsen, *Sydney Morning Herald*,
'Sayings of the Week', 10 September 1988

3 An economist is a man who knows 100
ways of making love but doesn't know any
women.
Art Buchwald, attributed

4 But the age of chivalry is gone. That of
sophisters, economists, and calculators, has
succeeded; and the glory of Europe is
extinguished for ever.
Edmund Burke (1729–1797), *Reflections
on the Revolution in France*, 1790

5 Most of the simplest things in economics
have never been put in such a way as to
carry conviction to the mind of the sort of
person who is in the great majority of every
public, and the blame is not altogether to be
put on his feeble mind, but in large measure
on the unnecessarily complicated
expositions offered by economists.
Edwin Cannan (1861–1935), 'The Need for
Simpler Economics', *Economic Journal*,
September 1933, p. 367

6 Economists are like Bangkok taxi drivers:
put two of them together and you will have
four opinions, any of which will take you
careering in the wrong direction at great
expense.
Mike Carlton, *Sydney Morning Herald*,
'Sayings of the Week', 21 June 1986

7 Any man who is only an economist is
unlikely to be a good one.
F.A. Hayek, lecture, 1962, *The Times*,
9 May 1985

8 Please find me a one-armed economist so we
will not always hear 'On the other hand . . .'
Herbert Hoover (1874–1964), attributed

9 Old economists never die, they just change
their assumptions.
Sir Geoffrey Howe, *Sunday Times*, 29
January 1989

10 Woman is a natural economist.
Elbert Hubbard (1856–1915), *Notebook*,
1927, p. 44

11 The ideas of economists and political
philosophers, both when they are right and
when they are wrong, are more powerful
than is commonly understood. Indeed the
world is ruled by little else. Practical men,
who believe themselves to be quite exempt
from any intellectual influences, are usually
the slaves of some defunct economist.
John Maynard Keynes (1883–1946), *A
General Theory of Employment Interest and
Money*, 1936, bk. VI, ch. 24

12 I am an economist and have tried to give
you an economic solution for an economic
problem. Please do not argue that I am a
rotten economist on the grounds that the
economic solution is politically
unacceptable.
James E. Meade, 'Stagflation in the United
Kingdom', *Atlantic Economic Journal*,
December 1979, p. 9

13 It is not the business of economists to teach
woollen manufacturers how to make and
sell wool, or brewers how to make and sell
beer, or any other business men how to do
their job.
A.C. Pigou (1877–1959), 'Empty Economic
Boxes, A Reply', *The Economic Journal*,
1922

14 It has been well said by M. Say that it is not
the province of the Political Economist to
advise:— he is there to tell you how you

may become rich, but he is not to advise you to prefer riches to indolence, or indolence to riches.
David Ricardo (1772–1823), *Notes on Malthus*, in *Works*, ed. Sraffa. vol. II, p. 338

15 If all economists were laid end to end, they would not reach a conclusion.
George Bernard Shaw (1856–1950), attributed

16 President Reagan did a very wise thing — he dismissed all the academic economists in Washington.
Earl of Stockton (Harold Macmillan) (1894–1986), House of Lords, 23 January 1985

17 You and I come by road or rail — but economists travel on infrastructure.
Margaret Thatcher, *Observer*, 'Sayings of the Week', 26 May 1985

---

67 ECONOMY

---

1 Economy is how to spend your money without enjoying it.
Anonymous

2 Economy, *n*. Purchasing the barrel of whisky that you do not need for the price of the cow that you cannot afford.
Ambrose Bierce (1842–1914?), *The Devil's Dictionary*, 1911

3 As gold itself may be bought too dear, so may economy; money may be saved at too high a price.
Henry Peter Brougham (1778–1868), House of Commons, 7 February 1828

4 Everybody is always in favour of general economy and particular expenditure.
Sir Anthony Eden (1897–1977), *Observer*, 17 June 1956

5 Economy is going without something you do want in case you should, some day, want something you probably won't want.
Anthony Hope (1863–1933), *The Dolly Dialogues*, 1919, 12

6 Take care of the pence, and the pounds will take care of themselves.
William Lowndes (1652–1724), attributed

7 He who is taught to live upon little owes more to his father's wisdom than he that has

a great deal left him does to his father's care.
William Penn (1644–1718) in Tryon Edwards, *The New Dictionary of Thoughts*

8 It is not economical to go to bed early to save the candles if the results are twins.
Proverb, Chinese

9 Economy is too late at the bottom of the purse.
Seneca (*c*.4 BC–AD 65), *Epistulae ad Lucilium*, epis. i, sec. 5

10 Economy is the art of making the most of life.
George Bernard Shaw (1856–1950), *Maxims for Revolutionists*, 1903

11 The love of economy is the root of all virtue.
George Bernard Shaw (1856–1950), *ibid.*

12 Economy is half the battle of life; it is not so hard to earn money, as to spend it well.
Charles Haddon Spurgeon (1834–1892) in Tryon Edwards, *The New Dictionary of Thoughts*

---

68 EDUCATION

---

1 There are obviously two educations. One should teach us how to make a living and the other how to live.
James Truslow Adams (1878–1949) in Tryon Edwards, *The New Dictionary of Thoughts*

2 Academic staff rather enjoy coming to conclusions, but they don't like coming to decisions at all.
Lord Annan, *Observer*, 'Sayings of the Week', 8 February 1981

3 Old professors don't die: they just lose their faculties.
Anonymous

4 For the wisdom of business, wherein man's life is most conversant, there be no books of it . . . if books were written of this . . . I doubt not but learned men with mean experience, would far excel men of long experience without learning, and outshoot them in their own bow.
Francis Bacon (1561–1626), *The Advancement of Learning*, 1605, bk. II, XXIII, 4

5 When Sir Peter Swinnerton-Dyer suggested

that it was ludicrous that a professor of theology should be paid the same as a professor of business studies, he was making an astute point. The business studies don has always had all kinds of opportunities for contracts, consultancies, and advisory fees which make it unnecessary for him to be paid nearly as much as the theologian.
Rodney Barker, *The Times Higher Education Supplement*, 21 February 1986

6 Education, *n*. That which discloses to the wise and disguises from the foolish their lack of understanding.
Ambrose Bierce (1842–1914?), *The Devil's Dictionary*, 1911

7 Hell hath no fury like a wallflower with a sociology degree.
Julie Burchill, *Sydney Morning Herald*, 'Sayings of the Week', 5 April 1986

8 He is to be educated not because he is to make shoes, nails, and pins, but because he is a man.
William Ellery Channing (1780–1842) in Tryon Edwards, *The New Dictionary of Thoughts*

9 The men who control Harvard today are very little else than businessmen running a large department store which dispenses education to the millions.
John Jay Chapman in Laurence J. Veysey, *The Emergence of the American University*, 1965, p. 346

10 The chief object of education is not to learn things but to unlearn things.
G.K. Chesterton (1874–1936) in Rudolf Flesch, *The Book of Unusual Quotations*, 1959

11 Education is a rite of initiation into the prevalent 'thing' of any generation. The trouble now is that there is no prevalent 'thing'.
Manning Clark, *Sydney Morning Herald*, 'Sayings of the Week', 26 March 1987

12 A lecturer is a sound scholar, who is chosen to teach on the ground that he was once able to learn.
F.M. Cornford (1874–1943), *Microcosmographia Academica*, 1908, V

13 Upon the education of the people of this country the fate of this country depends.
Benjamin Disraeli (1804–1881), House of Commons, 15 June 1874

14 Technical education is the exaltation of manual labour, the bringing of manual labour up to the highest excellence of which it is susceptible.
W.E. Gladstone (1809–1898), Speech, 12 September 1890

15 A college education shows a man how little other people know.
Thomas C. Haliburton (1796–1865) in Tryon Edwards, *The New Dictionary of Thoughts*

16 The truly educated man is the useful man.
Elbert Hubbard (1856–1915), *Notebook*, 1927, p. 29

17 To work intelligently is education.
Elbert Hubbard (1856–1915), *ibid.*, p. 144

18 After a feller gits out o' th' school o' experience it's too late t' git t' th' front.
Frank McKinney Hubbard (1868–1930), *New Sayings by Abe Martin*, 1917

19 College: A place where you have to go in order to find out that there's nothing in it.
Frank McKinney Hubbard (1868–1930), *The Roycroft Dictionary*, 1923

20 Teacher: . . . One who makes two ideas grow where only one grew before.
Frank McKinney Hubbard (1868–1930), *ibid.*

21 University: . . . A place where rich men send their sons who have no aptitude for business.
Frank McKinney Hubbard (1868–1930), *ibid.*

22 Better unborn than untaught.
James Kelly, *Scottish Proverbs*, 1721, B, no. 72

23 It is not possible to claim that more education will lead to economic growth. It is not that simple, but growth does require education to sustain it.
Thomas Kempner, *The Times*, 5 September 1985

24 Australia may be the only country in the world in which the word academic is regularly used as a term of abuse.
Dame Leonie Kramer, *Sydney Morning Herald*, 'Sayings of the Week', 29 March 1986

25 Why are institutions of learning so often run

by unspeakable barbarians?
Bernard Levin in C. Bingham, *Wit and Wisdom*, 1982

26 Americans seem to have forsaken the goal of a decent mathematical education for all. Only gamblers, apparently, retain any notion of what a probability is.
Harold W. Lewis, *International Herald Tribune*, 2 September 1985

27 A human being is not, in any proper sense, a human being till he is educated.
Horace Mann (1796–1859) in Tryon Edwards, *The New Dictionary of Thoughts*

28 My mother wanted me to have an education, so she got me out of school.
Margaret Mead (1901–1978) in C. Bingham, *Wit and Wisdom*, 1982

29 Huge numbers of students are being influenced by the biased one-sidedness of contemporary sociology. They are being systematically de-skilled for effective work and trained to be nothing better than critical saboteurs.
David Marsland, *Observer*, 'Sayings of the Week', 19 July 1987

30 If you think law is just something to enable you to get a Volvo while you are waiting for your parents to die and leave you with their superfluous wealth, then you should really be doing something else.
Chris Murphy (address to law students), *Sydney Morning Herald*, 'Sayings of the Week', 24 September 1988

31 That's what education means — to be able to do what you've never done before.
George Herbert Palmer (1842–1933), *Life of Alice Freeman Palmer*, 1908

32 Exporting higher education is not the same as exporting tea.
I.G. Patel, *Independent*, 25 July 1988

33 The best education in the world is that got by struggling to get a living.
Wendell Phillips (1811–1884) in Tryon Edwards, *The New Dictionary of Thoughts*

34 There is no more sense in students participating in the management of universities than there would be in a union of housewives participating in the management of Marks and Spencer's stores.
Enoch Powell, *Observer*, 'Sayings of the Week', 15 March 1970

35 Of all human activities, education is the one most likely to give rise to cant, pomposity and fraudulent expertise.
John Rae, *Observer*, 'Sayings of the Week', 12 June 1983

36 This country [UK] is really bad at appreciating the importance of education. It is the only country where it is no stigma to be ignorant.
Baroness Seear, *Daily Telegraph*, 31 March 1986

37 With education, as with other things, price is a tolerably safe index of value.
Herbert Spencer (1820–1903), *Social Statics*, 1970, pt. III, ch. XXVI, sec. V

38 All the world over there is a realisation that only through right education can a better order of society be built up.
Rabindranath Tagore (1861–1941) in N.B. Sen, *Wit and Wisdom of India*, 1961

39 Our modern system of popular Education . . . produced a vast population able to read but unable to distinguish what is worth reading, an easy prey to sensations and cheap appeals.
George Macaulay Trevelyan (1876–1962), *English Social History*, 1942, ch. XVIII

40 The School of Hard Knocks, beloved of businessmen, is a somewhat unstructured comprehensive.
Lord Vaizey, *Observer*, 'Sayings of the Week', 12 June 1983

41 Nearly all educated at the best public schools and Oxbridge, bishops, deans and dons found it natural to look with distaste and disapproval upon the world of commerce and industry. Such an inclination could flourish in them unchecked by the practical necessity, often forced upon many of their fellows, of making a living in the world.
Martin J. Wiener, *English Culture and the Decline of the Industrial Spirit 1850–1980*, 1981, ch. 6

42 Education is an admirable thing, but it is well to remember from time to time that nothing that is worth knowing can be taught.
Oscar Wilde (1854–1900), *The Critic as Artist*, 1891

43 We don't have, but we desperately need, a training culture.
Norman Willis, 'A Worker's Right to Train', *National Westminster Bank Quarterly Review*, February 1989

44 Scholarship is important to more effective management, but doesn't make more effective managers *per se*.
Gordon Wills, *Sunday Times*, 29 September 1985

69 EFFICIENCY

1 Do it now.
Anonymous

2 You have to be efficient if you're going to be lazy.
Shirley Conran, *Superwoman*, 1975

3 Have you ever noticed what happens when something becomes efficient? It invariably gets worse. Efficiency, you see, is never efficient for us, it's always efficiency for them. Having a conductor to come and collect your fare on a bus or tram is inefficient; having you stand in a queue to buy your ticket, that's efficient.
Robert Haupt, *Sydney Morning Herald Magazine*, 20 July 1985

4 This Modern Efficiency you are hearing about is the same old Hard Work your grandfather dreaded.
E.W. Howe (1853–1937), *Sinner Sermons*, 1926

5 It's pretty hard to be efficient without being obnoxious.
Frank McKinney Hubbard (1868–1930) in Rudolf Flesch, *The Book of Unusual Quotations*, 1959

6 Obviously, the highest type of efficiency is that which can utilize existing material to the best advantage.
Jawaharlal Nehru (1889–1964) in N.B. Sen, *Wit and Wisdom of India*, 1961

7 It is more than probable that the average man could, with no injury to his health, increase his efficiency fifty per cent.
Walter Dill Scott (1869–1955) in Tryon Edwards, *The New Dictionary of Thoughts*

8 There are only two qualities in the world: efficiency and inefficiency, and only two sorts of people; the efficient and the inefficient.
George Bernard Shaw (1856–1950), *John Bull's Other Island*, 1909, act IV

70 EMPLOYEES
See also 108 LABOUR, 215 WORKERS

1 There is not one whom we employ who does not, like ourselves, desire recognition, praise, gentleness, forbearance, patience.
Henry Ward Beecher (1813–1887), *Proverbs from Plymouth Pulpit*, 1887

2 Employees during working hours are the classic captive audience.
Earl Warren, *NLRB* v. *United Steelworkers*, 1958

71 EMPLOYERS
See also 21 BOSSES, 117 MANAGEMENT

1 A good paymaster never wants workmen.
Thomas Fuller (1654–1734), *Gnomologia*, 1732, no. 168

2 The employer has a duty to perform, too, when a helper errs.
Elbert Hubbard (1856–1915), *Notebook*, 1927, p. 36

3 Forget the paternity leave; most bosses would look askance if [their male employees] asked to leave work early to take their children to the dentist. The immediate assumption would be that their wife must just have died.
Penelope Leach, *Independent*, 'Quote Unquote', 29 October 1988

4 There could be no worse friend to labour than the benevolent, philanthropic employer who carries his business on in a loose, lax, manner, showing 'kindness' to his employees; because, as certain as that man exists, because of his looseness and laxness and because of his so-called kindness, benevolence, and lack of business principles, sooner or later he will be compelled to close.
W.H. Lever (Lord Leverhulme) in Charles Wilson, *The History of Unilever*, vol. 1, 1951, p. 143

72 EMPLOYMENT

See also 70 EMPLOYEES, 108 LABOUR,
215 WORKERS

1 I will undoubtedly have to seek what is
happily known as gainful employment,
which I am glad to say does not describe
holding public office.
Dean Acheson (1893–1971), attributed

2 If it's a job at any price, the answer is we
don't want a job at all.
Anonymous shop steward at Swan Hunter,
Sydney Morning Herald, 'Sayings of the
Week', 12 April 1986

3 It is all one to me if a man comes from Sing
Sing or Harvard. We hire a man, not his
history.
Henry Ford (1863–1947) in S. Diamond,
*The Reputation of the American
Businessman*, 1955, p. 157

4 There must be something wrong with a
system where it pays to be sacked.
Joe Grimond, *Observer*, 'Sayings of the
Week', 1 May 1983

5 A man who qualifies himself well for his
calling never fails of employment in it.
Thomas Jefferson (1743–1826), letter to
Peter Carr, 1792

6 The behaviour of each individual firm in
deciding its daily output will be determined
by its *short-term expectations* . . . It is upon
these various expectations that the amount
of employment which the firms offer will
depend.
John Maynard Keynes (1883–1946), *The
General Theory of Employment, Interest and
Money*, 1936, bk. II, ch. 4

7 The social hygiene of full employment.
Abba P. Lerner, 'Employment Theory and
Employment Policy', *American Economic
Review*, 1967, p. 17

8 Employment is a source of happiness,
especially when you are usefully employed.
An industrious person is always a happy
person, provided he is not obliged to work
too hard; and even where you have cause for
unhappiness, nothing makes you forget it so
soon as occupation.
Captain Marryat (1792–1848), *Masterman
Ready*, 1841, ch. XXXV

9 Aim at employment and you head for
disaster. Aim at prosperity and employment
will be a by-product.
C. Northcote Parkinson in Ray Wild, *How
to Manage*, 1982, p. 174

10 What employment have we here?
William Shakespeare (1564–1616), *Twelfth
Night*, 1599–1600, act II, sc. V

11 In the advanced state of society . . . they are
all very poor people who follow as a trade,
what other people pursue as a pastime.
Adam Smith (1723–1790), *Wealth of
Nations*, 1776, vol. I, bk. I, ch. X

12 To judge whether [a workman] is fit to be
employed, may surely be trusted to the
discretion of the employers whose interest it
so much concerns. The affected anxiety of
the law-giver lest they should employ an
improper person, is evidently as impertinent
as it is oppressive.
Adam Smith (1723–1790), *ibid.*

13 The real and effectual discipline which is
exercised over a workman, is . . . that of his
customers. It is the fear of losing their
employment which restrains his frauds and
corrects his negligence.
Adam Smith (1723–1790), *ibid.*

14 My observation on every employment in life
is, that, wherever and whenever one person
is found adequate to the discharge of a duty
by close application thereto, it is worse
executed by two persons, and scarcely done
at all if three or more are employed therein.
George Washington (1732–1799), letter to
Henry Knox, 24 September 1792

73 ENGINEERS

1 When the Waters were dried an' the Earth
           did appear,
('It's all one,' says the Sapper),
The Lord He created the Engineer,
Her Majesty's Royal Engineer,
With the rank and pay of a Sapper.
Rudyard Kipling (1865–1936), *Sappers*

2 It has been said that an engineer is a man
who can do for ten shillings what any fool
can do for a pound.
Nevil Shute (1899–1960), *Slide Rule*, 1954,
ch. 3

74 ENTERPRISE
See also 25 BUSINESS, 41 COMMERCE,
159 PUBLIC ENTERPRISE

1 If Enterprise is afoot, wealth accumulates
whatever may be happening to Thrift; and if
Enterprise is asleep, wealth decays whatever
Thrift may be doing.
John Maynard Keynes (1883–1946), *A
Treatise on Money*, 1930, vol. II, bk. VI,
ch. 30

2 The successful conduct of an industrial
enterprise requires two quite distinct
qualifications: fidelity and zeal.
John Stuart Mill (1806–1873), *Principles
of Political Economy*, 1848, bk. I, ch. IX,
2, p. 139

3 Enterprise does not have to be private in
order to be enterprise.
Herbert Morrison (1888–1965), *Observer*,
'Sayings of the Week', 27 December
1942

4 A program whose basic thesis is not that the
system of free private enterprise for profit
has failed in this generation, but that it has
not yet been tried.
Franklin D. Roosevelt (1882–1945),
Message on Concentration of Economic
Power, 29 April 1938

5 The very life-blood of our enterprise.
William Shakespeare (1564–1616), *Henry
IV, Pt. I*, 1597–8, act IV, sc. I

6 Beware of all enterprises that require new
clothes.
Henry David Thoreau (1817–1862),
Walden, 1854, I, 'Economy'

7 Every enterprise that does not succeed is a
mistake.
Eleutherios Venizelos (1864–1936) in C.
Bingham, *Wit and Wisdom*, 1982

8 The whole thrust of changes in our economy
since the late nineteenth century has been
anti-enterprise.
Lord Young, *Observer*, 'Sayings of the
Year', 28 December 1986

9 We must have an enterprise culture, not a
dependency culture.
Lord Young, *Observer*, 'Sayings of the
Week', 6 March 1988

75 ENTERTAINMENT
See also 64 DRINK, 89 GIFTS

1 There's no such thing as a free lunch.
Anonymous. There are several suggestions
as to the origin. One is an Italian immigrant
with a shoe-shine box outside Grand
Central Station, New York City. Another is
that it dates from the 1840s in America
where saloon keepers offered bits of food to
drinkers.

2 The mass production of distraction is now
as much a part of the American way of life
as the mass production of automobiles.
C. Wright Mills, *Power, Politics and People*,
1963

3 A dinner lubricates business.
William Scott, Baron Stowell (1745–1836),
in Boswell's *Life of Johnson*, 1781

4 I have very poor and unhappy brains for
drinking: I could well wish courtesy would
invent some other custom of entertainment.
William Shakespeare (1564–1616),
Othello, 1604–5, act II, sc. III

76 ENTREPRENEURS
See also 27 BUSINESSMEN, 205 TRADERS

1 Entrepreneurs come in all shapes and sizes.
They straddle every class and every system
of education. The common theme that links
them is sound judgement, ambition,
determination, capacity to assess and take
risks, hard work, greed, fear and luck. The
most dangerous entrepreneur is the self
righteous one who preaches morality and
pretends that he is doing it for the good of
others. That kind of entrepreneur usually
ends up bust, having dilapidated the savings
of those who invested in him.
Sir James Goldsmith in Ray Wild, *How to
Manage*, 1982, pp. 185–6

2 I reckon one entrepreneur can recognize
another at 300 yards on a misty day.
Sir Peter Parker in Ray Wild, *How to
Manage*, 1982, p. 2

3 Entrepreneurial profit . . . is the expression
of the value of what the entrepreneur
contributes to production.
J.A. Schumpeter (1883–1950), *The Theory
of Economic Development*, 1934, ch. 4

77 EQUAL OPPORTUNITIES

See also 32 CAREERS, 153 PROMOTION,
193 SUCCESS

1 Men their rights and nothing more; women
their rights and nothing less.
Susan B. Anthony (1820–1906), motto of
The Revolution, 1868

2 Make [your employers] understand that you
are in their service as workers, not as
women.
Susan B. Anthony (1820–1906), *The
Revolution*, 8 October 1868

3 Join the union, girls, and together say *Equal
Pay for Equal Work*.
Susan B. Anthony (1820–1906), *ibid*., 18
March 1869

4 The male is by nature superior, and the
female inferior: the one rules and the other
is ruled.
Aristotle (384–322 BC), *Politics*, bk. I, ch. 5

5 No man naturally can imagine any more
compelling business for a woman than being
interested in him.
Mary Austin (1868–1934), *A Woman of
Genius*, 1912, bk. IV, ch. VI

6 Errors are notoriously hard to kill, but an
error that ascribes to a man what was
actually the work of a woman has more lives
than a cat.
Hertha Ayrton (1854–1923) (referring to
the assertion that Pierre and not Marie
Curie discovered radium), *Westminster
Gazette*, 14 March 1909

7 The feminist pendulum will swing too far.
Pendulums always do. (That is why clocks
go.) As I have before indicated, it is already
dangerous in certain circles to doubt
whether anything that is possible to men is
impossible to women.
Arnold Bennett (1867–1931), *Our Women*,
1920, ch. IV

8 That she is not his peer in all intellectual and
moral capabilities, cannot at least be very
well provided until she is allowed an equally
untrammelled opportunity to test her own
strength.
Antoinette Brown Blackwell (1825–1921),
The Sexes Throughout Nature, 1875

9 Men are vain, but they won't mind women

working so long as they get smaller salaries
for the same job.
Irvin Shrewsbury Cobb (1876–1944) in N.
Bentley and E. Esar, *The Treasury of
Humorous Quotations*

10 The pressure of male trade unions appears
to be largely responsible for that crowding
of women into comparatively few
occupations, which is universally recognised
as a main factor in the depression of their
wages.
F.Y. Edgeworth (1845–1926), 'Equal Pay
to Men and Women for Equal Work',
Economic Journal, December 1922

11 It is folly to imagine that there can be
anything very bad in the position of woman
compared with that of man, at any time: for
since every woman is a man's daughter, and
every man is a woman's son, every woman is
too near to man, was too recently a man,
than that possibly any wide disparity can be.
As is the man will be the woman; and as is
the woman the man.
Ralph Waldo Emerson (1803–1882),
Journal, 1843

12 The Paula Principle ensures that women stay
below their level of competence, because
they hold back from promotion.
Liz Filkin, quoted by Katharine Whitehorn,
Observer, 19 October 1986. See also the
Peter Principle 153.6.

13 The male human being is thousands of years
in advance of the female in economic status.
Charlotte Perkins Gilman (1860–1935),
Women and Economics, 1898, ch. 1

14 Now I came to power and I said: 'Look, this
is nonsense, we are great people, we
Australians.' Employers are great blokes,
workers are great blokes, farmers are great
blokes — and I use the term blokes to
encompass men and women.
Bob Hawke, *Sydney Morning Herald*,
'Sayings of the Year', 31 December 1988

15 Women have no need to prove their
manhood.
Wilma Scott Heide in Lisa Leghorn and
Katherine Parker, *Sexual Economics and the
World of Men*

16 When women ask for equality, men take
them to be demanding domination.
Elizabeth Janeway, *Man's World, Woman's
Place*, 1971, ch. 19

17 The percentage of women in management has stuck at between one and two per cent for thirty years. Employers plainly do not think women are a good investment.
Thomas Kempner, *The Times*, 10 February 1983

18 Men are made to be managed, and women are born managers.
George Meredith (1828–1909), *The Ordeal of Richard Feverel*, 1859, ch. 34

19 The legend of the jungle heritage and the evolution of man as a hunting carnivore has taken root in man's mind . . . He may even believe that equal pay will do something terrible to his gonads.
Elaine Morgan, *The Descent of Woman*, 1972, ch. 1

20 More women than ever before in our history are relying on themselves instead of Prince Charming. Work is the vehicle that permits this.
Elizabeth Nickles and Laura Ashcraft, *The Coming Matriarchy*, 1981, ch. 1

21 It was rapidly becoming clear to my mind that men regarded women as a servant class in the community, and that women were going to remain in the servant class until they lifted themselves out of it.
Emmeline Pankhurst (1858–1928), *My Own Story*, 1914

22 A woman is like a teabag — only in hot water do you realize how strong she is.
Nancy Reagan, *Observer*, 'Sayings of the Week', 3 January 1982

23 No one asks a man how his marriage survives if he's away a lot.
Angela Rippon, *Observer*, 'Sayings of the Week', 27 September 1981

24 We hold these truths to be self-evident: that all men and women are created equal.
Elizabeth Cady Stanton (1815–1902), Declaration of Sentiments, First Woman's Rights Convention, Seneca Falls, New York, July 1848

25 The corset is, in economic theory, substantially a mutilation, undergone for the purpose of lowering the subject's vitality and rendering her permanently and obviously unfit for work.
Thorstein Veblen (1857–1929), *Theory of the Leisure Class*, 1899, ch. 7

26 Whatever women do they must do twice as well as men to be thought half as good. Luckily this is not difficult.
Charlotte Whitton (1896–1975), M. Rogers, *Contradictory Quotations*

27 It cannot be demonstrated that woman is essentially inferior to man because she has always been subjugated.
Mary Wollstonecraft (1759–1797), *A Vindication of the Rights of Women*, 1792, ch. II

28 The history of men's opposition to women's emancipation is more interesting perhaps than the story of that emancipation itself.
Virginia Woolf (1882–1941), *A Room of One's Own*, 1929

78 EXCHANGE

1 Nothing is to be had for nothing.
Epictetus (*fl.* AD 100), *Discourses*, bk. IV, ch. 10

2 Exchange can . . . bring about co-ordination without coercion.
Milton Friedman, *Capitalism and Freedom*, 1962, ch. I

3 The practical application of the principle of individualism is entirely dependent on the practice of exchange.
R.G. Hawtrey (1879–1971), *The Economic Problem*, 1926, ch. III, p. 13

4 A fair exchange is no robbery.
Proverb, 16th century

5 Man might be defined as 'An animal that makes exchanges'.
Richard Whately (1787–1863), attributed

6 Each of us puts in what he has at one point of the circle of exchange and takes out what he wants at another.
P.H. Wicksteed (1844–1927), 'The Scope and Method of Political Economy', *Economic Journal*, March 1914

79 EXPENSES

1 For your expenses.
William Shakespeare (1564–1616), *Henry VI, Pt. I*, 1589–90, act V, sc. V

2 Hold, there's expenses for thee.
   William Shakespeare (1564–1616), *Twelfth Night*, 1599–1600, act III, sc. I

---

80 EXPORTS

1 If we take care of our imports, our exports will take care of themselves.
   Anonymous

2 How many people in Britain recognise that we export as a percentage of our total production twice as much as the Japanese.
   Sir Raymond Pennock, *Observer*, 'Sayings of the Year', 3 January 1982

---

81 FACTORIES
   See also 99 INDUSTRY

---

1 The factory, for Taylor, was not only an instrument for the production of goods and profit, it was also a moral gymnasium for the exercise of character.
   Samuel Haber, *Efficiency and Uplift*, 1964

2 There is a disease known as factory melancholia. If there is a depression of spirit in the front office it goes out through the foreman, the superintendent, and reaches everybody in the employ of the institution.
   Elbert Hubbard (1856–1915), *Notebook*, 1927, p. 118

---

82 FASHION
   See also 6 ADVERTISING, 119 MARKETING, 169 RETAILING, 172 SALES, 179 SELLING

---

1 We don't want to push our ideas on to customers, we simply want to make what *they* want.
   Laura Ashley (1925–1985), *Sunday Times*, 22 September 1985

2   Nothing is thought rare
   Which is not new, and follow'd; yet we know
   That what was worn some twenty years ago
   Comes into grace again.
   Francis Beaumont (1584–1616) **and John Fletcher** (1579–1625), *The Noble Gentleman*, 1626, prologue

3 Tailors and writers must mind the fashion.
   Thomas Fuller (1654–1734), *Gnomologia*, 1732, no. 4301

4 Fashion is a substitute for taste.
   R.G. Hawtrey (1879–1971), *The Economic Problem*, 1926, ch. XVIII

5 Fashion: A barricade behind which men hide their nothingness.
   Frank McKinney Hubbard (1868–1930), *The Roycroft Dictionary*, 1923

6 A top of fashion is the mercer's friend, the tailor's fool, and his own foe.
   John Caspar Lavater (1741–1801) in Tryon Edwards, *The New Dictionary of Thoughts*

7 Thou knowest that the fashion of a doublet, or a hat, or a cloak is nothing to a man.
   William Shakespeare (1564–1616), *Much Ado About Nothing*, 1598–9, act III, sc. III

8 The fashion wears out more apparel than the man.
   William Shakespeare (1564–1616), *ibid.*

9 Report of fashions in proud Italy,
   Whose manners still our tardy apish nation
   Limps after, in bare imitation.
   William Shakespeare (1564–1616), *Richard II*, 1595–6, act II, sc. I

10 These fashion-mongers.
   William Shakespeare (1564–1616), *Romeo and Juliet*, 1595–6, act II, sc. IV

11   Not acquainted
   With shifting change, as is false women's fashion.
   William Shakespeare (1564–1616), *Sonnets*, XX

12 You cannot be both fashionable and first-rate.
   Logan Pearsall Smith (1865–1946), *Afterthoughts*, 1931

13 He who goes against the fashion is himself its slave.
   Logan Pearsall Smith (1865–1946) in Rudolf Flesch, *The Book of Unusual Quotations*, 1959

14 Fashion is intrinsically imitative. Imitation may result from two widely divergent motives. It may be prompted by reverence for one imitated, or it may be prompted by the desire to assert equality with him.

Herbert Spencer (1820–1903), *Principles of Sociology*, 1893, pt. IV, ch. XI

15 Fashion, the arbiter, and rule of right.
Sir Richard Steele (1672–1729), *The Spectator*, 1712, no. 478

16 A love of fashion makes the economy go round.
Liz Tilberis, *Observer*, 'Sayings of the Week', 30 August 1987

83 FINANCE
See also 16 BANKING, 37 THE CITY

1 Finance, *n*. The art or science of managing revenues and resources for the best advantage of the manager.
Ambrose Bierce (1842–1914?), *The Devil's Dictionary*, 1911

2 I would rather see Finance less proud and Industry more content.
Sir Winston Churchill (1874–1965) in D.E. Moggridge, *The Return to Gold*

3 Financial sense is knowing that certain men will promise to do certain things and fail.
E.W. Howe (1853–1937), *Sinner Sermons*, 1926

4 I'm old enough to know that to give financial advice is the quickest way of making enemies.
Hammond Innes, *The White South*, 1949, ch. IV

5 London would have to work pretty hard to destroy itself as a financial centre.
Scott Lowry, *The Times*, 2 May 1986

6 [The financial establishment] . . . the bankers, the Bank of England, what are called the experts, and the writers in financial papers — all those great world commentators who always know best but happily forget later what it was they recommended.
Earl of Stockton (Harold Macmillan) (1894–1986), House of Lords, 23 January 1985

7 Personal financial planning is of very little use to people without any money.
Maurice Thompsett, *Observer*, 14 June 1987

84 FORECASTING

1 All forecasting is in an important sense *backward*-looking — vividly compared to steering a ship by its wake.
Ralph Harris, 'Models or Markets' in James B. Ramsey, *Economic Forecasting — Models or Markets?*, 1977, p. 86

2 FORECAST: A pretence of knowing what would have happened if what does happen hadn't.
Ralph Harris, 'Everyman's Guide to Contemporary Economic Jargon', *Growth, Advertising and the Consumer*, 1964, p. 22

3 Forecast: To observe that which has passed, and guess it will happen again.
Frank McKinney Hubbard (1868–1930), *The Roycroft Dictionary*, 1923

4 The weather forecast has no effect on the weather but the economics forecast may well affect the economy.
Sir John Mason, Presidential Address to the British Association, 1983

85 FRAUD
See also 54 CORRUPTION

1 Great firms, with a reputation which they have received from the past, and which they wish to transmit to the future, cannot be guilty of small frauds. They live by a *continuity* of trade, which detected fraud would spoil.
Walter Bagehot (1826–1877), *Lombard Street*, 1873, ch. 1

2 Like a gun that fires at the muzzle and kicks over at the breach, a cheating transaction hurts the cheater as much as the man cheated.
Henry Ward Beecher (1813–1887), *Proverbs from Plymouth Pulpit*, 1887

3 There are some frauds so well conducted, that it would be stupidity *not* to be deceived by them.
C.C. Colton (1780–1832), *Lacon*, 1820, vol. I, XCVI

4 Some frauds succeed from the apparent candour, the open confidence, and the full

blaze of ingenuousness that is thrown around them. The slightest mystery would excite suspicion, and ruin all. — Such stratagems may be compared to the stars, they are discoverable by *darkness*, and hidden by light.
C.C. Colton (1780–1832), *ibid.*, LXIX

5 He that's cheated twice by the same man, is an accomplice with the cheater.
Thomas Fuller (1654–1734), *Gnomologia*, 1732, no. 2281

6 Fraud is infinite in variety; sometimes it is audacious and unblushing; sometimes it pays a sort of homage to virtue, and then it is modest and retiring; it would be honesty itself if it could only afford it. But fraud is fraud all the same.
Lord Macnaghten (1830–1913), *Reddaway v. Banham*, 1896

---

86 FREE TRADE
See also 109 LAISSEZ-FAIRE

---

1 We [the candlemakers] are suffering from the intolerable competition of a foreign rival, who is placed . . . in a condition so infinitely superior to ours for the production of light, that he *inundates* our *national market* at a marvellously reduced price . . . This rival . . . is no other than the sun . . . We pray that you will be pleased to make a law ordering that all windows, skylights, inside and outside shutters, curtains, fan-lights, bulls'-eyes, carriage-blinds, in short that all openings, holes, chinks, and crevices should be closed by which the light of the sun can penetrate into houses, to the injury of the flourishing trade with which we have endowed our country.
Frédéric Bastiat (1801–1850), *Sophismes Économiques*, 1846, ch. VII

2 We advocate nothing but what is agreeable to the highest behests of Christianity — to buy in the cheapest market and sell in the dearest.
Richard Cobden (1804–1865) in Miriam Beard, *A History of Business*, vol. II, p. 141

3 In the long run, free trade benefits everyone; in the short run it is bound to produce much pain.
Henry Hobhouse, *Seeds of Change*, 1985, p. 210

4 Free trade, one of the greatest blessings which a government can confer on a people, is in almost every country unpopular.
Lord Macaulay (1800–1859), *Essay on Mitford's History of Greece*, 1824

5 If we will not buy, we cannot sell.
William McKinley (1843–1901) in Ludwell Denny, *America Conquers Britain*, 1930

6 It is the maxim of every prudent master of a family, never to attempt to make at home what it will cost him more to make than to buy . . . What is prudence in the conduct of every private family, can scarce be folly in that of a great kingdom. If a foreign country can supply us with a commodity cheaper than we ourselves can make it, better buy it of them with some part of the produce of our own industry, employed in a way in which we have some advantage.
Adam Smith (1723–1790), *Wealth of Nations*, 1776, vol. I, bk. IV, ch. II

---

87 FUNERAL DIRECTORS

---

1 We're not the nicest people in town, but we're the last ones to let you down.
Anonymous funeral director at the undertakers' conference in Melbourne in March 1985, *Sydney Morning Herald*, 'Sayings of 1985', 28 December 1985

---

88 GAMBLING
See also 186 SPECULATION

---

1 The gambling known as business looks with austere disfavour upon the business known as gambling.
Ambrose Bierce (1842–1914?), *The Devil's Dictionary*, 1911

2 A gambler knows when to play his luck and when not to, when to keep on and when to give up, and that is a good thing for a businessman.
Sir James Goldsmith in Geoffrey Wansell, *Sir James Goldsmith*, 1982, ch. 14

3 For the average person the way to look at gambling is as a recreation which usually

costs money, and not a way to retire.
Darwin Ortiz (US gambling consultant),
Financial Review, 'Quotes of the Week', 11
April 1986

4   Don't gamble; take all your savings and buy
some good stock, and hold it till it goes up,
then sell it. *If it don't go up, don't buy it!*
Will Rogers (1879–1935) in Donald Day,
Will Rogers: A Biography, 1962, ch. 26

5   In gambling the many must lose in order
that the few may win.
George Bernard Shaw (1856–1950), 'The
Economic Basis of Socialism', *Fabian
Essays*, 1889

6   Avoid Gaming. This is a vice which is
productive of every possible evil; equally
injurious to the morals and health of its
votaries. It is the child of avarice, the
brother of iniquity, and the father of
mischief.
George Washington (1732–1799), Letter to
Bushrod Washington, 15 January 1783

7   All Gaming, since it implies an desire to
profit at the expense of another, involves a
breach of the tenth Commandment.
Richard Whately (1787–1863), *Thoughts
and Apophthegms*, 1856, pt. VI

---

89 GIFTS
See also 75 ENTERTAINMENT

---

1   Thou shalt take no gift: for the gift blindeth
the wise, and perverteth the words of the
righteous.
Bible, Authorized Version, Exodus 23:8

2   You cannot afford to have things given to
you.
E.W. Howe (1853–1937), *Country Town
Sayings*, 1911

3   There are no real free gifts in this world,
only deferred payments.
Warren Tute, *The Golden Greek*, 1960,
ch. 7

4   Do not trust the horse, Trojans. Whatever it
is, I fear the Greeks even when they bring
gifts.
Virgil (70–19 BC), *Aeneid*, bk. II, l. 49

---

90 GOLD
See also 124 MONEY

---

1   You shall not press down upon the brow of
labor this crown of thorns, you shall not
crucify man upon a cross of gold.
William Jennings Bryan (1860–1925),
speech at the National Democratic
Convention, Chicago, 1896. He had made a
similar statement in the House of
Representatives in December 1894

2   O Gold! I still prefer thee unto paper
Which makes bank credit like a bank of
            vapour.
Lord Byron (1788–1824), *Don Juan*, canto
XII, 1823, st. IV

3   [Gold] which does not change its nature,
which has no nationality, which is eternally
and universally accepted as the unalterable
fiduciary value par excellence.
Charles de Gaulle (1890–1970), press
conference, 1965, *Economist*, 22 March
1975, 'Survey', p. 4

4   When every blessed thing you hold
Is made of silver, or of gold,
    You long for simple pewter.
When you have nothing else to wear
But cloth of gold and satins rare,
For cloth of gold you cease to care —
    Up goes the price of shoddy.
W.S. Gilbert (1836–1911), *The Gondoliers*,
1899, act II

5   Gold! Gold! Gold! Gold!
Bright and yellow, hard and cold,
Molten, graven, hammer'd and roll'd;
Heavy to get, and light to hold;
Hoarded, barter'd, bought and sold,
Stolen, borrow'd, squander'd, doled:
Spurn'd by the young, but hugg'd by the old
To the very verge of the churchyard mould;
Price of many a crime untold:
Gold! Gold! Gold! Gold!
Good or bad a thousand-fold!
How widely its agencies vary —
To save — to ruin — to curse — to bless —
As even its minted coins express,
Now stamp'd with the image of Good
            Queen Bess,
And now of a Bloody Mary.
Thomas Hood (1799–1845), *Miss
Kilmansegg*, 1841–3, *Her Moral*

6 Gold is good but may be dear bought.
James Kelly, *Scottish Proverbs*, 1721, G, No. 4

7 Dr Freud relates that there are peculiar reasons deep in our subconsciousness why gold in particular should satisfy strong instincts and serve as a symbol.
John Maynard Keynes (1883–1946), 'The Return to Gold', *Essays in Persuasion*, 1933, pt. III, p. 182

8 Gold and silver, like all other commodities, are valuable only in proportion to the quantity of labour necessary to produce them, and bring them to market.
David Ricardo (1772–1823), *Principles of Political Economy and Taxation*, 1817, ch. XXVII

9 All that glisters is not gold, —
Often have you heard that told;
Many a man his life hath sold
But my outside to behold;
Gilded tombs do worms infold.
William Shakespeare (1564–1616), *The Merchant of Venice*, 1596–7, act II, sc. VII

10 *Alcibiades*: Here is some gold for thee.
Timon: Keep it, I cannot eat it.
William Shakespeare (1564–1616), *Timon of Athens*, 1607–8, act IV, sc. III

11 Commerce has set the mark of selfishness,
The signet of its all-enslaving power
Upon a shining ore, and called it gold;
Before whose image bow the vulgar great,
The vainly rich, the miserable proud,
The mob of peasants, nobles, priests, and
        kings,
And with blind feelings reverence the power
That grinds them to the dust of misery.
But in the temple of their hireling hearts
Gold is a living god, and rules in scorn
All earthly things but virtue.
Percy Bysshe Shelley (1792–1822), *Queen Mab*, 1813, pt. V

91 GOODWILL

1 It is very difficult to gain good-will; but once you have it, it is easy to keep it.
Baltasar Gracián (1601–1658), *The Art of Worldly Wisdom*, 1647, CXII

2 Good will should be taken for part payment.
James Kelly, *Scottish Proverbs*, 1721, G, no. 36

92 GOVERNMENT

See also 24 BUREAUCRACY, 38 CIVIL SERVICE, 49 CONGRESS, 133 PARLIAMENT, 142 POLITICS

1 The foundation of every government is some principle or passion in the minds of the people.
John Adams (1735–1826), *Thoughts on Government*, 1776

2 The essence of a free government consists in an effectual control of rivalries.
John Adams (1735–1826), *Discourses on Davila*, 1789

3 All governments like to interfere; it elevates their position to make out that they can cure the evils of mankind.
Walter Bagehot (1826–1877), *Economic Studies*, ed. Hutton, 1880, I, p. 5

4 Nothing can be more surely established than that a Government which interferes with any trade injures that trade.
Walter Bagehot (1826–1877), *Lombard Street*, 1873, ch. 4

5 Government is the great fiction, through which everybody endeavours to live at the expense of everybody else.
Frédéric Bastiat (1801–1850), *Essays on Political Economy*, 1872, pt. III

6 The perverts and maniacs who might succeed as monarchs could never, even in the renaissance, manage a cloth factory.
Miriam Beard in E.C. Bursk, D.T. Clark and R.W. Hidy, *The World of Business*, 1962, vol. 1, p. 24

7 Accountancy — that is government.
Louis D. Brandeis (1856–1941), statement before the House Committee on Interstate and Foreign Commerce, 30 January 1918

8 Though the people support the government, the government should not support the people.
Grover Cleveland (1837–1908) in Tryon Edwards, *The New Dictionary of Thoughts*

9 The point to remember is that what the government gives it must first take away.
John S. Coleman (1897–1958) in *The International Thesaurus of Quotations*

10 When governments cannot be changed, governments' minds are unlikely to change much, either.
Economist, 5 December 1987

11 Government has been a fossil; it should be a plant.
Ralph Waldo Emerson (1803–1882), *The Young American*, 1844

12 Whereas the Prime Minister's authority is anchored in the powers of patronage which go with her office, the Chancellor has all the job security of a First Division football manager: he is entirely dependent on results.
Robert Harris, *Observer*, 28 August 1988

13 The more the state 'plans' the more difficult planning becomes for the individual.
F.A. Hayek, *The Road to Serfdom*, 1944, ch. VI

14 Frankly, I'd like to see the government get out of war altogether and leave the whole field to private industry.
Joseph Heller, *Catch-22*, 1955, ch. 24

15 Democratic governments, by their nature, are pressure-responders rather than problem anticipators.
Walter W. Heller, 'What's Right with Economics?', *American Economic Review*, March 1975, p. 18

16 Government: A kind of legalized pillage.
Frank McKinney Hubbard (1868–1930), *The Roycroft Dictionary*, 1923

17 People and politicians are dominated by quite excessive expectations as to what can possibly, or practicably, be delivered by governmental economic policies.
T.W. Hutchison, *Knowledge and Ignorance in Economics*, 1977, ch. 1

18 Many journalists have fallen for the conspiracy theory of government. I do assure you that they would produce more accurate work if they adhered to the cock-up theory.
Bernard Ingham (press secretary to the Prime Minister), *Observer*, 'Sayings of the Week', 17 March 1985

19 I have no ambition to govern men. It is a painful and thankless office.
Thomas Jefferson (1743–1826), letter to John Adams, 1796

20 We must aim at separating those services which are *technically social* from those which are *technically individual* . . . The important thing for Government is not to do things which individuals are doing already, and to do them a little better or a little worse; but to do those things which at present are not done at all.
John Maynard Keynes (1883–1946), *The End of Laissez-Faire*, 1926, pt. IV

21 Most of the serious errors in economic policy committed by governments throughout the ages, and most of the layman's errors in thinking about economic affairs, flow from a failure (sometimes useful, often not) to consider the second order or third order effects of policies over time.
Irving Kristol, 'Rationalism in Economics' in D. Bell and I. Kristol (eds.), *The Crisis in Economic Theory*, 1981, p. 205

22 The Conservative Party has never believed that the business of government is the government of business.
Nigel Lawson, House of Commons, 10 November 1981

23 No man is good enough to govern another man without that other's consent.
Abraham Lincoln (1809–1865), speech, 16 October 1854

24 Government creates scarcely anything . . . A Government could print a good edition of Shakespeare's works, but it could not get them written.
Alfred Marshall (1842–1924), 'The Social Possibilities of Economic Chivalry', *Economic Journal*, March 1907, pp. 21–2

25 Government management is, indeed, proverbially jobbing, careless, and ineffective, but so likewise has generally been joint-stock management. The directors of a joint-stock company, it is true, are always shareholders; but also the members of a government are invariably taxpayers.
John Stuart Mill (1806–1873), *Principles of Political Economy*, 1848, bk. V, ch. XI, 5

26 Above any other position of eminence, that of Prime Minister is filled by fluke.
Enoch Powell, *Observer*, 'Sayings of the Week', 8 March 1987

27 Government should see that the economic game is played vigorously and according to the rules. But the referee cannot also play, for who will then referee the referee?
James B. Ramsey, *Economic Forecasting — Models or Markets?*, 1977, p. 76

28 For three long years I have been going up and down this country preaching that government costs too much. I shall not stop that preaching.
Franklin D. Roosevelt (1882–1945), speech of acceptance of the US Presidency, 2 July 1932

29 Englishmen never will be slaves: they are free to do whatever the Government and public opinion allow them to do.
George Bernard Shaw (1856–1950), *Man and Superman*, 1903, act III

30 The uniform, constant and uninterrupted effort of every man to better his condition, the principle from which public and national, as well as private opulence is originally derived, is frequently powerful enough to maintain the natural progress of things toward improvement, in spite both of the extravagance of government, and of the greatest errors of administration. Like the unknown principle of animal life, it frequently restores health and vigour to the constitution, in spite, not only of the disease, but of the absurd prescriptions of the doctor.
Adam Smith (1723–1790), *Wealth of Nations*, 1776, vol. I, bk. II, ch. III

31 As we know well, price policies and wage control policies do not succeed; they just create a dam which, when it bursts, creates something worse than existed before.
Earl of Stockton (Harold Macmillan) (1894–1986), House of Lords, 23 January 1985

32 That government is best which governs not at all.
Henry D. Thoreau (1817–1862), *Resistance to Civil Government*, 1849

33 That's the difference between governments and individuals. Governments don't care, individuals do.
Mark Twain (1835–1910), *A Tramp Abroad*, 1880, vol. 2, ch. 10

34 Candor is not a more conspicuous trait in the character of governments than it is in individuals.
George Washington (1732–1799), letter to Timothy Pickering, 29 August 1797

93 HEALTH
See also 122 MEDICINE

1 Executives should not worry about insomnia — it only keeps them awake.
Anonymous

2 Hard work never killed anybody but worrying about it did.
Anonymous

3 Obesity is a huge problem.
Anonymous

4 One lesson a man learns in the Harvard Business School is that an executive is only as good as his health.
Jeffrey Archer, *Not a Penny More, Not a Penny Less*, 1976, ch. 2

5 It is not work that kills men, it is worry. Work is healthful, worry is rust upon the blade.
Henry Ward Beecher (1813–1887), *Proverbs from Plymouth Pulpit*, 1887

6 Good Christian people who would not dream of misbehaving will not catch Aids. My message to the businessmen of this country when they go abroad on business is, there is one thing above all they can take with them to stop them catching Aids and that is the wife.
Edwina Currie, *Sunday Times*, 15 February 1987

7 The first wealth is health.
Ralph Waldo Emerson (1803–1882), *The Conduct of Life*, 1860, 'Power'

8 Exercise is bunk. If you are healthy, you don't need it: if you are sick, you shouldn't take it.
Henry Ford (1863–1947), attributed

9 It is health which is real wealth and not pieces of gold and silver.
Mahatma Gandhi (1869–1948) in N.B. Sen, *Wit and Wisdom of India*, 1961

10 Take care of your health; you have no right
    to neglect it, and thus become a burden to
    yourself, and perhaps to others.
    William Hall (1748–1825) in Tryon
    Edwards, *The New Dictionary of Thoughts*

11 I was told to avoid stress, but that's a laugh
    in my job [Attorney-General], how can you
    avoid it?
    Sir Michael Havers, *Observer*, 'Sayings of
    the Week', 8 February 1987

12 In the health service itself, the fundamental
    fallacy is that the more efficient it becomes,
    the less money it will need. This is fantastic
    nonsense.
    Edward Heath, *Independent*, 'Quote
    Unquote', 29 October 1988

13 Middle age is when your age starts to show
    around your middle.
    Bob Hope in James Beasley Simpson, *Best
    Quotes of '54, '55, '56*, 1957

14 The feeling of health can only be gained by
    sickness.
    Georg Christoph Lichtenberg (1742–1799)
    in Rudolf Flesch, *The Book of Unusual
    Quotations*, 1959

15 The biggest danger to the human being is
    the knife and fork. Obesity kills more people
    than anything in the world.
    Gary Player, *Sydney Morning Herald*,
    'Sayings of the Week', 3 May 1986

16 Mr Speaker, Sir, we have ante-natal
    treatment and we have post-natal treatment:
    but we still have these appalling figures.
    Eleanor Rathbone (*c*.1930s), A.P. Herbert,
    Independent Member, ch. 5

17 In theory people having private health care
    either die, or get better, or run out of money
    but they seldom seem to do the last thing.
    Mike Rogers, *Guardian*, 30 July 1988

---

94 HONESTY

---

1 What is honest is not dishonest.
   Lord Justice Bowen (1835–1894), *Angus* v.
   Clifford, 1891

2 Honesty consists not in never stealing but in
   knowing where to stop in stealing, and how
   to make good use of what one does steal.
   Samuel Butler (1835–1902), *Note Books*,
   ed. Festing Jones, 1912, ch. VIII

3 'Tis my opinion every man cheats in his
   way, and he is only honest who is not
   discovered.
   Susannah Centlivre (1667?–1723), *The
   Artifice*, 1710, act V

4 He that resolves to deal with none but
   honest men, must leave off dealing.
   Thomas Fuller (1654–1734), *Gnomologia*,
   1732, no. 2267

5 He's not honest, whom the lock only makes
   honest.
   Thomas Fuller (1654–1734), *ibid.*, no.
   2466

6 Honesty is the best policy.
   Thomas Fuller (1654–1734), *ibid.*, no.
   2534

7 Our great error is that we suppose mankind
   more honest than they are.
   Alexander Hamilton (1757–1804), speech,
   22 June 1787

8 Men are disposed to live honestly, if the
   means of doing so are open to them.
   Thomas Jefferson (1743–1826), letter to
   M. de Marbois, 1817

9 A nod of an honest man is good enough.
   James Kelly, *Scottish Proverbs*, 1721, A, no.
   21

10 I do not remember that in my whole life I
   ever wilfully misrepresented anything to
   anybody at any time. I have never
   knowingly had connection with a fraudulent
   scheme.
   John Pierpont Morgan (1837–1913),
   attributed, 1910

11 It is not true that honesty, as far as material
   gain is concerned, profits individuals. A
   clever and cruel knave will in a mixed
   society always be richer than an honest
   person can be.
   John Ruskin (1819–1900), *Munera
   Pulveris*, 1862, IV

12 Rich honesty dwells like a miser, sir, in a
   poor house; as your pearl in a foul oyster.
   William Shakespeare (1564–1616), *As You
   Like It*, 1596–1600, act I, sc. IV

13 Ay, sir; to be honest, as this world goes, is to
   be one man picked out of ten thousand.
   William Shakespeare (1564–1616),
   Hamlet, 1599–1600, act II, sc. II

14 It is an old adage, that *honesty is the best*

policy. This applies to public as well as private life, to states as well as individuals.
George Washington (1732–1799), letter to James Madison, 30 November 1785

15 'Honesty is the best policy'; but he who acts on that principle is not an honest man.
Richard Whately (1787–1863), *Thoughts and Apophthegms*, 1856, pt. II, ch. XVIII

95 INCENTIVES

1 If the condition of the industrious were not better than the condition of the idle, there would be no reason for being industrious.
Jeremy Bentham (1748–1832), *Principles of the Civil Code*, 1838, pt. I, ch. 3

2 The efficiency of industry may be expected to be great, in proportion as the fruits of industry are insured to the person exerting it.
John Stuart Mill (1806–1950), *Principles of Political Economy*, 1848, bk. I, ch. VII, 6

3 As a general view, remuneration by fixed salaries does not in any class of functionaries produce the maximum amount of zeal.
John Stuart Mill (1806–1873), *ibid.*, bk. II, ch. I, 3

4 If a man is producing nothing, nobody can be the worse for a reduction of his incentive to produce.
George Bernard Shaw (1856–1950), 'Socialism and Superior Brains', *The Fortnightly Review*, April 1894

96 INCOME
See also 150 PROFIT, 212 WAGES

1 A large income is the best recipe for happiness I ever heard of.
Jane Austen (1775–1817), *Mansfield Park*, 1816, ch. 22

2 Income, *n.* The natural and rational gauge and measure of respectability.
Ambrose Bierce (1842–1914?), *The Devil's Dictionary*, 1911

3 All progress is based upon a universal innate desire on the part of every organism to live beyond its income.
Samuel Butler (1835–1902), *Note Books*, ed. Festing Jones, 1912

4 A business with an income at its heels Furnishes always oil for its own wheels.
William Cowper (1731–1800), *Retirement*, 1782

5 Income is a series of events.
Irving Fisher (1867–1947), *The Theory of Interest*, 1930, ch. I, p. 3

6 We ought to define a man's income as the maximum value which he can consume during a week, and still expect to be as well off at the end of the week as he was at the beginning.
J.R. Hicks, *Value and Capital*, 2nd ed., 1946, pt. III, ch. XIV

7 Few people would assert that a man with fifty thousand a year is likely to have a very much happier life than if he had only a thousand.
Alfred Marshall (1842–1924), 'The Social Possibilities of Economic Chivalry', *Economic Journal*, March 1907

8 All decent people live beyond their income nowadays, and those who aren't respectable live beyond other people's.
Saki [Hector Hugh Munro, 1870–1916], 'The Matchmaker', *The Chronicles of Clovis*, 1911

9 Personal income connotes, broadly, the exercise of control over the use of society's scarce resources. It has to do not with sensations, services or goods but rather with rights which command prices (or to which prices may be imputed).
H.C. Simons (1899–1946), *Personal Income Taxation*, 1938, ch. 2

10 Personal income may be defined as the algebraic sum of (a) the market value of rights exercised in consumption and (b) the change in the value of the store of property rights between the beginning and end of the period in question.
H.C. Simons (1899–1946), *ibid.*

11 There are few sorrows, however poignant, in which a good income is of no avail.
Logan Pearsall Smith (1865–1946), *Afterthoughts*, 1931

12 Solvency is entirely a matter of temperament and not of income.
Logan Pearsall Smith (1865–1946), *ibid.*

97 INDUSTRIAL RELATIONS
See also 40 COLLECTIVE BARGAINING, 81 FACTORIES, 117 MANAGEMENT, 129 NEGOTIATIONS, 138 PERSONNEL MANAGEMENT, 206 TRADE UNIONS

1 The measure of labour relations is labour turnover.
Anonymous, 'Political and Economic Planning', *Attitudes in British Management*, 1966, ch. 5

2 Management and union may be likened to that serpent of the fables who on one body had two heads that fighting each other with poisoned fangs, killed themselves.
Peter Drucker, *The New Society*, 1951, ch. 14, p. 129

3 Industrial relations are like sexual relations. It's better between two consenting parties.
Baron (Vic) Feather (1908–1976), *Guardian Weekly*, 8 August 1976

4 Industrial relations are human relations.
Edward Heath, attributed

5 All of you who have read trade union literature know that there are not only trade unions in England, but also alliances between workers and capitalists in a particular industry for the purpose of raising prices and of robbing everybody else.
V.I. Lenin (1870–1924), *Selected Works*, vol. 7, p. 419

6 In . . . disputes the masters can hold out much longer . . . In the long-run the workman may be as necessary to his master as his master is to him, but the necessity is not so immediate.
Adam Smith (1723–1790), *Wealth of Nations*, 1776, vol. I, bk. I, ch. VII

98 INDUSTRIAL REVOLUTION

1 The Industrial Revolution was not indeed an episode with a beginning and an end . . . It is still going on.
E.J. Hobsbawm, *The Age of Revolution, 1789–1848*, 1962, ch. 2, p. 46

2 The elemental truth must be stressed that the characteristic of any country before its industrial revolution and modernization is poverty.
Peter Mathias, *The First Industrial Revolution*, 1969, ch. 1

3 It is possible to identify all societies in their economic dimensions, as lying within one of five categories: the traditional society, the preconditions for take-off, the take off, the drive to maturity, and the age of high mass-consumption.
W.W. Rostow, *The Stages of Economic Growth*, 1960, ch. 2

4 The Industrial Revelation.
W.C. Sellar (1898–1951) **and R.J. Yeatman** (1897–1968), *1066 and All That*, 1930, ch. 49

5 The essence of the Industrial Revolution is the substitution of competition for the mediaeval regulations which had previously controlled the production and distribution of wealth.
Arnold Toynbee (1852–1883), *Lectures on the Industrial Revolution of the Eighteenth Century in England*, 1884, ch. 8

99 INDUSTRY
See also 81 FACTORIES, 97 INDUSTRIAL RELATIONS

1 England . . . owes her great influence not to military success, but to her commanding position in the arena of industry and commerce. If she forgets this, she is lost.
Anonymous, *Annual Register*, 1867

2 That *rara avis*, a successful manufacturer who is fit for something besides manufacturing.
A.J. Balfour (1848–1930) in Kenneth Young, *Balfour*, 1963, p. 126

3 In developing our industrial strategy for the period ahead, we have had the benefit of much experience. Almost everything has been tried at least once.
Tony Benn, *Observer*, 'Sayings of the Week', 17 March 1974

4 The Manchester School will tell you that the destiny of this country is to become 'The

Workshop of the World'. I say that is not true; and that it would be a thing to deplore if it were true.
Robert Blatchford (1851–1943), *Merrie England*, 1894

5 The pursuit of alibis for poor industry performance is one of the great Australian art forms.
John Button, *Sydney Morning Herald*, 'Sayings of the Week', 5 July 1986

6 Captains of Industry.
Thomas Carlyle (1795–1881), *Past and Present*, 1843, bk. IV, ch. IV, title

7 I cannot consent that the laws regulating the industry of a great nation should be made the shuttlecock of party strife.
Benjamin Disraeli (1804–1881), House of Commons, 11 February 1851

8 Industry must manage to keep wages high and prices low. Otherwise it will limit the number of its customers. One's own employees should be one's best customers.
Henry Ford (1863–1947) in Clifton Fadiman, *The American Treasury 1455–1955*, 1955

9 Avarice, the spur of industry.
David Hume (1711–1776), *Essays*, 1741–2, 'Of Civil Liberty'

10 The whole episode which made England the workshop of the world was alien to the spirit and character of the English people.
William Ralph Inge (1860–1954), *The Fall of the Idols*, 1940, p. 150

11 The difficulty is that we have an industrial base with so many characteristics of an industrial museum or of an industrial hospital.
Barry Jones, *Sydney Morning Herald*, 'Sayings of the Week', 12 July 1986

12 Industry is limited by capital.
John Stuart Mill (1806–1873), *Principles of Political Economy*, 1848, bk. I, ch. V, 1

13 It takes more than industry to industrialize.
W.W. Rostow, *The Stages of Economic Growth*, 1960, ch. 3

14 Life without industry is guilt, industry without art is brutality.
John Ruskin (1819–1900), *Lectures on Art*, 1870

15 Rough, honest, industry, and smiling peace,
Thus plant, thus build, and give the land encrease.
Richard Savage (*c.*1697–1743), *Of Public Spirit*, 1736

16 The sweat of industry would dry and die But for the end it works to.
William Shakespeare (1564–1616), *Cymbeline*, 1609–10, act III, sc. VI

17 Industry keeps the body healthy, the mind clear, the heart whole, and the purse full.
Charles Simmons (1798–1856) in Tryon Edwards, *The New Dictionary of Thoughts*

18 Industry does nothing but produce scarce things.
Léon Walras (1834–1910), *Elements of Pure Economics*, trans. W. Jaffé, pt. I, Lesson 4

19 The two sides of industry have traditionally always regarded each other in Britain with the greatest possible loathing, mistrust and contempt. They are both absolutely right.
Auberon Waugh, *Private Eye*, no. 574, 16 December 1983

20 The industrial world is a spontaneous organisation for transmuting what every man has into what he desires, wholly irrespective of what his desires may be.
Philip H. Wicksteed (1844–1927), *The Common Sense of Political Economy*, 1933

21 Industry is the root of all ugliness.
Oscar Wilde (1854–1900), *Phrases and Philosophies for the Use of the Young*, 1891

---

100 INFLATION

---

1 Inflation means that your money won't buy as much today as it did when you didn't have any.
Anonymous, M.Z. Hepker, *A Modern Approach to Tax Law*, 1973

2 Inflation occurs when too much money is chasing too few goods.
Anonymous

3 *Question*: What sex is to the novelist, inflation is to the economist. Discuss.
Answer: I am not sure how I am supposed

to answer this question but it may be said that both inflation and sex are characterised by a rising rate of interest.
Anonymous

4 Inflation is repudiation.
Calvin Coolidge (1872–1933), speech, 11 January 1922

5 Bolshevism was caused largely by the changes in the buying power of money.
Lord D'Abernon (1857–1941) in Irving Fisher, *The Money Illusion*, 1928

6 Inflation might almost be called legal counterfeiting.
Irving Fisher (1867–1947), *Stabilizing the Dollar*, 1920, ch. II

7 Inflation is always and everywhere a monetary phenomenon.
Milton Friedman, Wincott Memorial Lecture, London, 16 September 1970

8 Inflation is like sin; every government denounces it and every government practises it.
Sir Frederick Leith-Ross (1887–1968), *Observer*, 30 June 1957

9 Among the many disadvantages arising from alteration of the coinage which affect the whole community is . . . that the prince could thus draw to himself almost all the money of the community and impoverish his subjects. And as some chronic illnesses are more dangerous than others because they are less perceptible, so such an exaction is the more dangerous the less obvious it is.
Nicholas Oresme (1320?–1382), *The Origin, Nature, Law and Alterations of Money*, c.1360

10 Imagine believing in the control of inflation by curbing the money supply! That is like deciding to stop your dog fouling the sidewalk by plugging up its rear end. It is highly unlikely to succeed, but if it does it kills the hound.
Michael D. Stephens, 'On Sinai, There's No Economics', *New York Times*, 13 November 1981

11 The consumer price index includes meat and milk which have little relevance to a vegetarian or to a playboy who consumes wine, women and song.
Robert R. Sterling, *Theory of the Measurement of Enterprise Income*, 1970, p. 339

12 From now on the pound abroad is worth 14 per cent or so less in terms of other currencies. It does not mean, of course, that the pound here in Britain, in your pocket or purse, or in your bank has been devalued.
Harold Wilson, broadcast announcing devaluation, November 1967

101 INHERITANCE

1 An hereditary business of great magnitude is dangerous.
Walter Bagehot (1826–1877), *Lombard Street*, 1873, ch. 10

2 A good man leaveth an inheritance to his children's children: and the wealth of the sinner is laid up for the just.
Bible, Authorized Version, Proverbs 13:22

3 A son can bear with equanimity the loss of his father, but the loss of his inheritance may drive him to despair.
Niccolò Machiavelli (1469–1527), *The Prince*, 1513, XVII

102 INNOVATION
See also 105 INVENTIONS

1 One company's research is another's development.
Anonymous, 'Where Private Industry Puts its Research Money', *Business Week*, 28 June 1976

2 Time is the greatest innovator.
Francis Bacon (1561–1626), *Essays*, 1625, 'Of Innovations'

3 We must beware of needless innovations, especially when guided by logic.
Sir Winston Churchill (1874–1965) in Rudolf Flesch, *The Book of Unusual Quotations*, 1959

4 We ought not to be over anxious to encourage innovation, in case of *doubtful* improvement, for an old system must ever have two advantages over a new one; it is established, and it is understood.
C.C. Colton (1780–1832), *Lacon*, 1845, vol. I, DXXI

5 Innovations are dangerous.
Thomas Fuller (1654–1734), *Gnomologia*, 1732, no. 3103

6 As pragmatists — as our economic figures show — we are failing. It is essential for Australia to be a more productive and creative society. This is not possible unless there is respect in Australia for innovative culture.
Donald Horne, *Sydney Morning Herald*, 'Sayings of the Week', 12 November 1988

7 Every innovation has to fight for its life.
Elbert Hubbard (1856–1915), *Notebook*, 1927, p. 16

8 The most daring innovators are most often those most thoroughly steeped in tradition.
Henry Parris in C. Bingham, *Wit and Wisdom*, 1982

---

103 INSURANCE

---

1 Insurance, *n*. An ingenious modern game of chance in which the player is permitted to enjoy the comfortable conviction that he is beating the man who keeps the table.
Ambrose Bierce (1842–1914?), *The Devil's Dictionary*, 1911

2 The Act of God designation on all insurance policies; which means, roughly, that you cannot be insured for the accidents that are most likely to happen to you.
Alan Coren, *The Lady from Stalingrad Mansions*, 1977

3 How do you insure yourself against insurance premiums?
Peter Corris, *The Dying Trade*, 1980, ch. 5

4 A Life Assurance Office is at all times exposed to be practised upon by the most crafty and cruel of the human race.
Charles Dickens (1812–1870), *Hunted Down*, 1860, II

5 I understand your object. You want to save your funds, and escape from your liabilities; these are old tricks of trade [in insurance] with you Office-gentlemen.
Charles Dickens (1812–1870), *ibid.*, V

6 The chief value of life-insurance seems to be that it gives the man insured an increased capacity for meeting the natural and inevitable trials, difficulties and obstacles of life.
Elbert Hubbard (1856–1915), *Notebook*, 1927, p. 112

7 Fun is like life insurance; the older you get the more it costs.
Frank McKinney Hubbard (1868–1930), attributed

8 The underwriter knows nothing and the man who comes to him to ask him to insure knows everything.
Lord Justice Scrutton (1856–1934), *Rozanes* v. *Bowen*, 1928

9 This is a poor old ship, and ought to be insured and sunk.
Mark Twain (1835–1910), *Following the Equator*, 1897, vol. 2, ch. 2

10 An insurance policy is like old underwear. The gaps in its cover are only shown by accident.
David Yates, *Sunday Times*, 21 October 1984

---

104 INTEREST
See also 57 CREDIT

---

1 It is better to mitigate usury by declaration than to suffer it to rage by connivance.
Francis Bacon (1561–1626), *Essays*, 1625, 'Of Usury'

2 Since there must be borrowing and lending, and men are so hard of heart as they will not lend freely, usury must be permitted.
Francis Bacon (1561–1626), *ibid.*

3 Interest works night and day, in fair weather and in foul. It gnaws at a man's substance with invisible teeth. It binds industry with its film, as a fly is bound upon a spider's web.
Henry Ward Beecher (1813–1887), *Proverbs from Plymouth Pulpit*, 1887

4 Waiting necessarily commands a price.
Gustav Cassel (1866–1945), *The Nature and Necessity of Interest*, 1903, ch. VII

5 The sweet simplicity of the three per cents.
Benjamin Disraeli (1805–1881), *Endymion*, 1880, ch. XCVI

6 The rate of interest acts as a link between income-value and capital-value.
Irving Fisher (1867–1947), *The Nature of Capital and Income*, 1923, ch. XIII

7 Nothing is esteemed a more certain sign of
the flourishing condition of any nation than
the lowness of interest
David Hume (1711–1776), *Essays*,
1741–2, 'Of Interest'

8 The rate of interest is the reward for parting
with liquidity for a specified period.
John Maynard Keynes (1883–1946), *The
General Theory of Employment Interest and
Money*, 1936, bk. IV, ch. 13

9 High usury and bad security generally go
together.
Lord Macaulay (1800–1859), *Warren
Hastings*, 1841

10 Interest always carrieth with it an ensurance
praemium.
Sir William Petty (1623–1687),
'Quantulumcunque concerning Money',
1682, in *The Writings of Sir William Petty*,
ed. Hull, vol. II, p. 447

11 The Indian who sold Manhattan for $24.00
was a sharp salesman. If he had put his $24
away at 6% compounded semiannually, it
would now be $9.5 billion and he could buy
most of the now-improved land back.
S. Branch Walker, *Life*, 31 August 1959

105 INVENTIONS
See also 102 INNOVATION

1 Inventions, and mechanical arts are not
working half so much for the rich, the strong
and the wise, as they are for the poor, the
weak and the ignorant.
Henry Ward Beecher (1813–1887),
Proverbs from Plymouth Pulpit, 1887

2 Inventor, *n.* A person who makes an
ingenious arrangement of wheels, levers and
springs, and believes it civilization.
Ambrose Bierce (1842–1914?), *The Devil's
Dictionary*, 1911

3 Edison, whose inventions did as much as
any to add to our material convenience,
wasn't what we would call a scientist at all,
but a supreme 'do-it-yourself' man.
Sir Kenneth Clark (1903–1983),
Civilisation, 1969

4 Innovation depends on invention and
inventors should be treated as the pop stars
of industry.
Duke of Edinburgh, attributed

5 Anything that won't sell, I don't want to
invent.
Thomas Edison (1847–1931), attributed

6 In America, the geography is sublime, but
the men are not; the inventions are
excellent, but the inventors one is sometimes
ashamed of.
Ralph Waldo Emerson (1803–1882), *The
Conduct of Life*, 1860, 'Considerations by
the way'

7 Invention breeds invention.
Ralph Waldo Emerson (1803–1882),
Society and Solitude, 1870, 'Works and
Days'

8 Inventions that are not made, like babies
that are not born, are rarely missed.
John Kenneth Galbraith, *The Affluent
Society*, 1958, ch. 9, III

9 The brains of a thousand inventors have
seethed, dreamed, contrived, thought, so as
to bring me to my present form.
Elbert Hubbard (1856–1915), *Notebook*,
1927, p. 116

10 In an inventor's work there is required
something similar to that which the artist
brings to bear.
Elbert Hubbard (1856–1915), *ibid.*, p. 194

11 Time and space decreed his lot,
    But little Man was quick to note:
When Time and Space said man might not,
Bravely he answered, 'Nay! I mote!'
Rudyard Kipling (1865–1936), *The
Inventor*

12 The full importance of an epoch-making
idea is often not perceived in the generation
in which it is made . . . The mechanical
inventions of every age are apt to be
underrated relatively to those of earlier
times. For a new discovery is seldom fully
effective for practical purposes till many
minor improvements and subsidiary
discoveries have gathered themselves
around it.
Alfred Marshall (1842–1924), *Principles of
Economics*, 8th ed, 1920, bk. IV, ch. VI, 1,
p. 205, footnote

13 Necessity often mothers invention.
Ovid (43 BC–AD 17), *The Art of Love*, bk. II

14 I am not a management type. I am an inventor. I am awful at managing established businesses.
Sir Clive Sinclair, *Observer*, 'Sayings of the Week', 23 June 1985

15 Invention is the talent of youth, and judgement of age.
Jonathan Swift (1667–1745), *Thoughts on Various Subjects*, 1711

16 The great inventor is one who has walked forth upon the industrial world, not from universities, but from hovels; not as clad in silks and decked with honours, but as clad in fustian and grimed with soot and oil.
Isaac Taylor (1787–1865) in Tryon Edwards, *The New Dictionary of Thoughts*

17 The man with a new idea is a Crank until the idea succeeds.
Mark Twain (1835–1910), *Following the Equator*, 1897, vol. 1, ch. 32

18 If necessity is the mother of invention, what was papa doing?
Ruth Weekley in L.J. Peter, *Peter's Quotations*, 1977

106 INVENTORIES

1 To bear the inventory of thy shirts, as, one for superfluity, and one other for use.
William Shakespeare (1564–1616), *Henry IV, Pt. II*, 1597–8, act II, sc. II

2 Forsooth, an inventory, thus importing, — The several parcels of his plate, his treasure, Rich stuffs, and ornaments of household.
William Shakespeare (1564–1616), *Henry VIII*, 1612–13, act III, sc. II

3 Take an inventory of all I have,
To the last penny.
William Shakespeare (1564–1616), *ibid.*

4 I will give out divers schedules of my beauty. It shall be inventoried; and every particle and utensil labelled to my will: as, item, two lips indifferent red; item, two grey eyes with lids to them; item, one neck, one chin, and so forth.
William Shakespeare (1564–1616), *Twelfth Night*, 1599–1600, act I, sc. V

107 INVESTMENT

1 To understand economics the rational investor would be wise to understand ethics.
Jason Alexander, *Philosophy for Investors*, 1979, 'April'

2 The best investments are often those that looked dead wrong when they were made.
Anonymous Stock Market maxim

3 The social object of skilled investment should be to defeat the dark forces of time and ignorance which envelope our future.
John Maynard Keynes (1883–1946), *General Theory of Employment Interest and Money*, 1936, bk. IV, ch. 12, sec. V

4 There is no clear evidence from experience that the investment policy which is socially advantageous coincides with that which is most profitable.
John Maynard Keynes (1883–1946), *ibid.*

5 Most, probably, of our decisions to do something positive, the full consequences of which will be drawn out over many days to come, can only be taken as a result of animal spirits — of a spontaneous urge to action rather than inaction, and not as the outcome of a weighted average of quantitative benefits multiplied by quantitative probabilities.
John Maynard Keynes (1883–1946), *ibid.*

6 I would not, however, push the case for a sense of history quite so far as the History Fellow of an Oxford College who criticised the reasoning behind the Bursar's investment policy on the ground that the last two hundred years had been exceptional.
Donald MacDougall, 'In Praise of Economics', *Economic Journal*, December 1974, p. 781

7 Hell hath no fury like an investment analyst made to look foolish.
Robert Tyerman, *Sunday Telegraph*, 28 August 1988

108 LABOUR
See also 63 DIVISION OF LABOUR,
215 WORKERS

1 Human labour is not an *end* but a *means*.
Frédéric Bastiat (1801–1850), *Sophismes
Économiques*, 1846, ch. II, p. 21

2 What profit hath a man of all his labour
which he taketh under the sun?
Bible, Authorized Version, Ecclesiastes 1:3

3 The labourer is worthy of his hire.
Bible, Authorized Version, Luke 10:7

4 The labourer is worthy of his reward.
Bible, Authorized Version, 1 Timothy 5:18

5 Labor disgraces no man; unfortunately you
occasionally find men disgrace labor.
Ulysses S. Grant (1822–1885), speech,
1877

6 Labor is unpopular with all human beings,
and unnecessary labor, if recognized as such,
is the most hated.
Henry Hobhouse, *Seeds of Change*, 1985,
p. 153

7 O God! that bread should be so dear
And flesh and blood so cheap.
Thomas Hood (1799–1845), *The Song of
the Shirt*, 1843

8 Th' feller who raises a garden, like th' feller
who marries for money, never figures his
labor.
Frank McKinney Hubbard (1868–1930),
New Sayings by Abe Martin, 1917

9 Labour . . . is any painful exertion of mind
or body undergone partly or wholly with a
view to future good.
W. Stanley Jevons (1835–1882), *Theory
of Political Economy*, 4th ed., 1911,
ch.V

10 'Tis sweating labour.
William Shakespeare (1564–1616), *Antony
and Cleopatra*, 1606–7, act I, sc. III

11 Sir, I am a true labourer: I earn that I eat, get
that I wear; owe no man hate, envy no
man's happiness; glad of other men's good,
content with my harm; and the greatest of
my pride is, to see my ewes graze and my
lambs suck.
William Shakespeare (1564–1616), *As You
Like It*, 1596–1600, act III, sc. II

109 LAISSEZ-FAIRE
See also 86 FREE TRADE

1 The trouble about a free market economy is
that it requires so many policemen to make
it work.
Neal Ascherson, *Observer*, 26 May 1985,
p. 7

2 Let us remember, that it [laissez-faire] is a
practical rule, and not a doctrine of science;
a rule in the main sound, but like most other
sound practical rules, liable to numerous
exceptions; above all, a rule which must
never for a moment be allowed to stand in
the way of the candid consideration of any
promising proposal of social or industrial
reform.
J.E. Cairnes (1824–1875), *Essays in
Political Economy*, 1873, 'Political
Economy and Laissez-faire'

3 Laissez-faire, supply and demand, — one
begins to be weary of all that. Leave all to
egoism, to ravenous greed of money, of
pleasure, of applause; — it is the gospel of
despair.
Thomas Carlyle (1795–1881), *Past and
Present*, 1843

4 If freedom were not so economically
efficient it certainly wouldn't stand a
chance.
Milton Friedman, *Observer*, 'Sayings of the
Week', 1 March 1987

5 *Laissez-faire, laissez passer.*
Vincent de Gournay (1712–1759),
attributed

6 A considerable departure from laissez-faire
is necessary in order to realise the theoretical
results of laissez-faire.
Sir Hubert Henderson (1890–1952),
attributed

7 The principle of *laissez-faire* may be safely
trusted to in some things but in many more
it is wholly inapplicable; and to appeal to it
on all occasions savours more of the policy
of a parrot than of a statesman or a
philosopher.
J.R. McCulloch (1789–1864), *Treatise on
the Succession to Property Vacant by Death*,
1848

8 The man who accepts the laissez-faire
doctrine would allow his garden to run wild

so that the roses might fight it out with the weeds and the fittest might survive.
John Ruskin (1819–1900), attributed

9 The duty of the Government is to keep the peace, to protect all its subjects from the violence and fraud and malice of one another, and, having done so, to leave them to pursue what they believe to be their own interests in the way which they deem desirable.
Nassau Senior (1790–1864), *Lectures*, 1847–52, course 1, lecture 6

110 LAND

1 Land, *n.* A part of the earth's surface, considered as property. The theory that land is property subject to private ownership and control is the foundation of modern society, and is eminently worthy of the superstructure. Carried to its logical conclusion, it means that some have the right to prevent others from living; for the right to own implies the right exclusively to occupy; and in fact laws of trespass are enacted wherever property in land is recognised. It follows that if the whole area of *terra firma* is owned by A, B and C, there will be no place for D, E, F and G to be born, or, born as trespassers, to exist.
Ambrose Bierce (1842–1914?), *The Devil's Dictionary*, 1911

2 No land is bad, but land is worse. If a man owns land, the land owns him. Now let him leave home, if he dare.
Ralph Waldo Emerson (1803–1882), *The Conduct of Life*, 1860, 'Wealth'

3 The small landholders are the most precious part of a state.
Thomas Jefferson (1743–1826), letter to James Madison, 1785

4 No man made the land. It is the original inheritance of the whole species. Its appropriation is wholly a question of expediency. When private property in land is not expedient, it is unjust.
John Stuart Mill (1806–1873), *Principles of Political Economy*, 1848, bk. II, ch. II, 6

5 He that hath some land must have some labour.
John Ray (1627–1705), *English Proverbs*, 1670

6 Study how a society uses its land, and you can come to pretty reliable conclusions as to what its future will be.
E.F. Schumacher (1911–1977), *Small is Beautiful*, 1973, pt. II, ch. 2

7 I would give a thousand furlongs of sea for an acre of barren ground; long heath, brown furze, any thing.
William Shakespeare (1564–1616), *The Tempest*, 1611, act I, sc. I

111 LANDLORDS

1 I inhabit a weak, frail, decayed tenement; battered by the winds and broken in on by the storms, and, from all I can learn, the landlord does not intend to repair.
John Quincy Adams (1767–1848), attributed

2 Quick landlords make careful tenants.
Thomas Fuller (1654–1734), *Gnomologia*, 1732, no. 3994

3 There is a disadvantage belonging to land, compared with money. A man is not so much afraid of being a hard creditor as of being a hard landlord.
Samuel Johnson (1709–1784) in Boswell's *Life of Johnson*, 21 March 1783

4 The Lord giveth and the landlord taketh away.
John W. Raper (1870–1950), attributed

5 No one supposes, that the owner of urban land, performs *qua* owner, any function. He has a right of private taxation; that is all.
R.H. Tawney (1880–1962), *The Acquisitive Society*, 1921, ch. III

112 LAW
See also 113 LAWYERS, 115 LITIGATION

1 Every law has its loophole.
Anonymous

2 Law is a bottomless pit, it is a cormorant, a harpy, that devours everything.
John Arbuthnot (1667–1735), *Law is a Bottomless Pit*, 1712, pt. I, ch. VI

3 It makes no difference whether a good man defrauds a bad one, nor whether a man who commits an adultery be a good or a bad man; the law looks only to the difference created by the injury.
Aristotle (384–322 BC), *Nicomachean Ethics*, trans. Peters, bk. V, ch. 4

4 One of the Seven was wont to say 'that laws were like cobwebs; where the small flies are caught, and the great break through'.
Francis Bacon (1561–1626), *Apophthegms*, 1624

5 The law is of much interest to the layman as it is to the lawyer.
Lord Balfour (1848–1930), attributed

6 Organised business is a thing of law; and the law is always hard and unrelenting toward the weak.
Henry Ward Beecher (1813–1887), *Proverbs from Plymouth Pulpit*, 1887

7 A libel action is a toy that allows the rich to sue the rich, with the proceeds being trousered by the legal profession.
Marcel Berlins, *The Times*, 17 January 1987

8 The law is good, if a man use it lawfully.
Bible, Authorized Version, I Timothy 1:8

9 Lawful, *adj.* Compatible with the will of a judge having jurisdiction.
Ambrose Bierce (1842–1914?), *The Devil's Dictionary*, 1911

10 [Law is] . . . a species of knowledge in which the gentlemen of England have been more remarkably deficient than those of all Europe besides.
Sir William Blackstone (1723–1780), *Commentaries on the Laws of England*, 15th ed., 1809, vol. 1, p. 4

11 It is when merchants dispute about their own rules that they invoke the law.
Judge Brett (1815–1899), *Robinson* v. *Mollett*, 1875

12 Laws, like houses, lean on one another.
Edmund Burke (1729–1797), *Reflections on the Revolution in France*, 1790, para. 268

13 That which is law to-day is none to-morrow.
Robert Burton (1577–1640), *The Anatomy of Melancholy*, 1621, 'Democritus to the Reader'

14 'In my youth,' said his father, 'I took to the law,
And argued each case with my wife;
And the muscular strength, which it gave to my jaw,
Has lasted the rest of my life.'
Lewis Carroll (1832–1898), *Alice's Adventures in Wonderland*, 1865, ch. V

15 The great object of the law is to encourage commerce.
Judge Chambre (1739–1823), *Beale* v. *Thompson*, 1803

16 I am ashamed the law is such an ass.
George Chapman (*c.*1559–1634), *Revenge for Honour*, 1654, act III, sc. II. See also Dickens below.

17 The law, as manipulated by clever and highly respected rascals, still remains the best avenue for a career of honourable and leisurely plunder.
Gabriel Chevallier (1895–1969), *Clochemerle*, 1936, ch. 14

18 The meanest *English* plow-man studies law,
And keeps thereby magistrates in awe;
Will boldly tell them what they ought to do,
And sometimes punish their omissions too.
Daniel Defoe (*c.*1660–1731), *The True-Born Englishman*, 1701, pt. II

19 'The law supposes that your wife acts under your direction.' 'If the law supposes that,' said Mr Bumble, squeezing his hat emphatically with both hands, 'the law is a ass — a idiot. If that's the eye of the law, the law is a bachelor; and the worst I wish the law is, that his eye may be opened by experience — by experience.'
Charles Dickens (1812–1870), *Oliver Twist*, 1838, ch. LI. See also Chapman, above.

20 I think the navigation laws were not the most fortunate voyage.
Benjamin Disraeli (1804–1881), House of Commons, 13 February 1851

21 The law exists to protect us all, whether we are union members, union leaders, employers or merely long-suffering members of the public. We cannot do without it. But the law is not a one-way street. Part goes our way, part goes against us. We have either to accept it all or else to opt for anarchy.
Sir John Donaldson, *Con-Mech (Engineers) Ltd.* v. *AUEW*, 1973

22 The law is only a memorandum.
Ralph Waldo Emerson (1803–1882),
Essays, second series, 1844, 'Politics'

23 Where there is hunger, law is not regarded;
and where the law is not regarded, there will
be hunger.
Benjamin Franklin (1706–1790), *Poor
Richard's Almanac*, 1755

24 Much law, but little justice.
Thomas Fuller (1654–1734), *Gnomologia*,
1732, no. 3482

25 The more laws, the more offenders.
Thomas Fuller (1654–1734), *ibid.*,
no. 4663

26 Where there are many laws, there are many
enormities.
Thomas Fuller (1654–1734), *ibid.*,
no. 5672

27 The Law is the true embodiment
Of everything that's excellent.
It has no kind of fault or flaw,
And I, my Lords, embody the Law.
Sir W.S. Gilbert (1836–1911), *Iolanthe*,
1882, act I, 'Lord Chancellor's Song'

28 I know of no method to secure the repeal of
bad or obnoxious laws so effective as their
stringent execution.
Ulysses S. Grant (1822–1885), Inaugural
Address, 4 March 1869

29 I cannot resist saying that I regard our
profession [the law] as one of the obstacles
to national reform.
Lord Hailsham, *Observer*, 'Sayings of the
Week', 14 September 1986

30 I should regret to find that the law was
powerless to enforce the most elementary
principles of commercial morality.
Lord Herschell (1837–1899), *Reddaway* v.
Banham, 1896

31 Unnecessary laws are not good laws, but
traps for money.
Thomas Hobbes (1588–1679), *Leviathan*,
1651, pt. II, ch. XXVI

32 The most enlightened judicial policy is to let
people manage their own business in their
own way.
Oliver Wendell Holmes (1841–1935), *Dr
Miles Medical Co.* v. *Park & Sons Co.*, 1911

33 Laws for the regulation of trade should be
most carefully scanned. That which

hampers, limits, cripples and retards must
be done away with.
Elbert Hubbard (1856–1915), *Notebook*,
1927, p. 16

34 That ignorant, blundering, blind thing, the
law.
Elbert Hubbard (1856–1915), *ibid.*, p. 193

35 There is no ideal time for the consolidation
of companies' legislation. Company law is
not static, and if consolidation were to wait
until all the measures in the pipeline at that
time were enacted it would be delayed
almost indefinitely.
Lord Lucas, House of Lords, 7 February
1985

36 There are few Englishmen who will not
admit that the English law, in spite of
modern improvements, is neither so cheap
nor so speedy as might be wished. Still it is a
system which has grown up among us. In
some points, it has been fashioned to suit
our feelings; in others, it has gradually
fashioned our feelings to suit itself.
Lord Macaulay (1800–1859), *Warren
Hastings*, October 1841

37 Convenience is the basis of mercantile law.
Lord Mansfield (1705–1793), *Medcalf* v.
Hall, 1782

38 Judge — A law student who marks his own
papers.
H.L. Mencken (1880–1956), *Sententiae*

39 The Law . . . can be civil to you or
downright criminal.
Keith Miles, *The Finest Swordsman in all
France: A Celebration of the Cliché*, 1984

40 The laws do not undertake to punish
anything other than overt acts.
**Charles de Secondat, Baron de
Montesquieu** (1689–1755), *The Spirit of the
Laws*, 1748, bk. XII, 11

41 To me the law seems like a sort of maze
through which a client must be led to safety,
a collection of reefs, rocks and underwater
hazards through which he or she must be
piloted.
John Mortimer, *Clinging to the Wreckage*,
1982, ch. 7

42 The law is in another world; but it thinks it's
the *whole* world.
John Mortimer, *Rumpole of the Bailey*,
1978, 'Rumpole and the Alternative Society'

43 Please remember that law and sense are not
always the same.
Jawaharlal Nehru (1889–1964) in N.B.
Sen, *Wit and Wisdom of India*, 1961

44 One of the greatest delusions in the world is
the hope that the evils of this world can be
cured by legislation.
Thomas B. Reed (1839–1902), attributed

45 Laws describe constraint. Their purpose is
to control, not to create.
Tom Robbins, *Still Life with Woodpecker*,
1980, ch. 71

46 Still you keep o' the windy side of the law.
William Shakespeare (1564–1616), *Twelfth
Night*, 1599–1600, act III, sc. IV

47 When I hear any man talk of an unalterable
law, the only effect it produces on me is to
convince me that he is an unalterable fool.
Sydney Smith (1771–1845), *The Peter
Plymley Letters*, 1852, IV

48 As with forms of government, so with forms
of law; it is the national character which
decides.
Herbert Spencer (1820–1903), *Social
Statics*, 1870, pt. III, ch. XXI, sec. 6

49 If there be no law, there is no transgression.
Jonathan Swift (1667–1745), *Seasonable
Advice to the Grand Jury*, 1724

113 LAWYERS
See also 112 LAW, 115 LITIGATION

1 The body of the law is no less incumbered
with superfluous members, that are like
Virgil's army, which he tells us was so
crowded, many of them had not room to use
their weapons.
Joseph Addison (1672–1719), *The
Spectator*, no. 21, 24 March 1711

2 When Mr Justice was a counsellor, he would
never take less than a guinea for doing
anything, nor less than half a one for doing
nothing. He durst not if he would: among
lawyers, moderation would be infamy.
Jeremy Bentham (1748–1832), *Truth* v.
Ashhurst; or, Law As It Is, 1823

3 Woe unto you also, ye lawyers! for ye lade
men with burdens grievous to be borne, and
ye yourselves touch not the burdens with
one of your fingers.
Bible, Authorized Version, Luke 11:46

4 Woe unto you, lawyers! for ye have taken
away the key of knowledge: ye entered not
in yourselves, and them that were entering
in ye hindered.
Bible, Authorized Version, *ibid.*, 11:52

5 Lawyer, *n.* One skilled in circumvention of
the law.
Ambrose Bierce (1842–1914?), *The Devil's
Dictionary*, 1911

6 LL.D. Letters indicating the degree of
Legumptionorum Doctor, one learned in the
laws, gifted with legal gumption. Some
suspicion is cast upon this derivation by the
fact that the title was formerly ££.d., and
conferred only upon gentlemen
distinguished for their wealth.
Ambrose Bierce (1842–1914?), *ibid.*

7 A lawyer starts life giving $500 worth of law
for $5, and ends giving $5 worth for $500.
Benjamin H. Brewster (1816–1888),
attributed

8 A man must not think he can save himself
the trouble of being a sensible man and a
gentleman by going to his solicitor, any
more than he can get himself a sound
constitution by going to his doctor; but a
solicitor can do more to keep a tolerably
well-meaning fool straight than a doctor can
do for an invalid. Money is to the solicitor
what souls are to the parson or life to the
physician. He is our money-doctor.
Samuel Butler (1835–1902), *Note Books*,
ed. Festing Jones, 1912, ch. II

9 The laws I love, the lawyers I suspect.
Charles Churchill (1731–1764), *The
Farewell*, 1764

10 The trouble with law is lawyers.
Clarence Darrow (1857–1938), attributed

11 Next bring some lawyers to thy bar,
By innuendo they might all stand there;
There let them expiate their guilt,
And pay for all that blood their tongues ha'
    spilt,
These are the mountebanks of state.
Who by the slight of tongue can crimes
    create,
And dress up trifles in the robes of fate.
Daniel Defoe (*c.*1660–1731), *A Hymn to
the Pillory*, 1703

12 Words are the lawyer's tools of trade.
Lord Denning, *The Discipline of Law*, 1979, p. 5

13 The old woman hesitated, then cast a quick eye at a certain open box beside her roll-top desk and apparently decided that even lawyers can be thieves — a possibility few who have had to meet their fees would dispute.
John Fowles, *The French Lieutenant's Woman*, 1977, ch. 46

14 Lawyers don't love beggars.
Thomas Fuller (1654–1734), *Gnomologia*, 1732, no. 3151

15 I know you lawyers can, with ease,
Twist words and meanings as you please;
That language, by your skill made pliant,
Will bend to favour ev'ry client.
John Gay (1685–1732), *Fables*, 1728, vol. II, 1738, Fable I, 'The Dog and the Fox'

16 When I, good friends, was called to the bar,
I'd an appetite fresh and hearty,
But I was, as many young barristers are,
An impecunious party.
Sir W.S. Gilbert (1836–1911), *Trial by Jury*, 1875

17 That whether you're an honest man or
   whether you're a thief
Depends on whose solicitor has given me
   my brief.
Sir W.S. Gilbert (1836–1911), *Utopia Limited*, 1893, act I

18 There's no better way of using the imagination than the study of law. No poet ever interpreted nature as freely as a lawyer interprets truth.
Jean Giraudoux (1882–1944), *Tiger at the Gates*, 1935, trans. Christopher Fry

19 Lawyers are always more ready to get a man into troubles, than out of them.
Oliver Goldsmith (1728–1774), *The Good Natur'd Man*, 1768, act III

20 Lawyers do not take law reform seriously — there is no reason why they should. They think the law exists as the atmosphere exists, and the notion that it could be improved is too startling to entertain.
Lord Goodman, *Sydney Morning Herald*, 17 July 1982, p. 38

21 If the laws could speak for themselves they would complain of the lawyers in the first place.
Lord Halifax (1633–1695), *Political Thoughts and Reflexions*

22 I do not know a meaner or sadder portion of a man's existence, or one more likely to be full of impatient sorrow, than that which he spends in waiting at the offices of lawyers.
Sir Arthur Helps (1813–1875), *Companions of My Solitude*, 1851, ch. 1

23 Lawyer's houses are built on the heads of fools.
George Herbert (1593–1633), *Jacula Prudentum*, 1651

24 A British lawyer would like to think of himself as part of that mysterious entity called The Law; an American lawyer would like a swimming pool and two houses.
Simon Hoggart, *Observer*, 10 August 1986

25 The lawyers are a picked lot, 'first scholars' and the like, but their business is as unsympathetic as Jack Ketch's.
Oliver Wendell Holmes (1809–1894), *The Poet at the Breakfast-Table*, 1872

26 There are very few grave legal questions in a poor estate.
E.W. Howe (1853–1937) in Rudolf Flesch, *The Book of Unusual Quotations*, 1959

27 Every lawyer should be a conciliator.
Elbert Hubbard (1856–1915), *Notebook*, 1927, p. 120

28 Seventy per cent of the members of all our law-making bodies are lawyers. Very naturally, lawyers making laws favour laws that make lawyers a necessity. If that were not so, lawyers would not be human.
Elbert Hubbard (1856–1915), *ibid.*, p. 193

29 Lawyer . . . An unnecessary evil . . . The only man in whom ignorance of the law is not punished.
Frank McKinney Hubbard (1868–1930), *The Roycroft Dictionary*, 1923

30 Johnson observed, that 'he did not care to speak ill of any man behind his back, but he believed the gentleman was an *attorney*.'
Samuel Johnson (1709–1784) in Boswell's *Life of Johnson*, 1770

31 As it rarely happens that a man is fit to plead
his own cause, lawyers are a class of the
community, who, by study and experience,
have acquired the art and power of arranging
evidence, and of applying to the points at
issue what the law has settled. A lawyer is to
do for his client all that his client might fairly
do for himself, if he could.
Samuel Johnson (1709–1784), *ibid.*

32 I have ne'er been in a chamber with a lawyer
when I did not wish either to scream with
desperation or else fall into the deepest of
sleeps, e'en when the matter concern'd my
own future most profoundly.
Erica Jong, *Fanny*, 1980, bk. III, ch. XVI

33 Lawyers Can Seriously Damage Your
Health.
Michael Joseph, title of book, 1984

34 There are limits to permissible
misrepresentation, even at the hands of a
lawyer.
John Maynard Keynes (1883–1946),
quoted in Elizabeth S. Johnson, *The Shadow
of Keynes*, 1978, ch. 3, p. 33

35 Lawyers generally prefer not to rush things.
Justice Kirby (Australian Law Reform
Commission, on the 52 years it has taken for
lawyers to join scientists at ANZAAS),
Sydney Morning Herald, 'Sayings of the
Week', 15 May 1982

36 A certain young lawyer is said to criticise my
verses. I do not know his name, but if I find
out, lawyer, woe to you!
Martial (*c*. AD 40–*c*.104), *Epigrams*, bk. V,
epig. XXXIII

37 [Lawyers] . . . men that hire out words and
anger.
Martial (*c*. AD 40–*c*.104) in Joseph
Addison, *The Spectator*, no. 21

38 He had the prosperous look of a lawyer.
W. Somerset Maugham (1874–1966), *A
Writer's Notebook*, 1917

39 It is the curse, as well as the fascination of
the law, that lawyers get to know more than
is good for them about their fellow human
beings.
John Mortimer, *The Trials of Rumpole*,
1979, 'Rumpole and the Man of God'

40 The lawyer's is a manifold art.
Sir Frederick Pollock (1845–1937), *Oxford
Lectures*, 1890, p. 2

41 The practice of the law is a perfectly distinct
art.
Sir Frederick Pollock (1845–1937), *ibid.*

42 The lawyer has not reached the height of his
vocation who does not find therein . . .
scope for a peculiar but genuine artistic
function.
Sir Frederick Pollock (1845–1937), *ibid.*,
p. 100

43 'It is the act of lawyers', answered
Pantagruel, 'to sell words.'
François Rabelais (*c*.1494–1553),
Pantagruel, 1532, bk. IV, ch. LVI

44 A lawyer cannot be made honest by an act
of the Legislature. You've got to work on his
conscience, and his lack of conscience is
what made him a lawyer.
Will Rogers (1879–1935) in Donald Day,
Will Rogers: A Biography, 1962, ch. 22

45 Lawyers are brought up with an exaggerated
reverence for their system and, apart from a
few, they don't see what's wrong with it.
Tom Sargeant, *Observer*, 26 September
1982

46 With lawyers in the vacation; for they sleep
between term and term, and then they
perceive not how time moves.
William Shakespeare (1564–1616), *As You
Like It*, 1596–1600, act. III, sc. II

47 I will make
One of her women lawyer to me; for
I yet not understand the case myself.
William Shakespeare (1564–1616),
Cymbeline, 1609–10, act II, sc. III

48 Why may not that be the skull of a lawyer?
Where be his quiddits now, his quillets, his
cases, his tenures, his tricks?
William Shakespeare (1564–1616),
Hamlet, 1599–1600, act V, sc. I

49 *Dick*: The first thing we do, let's kill all the
lawyers.
Cade: Nay, that I mean to do. Is not this a
lamentable thing, that of the skin of an
innocent lamb should be made parchment?
that parchment being scribbled o'er, should
undo a man? Some say the bee stings; but I

say 'tis the bee's wax; for I did but seal once to a thing, and I was never mine own man since.
William Shakespeare (1564–1616), *Henry VI, Pt. II*, 1590–1, act IV, sc. II

50 Then 'tis like the breath of an unfee'd lawyer, — you gave me nothing for 't.
William Shakespeare (1564–1616), *King Lear*, 1605–6, act I, sc. IV

51 Lawyers' fingers, who straight dream on fees.
William Shakespeare (1564–1616), *Romeo and Juliet*, 1595–6, act I, sc. IV

52 Do as adversaries do in law, —
Strive mightily, but eat and drink as friends.
William Shakespeare (1564–1616), *The Taming of the Shrew*, 1593–4, act I, sc. II

53 There is a New Zealand attorney just arrived in London, with 6s.8d. tattooed all over his face.
Sydney Smith (1771–1845) in W. Jerrold, *Bon-Mots of Sydney Smith and R. Brinsley Sheridan*, p. 68

54 A lawyer's a man well trained in memory Of cases, precedent, repartee, speeches.
Stephen Spender, *Trial of a Judge*, 1938, act I

55 There was a society of men [lawyers] among us, bred up from their youth in the art of proving by words multiplied for the purpose, that *white* is *black*, and *black* is *white*, according as they are paid. To this society all the rest of the people are slaves.
Jonathan Swift (1667–1745), *Gulliver's Travels*, 1726, pt. IV, ch. V

56 I never heard a finer piece of satire against *lawyers*, than that of *astrologers*; when they pretend by rule of art to foretell in what time a suit will end, and whether to the advantage of the plaintiff or defendant: thus making the matter depend entirely upon the influence of the stars, without the least regard to the merits of the cause.
Jonathan Swift (1667–1745), *Thoughts on Various Subjects*, 1711

57 I have undertaken the duty of constituting myself one of the attorneys for the people in any court to which I can get entrance. I don't mean as a lawyer, for while I was a lawyer, I have repented.
Woodrow Wilson (1856–1924), speech, 2 September 1912

58 These are those lawyers who, by being in all causes, are in none.
William Wycherley (1640–1716), *The Plain-Dealer*, act III, sc. I

59 A man without money, needs no more fear a crowd of lawyers, than a crowd of pickpockets.
William Wycherley (1640–1716), *ibid.*

---

114 LENDING

See also 20 BORROWING, 57 CREDIT, 58 CREDITORS, 61 DEBT, 104 INTEREST

1

I had a		and a		as many of this land,
I lent my		to my		when he did it demand.
I sought my	penny	from my	friend	when he had kept it long,
I lost my		and my		and was not that a wrong?
Had I a		and a		as I have had before,
I wo'd keep my		and my		and play the fool no more.

James Kelly, *Scottish Proverbs*, 1721, L, no. 90

2 *Falstaff*: Will your lordship lend me a thousand pounds to furnish me forth?
Chief Justice: Not a penny, not a penny.
William Shakespeare (1564–1616), *Henry IV, Pt. II*, 1597–8, act I, sc. II

3 Lend less than thou owest.
William Shakespeare (1564–1616), *King Lear*, 1605–6, act I, sc. IV

4 I hate him for he is a Christian;
But more for that, in low simplicity,
He lends out money gratis, and brings down
The rate of usance here with us in Venice.
William Shakespeare (1564–1616), *The Merchant of Venice*, 1596–7, act I, sc. III

5 If thou wilt lend this money, lend it not
As to thy friends . . .
But lend it rather to thine enemy,
Who if he break, thou mayest with better face
Exact the penalty.
William Shakespeare (1564–1616), *ibid.*

6 I will not lend thee a penny.
William Shakespeare (1564–1616), *The Merry Wives of Windsor*, 1597–1601, act II, sc. II

7 This is no time to lend money; especially upon bare friendship, without security.
William Shakespeare (1564–1616), *Timon of Athens*, 1607–8, act III, sc. I

115 LITIGATION

See also 112 LAW, 113 LAWYERS

---

1 May you have a lawsuit in which you know you are in the right.
Anonymous gypsy curse in W.H. Auden and L. Kronenberger, *The Faber Book of Aphorisms*

2 Litigation, *n.* A machine which you go into as a pig and come out of as a sausage.
Ambrose Bierce (1842–1914?), *The Devil's Dictionary*, 1911

3 A law-suit is like an ill-managed dispute, in which the first object is soon out of sight, and the parties end upon a matter wholly foreign to that on which they began.
Edmund Burke (1729–1797), *A Vindication of Natural Society*, 1756

4 We may justly tax our wrangling lawyers, they do *consenescere in litibus* [grow old in lawsuits], are so litigious and busy here on earth, that I think they will plead their clients' causes hereafter, some of them in hell.
Robert Burton (1577–1640), *Anatomy of Melancholy*, 1621, 'Democritus to the Reader'

5 So he that goes to law, as the proverb is, holds a wolf by the ears, or, as a sheep in a storm runs for shelter to a briar.
Robert Burton (1577–1640), *ibid.*

6 There's only one motto I know of that's any good. 'Never go to law.'
Henry Cecil, *Brothers in Law*, 1955, ch. 5

7 It is ignorance of the law rather than knowledge of it that leads to litigation.
Cicero (106–43 BC), *De Legibus*, bk. I, ch. VI

8 *The Benefit of Going to Law*
Two beggars travelling along,
  One blind, the other lame,
Pick'd up an oyster on the way
  To which they both lay claim:
The matter rose so high, that they
  Resolv'd to go to law,
As often richer fools have done,
  Who quarrel for a straw.
A lawyer took it straight in hand,
Who knew his business was,
To mind nor one nor t'other side,
  But make the best o' th' cause;
As always in the law's the case
  So he his judgement gave,
And lawyer-like he thus resolv'd
  What each of them should have.
Blind plaintiff, lame defendant, share
The friendly law's impartial care,
A shell for him, a shell for thee,
The middle is the lawyer's fee.
Benjamin Franklin (1706–1790), *Poor Richard's Almanac*, 1733. (The last four lines are taken from Matthew Prior, 1664–1721, *The Lame and the Blind disputing the right to an Oyster found; The Lawyer decides the controversy*, 1720)

9 A petitioner at court that spares his purse, angles without bait.
Thomas Fuller (1654–1734), *Gnomologia*, 1732, no. 347

10 An indifferent agreement, is better than carrying a cause at law.
Thomas Fuller (1654–1734), *ibid.*, no. 637

11 Fools and obstinate men make lawyers rich.
Thomas Fuller (1654–1734), *ibid.*, no. 1, 565

12 Sue a beggar, and catch a louse.
Thomas Fuller (1654–1734), *ibid.*, no. 4285

13 Litigation: A form of hell whereby money is transferred from the pockets of the proletariat to that of lawyers.
Frank McKinney Hubbard (1868–1930), *The Roycroft Dictionary*, 1923

14 There is something sickening in seeing poor devils drawn into great expense about trifles by interested attorneys. But too cheap an access to litigation has its evils on the other hand, for the proneness of the lower classes to gratify spite and revenge in this way would be a dreadful evil were they able to endure the expense.
Sir Walter Scott (1771–1832), *Journal*, 12 December 1825

15 You never, but never, go to litigation if there is another way out. . . . Litigation only makes lawyers fat.
Wilbur Smith, *Hungry as the Sea*, 1979, p. 214

116 MACHINERY
See also 198 TECHNOLOGY

1 It is the Age of Machinery, in every outward and inward sense of that word.
Thomas Carlyle (1795–1881), *Signs of the Times*, 1829, vol. II

2 Man is a tool-using animal . . . Without tools he is nothing, with tools he is all.
Thomas Carlyle (1795–1881), *Sartor Resartus*, 1836, bk. I, ch. V

3 Machines are the produce of the mind of man; and their existence distinguishes the civilized man from the savage.
William Cobbett (1762–1835), *Letter to the Luddites of Nottingham*, 1816

4 The greatest task before civilization at present is to make machines what they ought to be, the slaves, instead of the masters of men.
Havelock Ellis (1859–1939), *Little Essays of Love and Virtue*, 1922, ch. 7

5 One machine can do the work of fifty ordinary men. No machine can do the work of one extraordinary man.
Elbert Hubbard (1856–1915), *The Philistine*, 1895–1915, vol. XVIII

6 It is never the machines that are dead. It is only the mechanically-minded men that are dead.
Gerald Stanley Lee (1862–1944), *Crowds*, 1913, pt. II, ch. V

7 The increase of net incomes, estimated in commodities, which is always the consequence of improved machinery, will lead to new accumulations. These savings are annual, and must soon create a fund much greater than the gross revenue originally lost by the discovery of the machine, when the demand for labour will be as great as before.
David Ricardo (1772–1823), *Principles of Political Economy*, 1817, XXXI

8 The worker who runs the machine knows its faults better than the intellectual who describes it.
Vital Roux (1760–1846), *De l'influence du gouvernement sur la prosperité du commerce*, 1800, p. 443

9 Men have become the tools of their tools.
Henry D. Thoreau (1817–1862), *Walden*, 1854

10 I see no reason to suppose that these machines [steam locomotives] will ever force themselves into general use.
Duke of Wellington (1769–1852) in J. Gere, *Geoffrey Madan's Notebooks*

11 The evil that machinery is doing is not merely in the consequences of its work but in the fact that it makes men themselves machines also.
Oscar Wilde (1854–1900), *Weekly Herald*, 22 March 1882

117 MANAGEMENT
See also 21 BOSSES, 71 EMPLOYERS,
118 MANAGEMENT CONSULTANCY,
138 PERSONNEL MANAGEMENT

1 The average vice-president is a form of executive fungus that attaches itself to a desk. On a boat this growth would be called a barnacle.
Fred Allen (1894–1956) in Clifton Fadiman, *The American Treasury 1455–1955*, 1955

2 Executive: An ulcer with authority.
Fred Allen (1894–1956), attributed

3 Management is the art of getting other people to do all the work.
Anonymous

4 A large business may be managed tolerably by a quiet group of second-rate men if these men be always the same; but it cannot be managed at all by a fluctuating body, even of the cleverest men.
Walter Bagehot (1826–1877), *Lombard Street*, 1873, ch. 9

5 Management seems to have concluded that the answer to most management problems lies with management itself.
Willard E. Bennett, *Manager Selection, Education and Training*, 1951, ch. 1

6 Demanding management is not necessarily bad management.
Geoffrey Boycott, *In the Fast Lane*, 1982, ch. 7

7 Running an air force in wartime is easier than running a corporation . . . the opportunity to threaten a few vice-presidents with a firing squad would have done wonders for Boeing and Lockheed when they were having their troubles.
Len Deighton, *Goodbye Mickey Mouse*, 1982, ch. 8

8 Managing a business requires a great deal of frankness and openness and you actually lead by being very honest with people.
Sir Michael Edwardes, *Observer*, 'Sayings of the Week', 19 June 1983

9 There is no merit in sowing dissension among subordinates; any beginner can do it.
Henri Fayol (1841–1925), *General and Industrial Management*, 1916, ch. IV

10 Dividing enemy forces to weaken them is clever, but dividing one's own team is a grave sin against the business.
Henri Fayol (1841–1925), *ibid.*

11 For any action whatsoever, an employee should receive orders from one superior only.
Henri Fayol (1841–1925), *ibid.*

12 Managerial skill can not be painted on the outside of executives — it has to go deeper than that.
Mary Parker Follett (1868–1933), *Freedom & Co-ordination*, 1949, ch. II

13 The modern corporate or joint-venture capitalism has largely replaced tycoon capitalism. The one-man-band owner-manager is fast being replaced by a new class of professional managers, dedicated more to the advancement of the company than to the enrichment of a few owners.
Henry Ford II, speech, 1955

14 Management: An activity or art where those who have not yet succeeded and those who have proved unsuccessful are led by those who have not yet failed.
Paulsson Frenckner, Address to the 7th Annual Congress of the European Accounting Association, Saint-Gall, Switzerland, 1984

15 An attack upon the trade unionists in this country [Australia] and upon the cost structure in this country is no excuse, no excuse at all, for management not getting off their sometimes lazy butt — their unimaginative butt.
Bob Hawke, *Sydney Morning Herald*, 'Sayings of the Week', 12 July 1986

16 Executive: A man who can make quick decisions and is sometimes right.
Frank McKinney Hubbard (1868–1930), *The Roycroft Dictionary*, 1923

17 Trade could not be managed by those who manage it, if it had much difficulty.
Samuel Johnson (1709–1784), letter to Mrs Thrale, 16 November 1779

18 Women managers are not viewed as one of the boys.
Jane Jordan, *Sydney Morning Herald*, 'Sayings of the Week', 7 September 1985

19 It is easier to talk about money — and much easier to talk about sex — than it is to talk about power. People who have it deny it; people who want it do not want to appear to hunger for it; and people who engage in its machinations do so secretly.
Rosabeth Moss Kanter, 'Power Failure in Management Circuits', *Harvard Business Review*, July–August 1979

20 We have a major problem in this country [Australia]: we have a management class which is, by and large, incompetent, by and large incapable of generating the level of investment and borrowings for this country.
Bill Kelty, *Sydney Morning Herald*, 'Sayings of the Week', 16 April 1986

21 To find men capable of managing business efficiently and secure to them the positions of responsible control is perhaps the most important single problem of economic organisation on the efficiency scale.
Frank H. Knight (1885–1972), *Risk, Uncertainty and Profit*, 1921, p. 283

22 Managing is the art of getting things done through and with people in formally organized groups. It is the art of creating an environment in which people can perform as individuals and yet co-operate towards the

attainment of group goals. It is the art of removing blocks to such performance.
Harold Koontz, 'Making Sense of Management Theory', *Harvard Business Review*, vol. 40, no. 4, 1962

23 The person who never makes a mistake works for someone who does.
Sir Hector Laing in Ray Wild, *How to Manage*, 1982, p. 39

24 Paternalism has become a nasty word, but it is by no means a defunct managerial philosophy.
D. McGregor, *The Human Side of Enterprise*, 1960, ch. 3

25 You can't run a business like a Communist cell.
Ian MacGregor, *Observer*, 'Sayings of the Week', 30 January 1983

26 Someone once defined the manager, only half in jest, as that person who sees the visitors so that everyone else can get the work done.
H. Mintzberg, *The Structure of Organizations*, 1979, ch. 2

27 Doing a job is more difficult than telling someone else how the job ought to be done.
C. Northcote Parkinson, *In-Laws and Outlaws*, 1959, ch. 4

28 Good management is not just a bright tool-kit of techniques and specifications, although the professional skills are essential. It involves the arts of entrepreneurship and leadership, it means managing change, including change itself.
Sir Peter Parker, *Sunday Times*, 6 October 1985

29 Management problems always turn out to be people problems.
John Peet, 'Management Consultancy', *Economist*, 13 February 1988

30 Managers may be born but they also have to be made.
Sir David Steel in Ray Wild, *How to Manage*, 1982, p. 34

31 It is time Britain paid less attention to its 'union problem' and far more to its 'management problem'.
Sunday Times, 1 September 1985

32 In a profit squeeze, management will come up with very creative reasons for changing the accounting system.
Robert Townsend, *Up the Organization*, 1971

33 Wise business management, and more particularly what is spoken of as safe and sane business management . . . reduces itself in the main to a sagacious use of sabotage.
Thorstein Veblen (1857–1929), *The Nature of the Peace*, 1919, ch. VII, p. 325

---

118 MANAGEMENT CONSULTANCY
See also 117 MANAGEMENT,
138 PERSONNEL MANAGEMENT

---

1 A management consultant is someone who tells management what it already knows but packages it differently.
Anonymous

2 Management consulting is an advisory service contracted for and provided to organisations by specially trained and qualified persons who assist, in an objective and independent manner, the client organisation to identify management problems, analyse such problems, recommend solutions to these problems and help, when requested, in the implementation of solutions.
Larry Greiner and Robert Metzger, *Consulting to Management*, 1983

3 Defining consultancy is a bit like defining the upper class: every possible candidate draws the line just below himself.
John Peet, 'Management Consultancy', *Economist*, 13 February 1988

4 [Management consultants] are the people who borrow your watch to tell you what time it is and then walk off with it.
Robert Townsend, *Up the Organization*, 1971

5 *Simon*: What's your husband do?
Jenny: He's a professional bullshit artist. A management consultant.
David Williamson, *Don's Party*, 1973, act 1

119 MARKETING
See also 6 ADVERTISING, 82 FASHION,
172 SALES, 179 SELLING

1 Exports are becoming obsolete, because
they are too slow. Marketers today must sell
the latest product everywhere at once —
and that means producing locally.
Carlo de Benedetti, *Observer*, 14 February
1988

2 Marketing is matter in motion.
**Paul D. Converse, Harvey W. Huegy and
Robert V. Mitchell**, *Elements of Marketing*,
6th ed., 1958, ch. 1

3 Marketing is simply sales with a college
education.
John Freund in Jim Fisk and Robert Barron,
Great Business Quotations, 1985

4 The successful company is the one which is
first to identify emerging consumer needs
and to offer product improvements which
satisfy those needs. The successful
marketeer spots a new trend early, and then
leads it.
Edward G. Harness in Ray Wild, *How to
Manage*, 1982, pp. 226–7

5 We shall be the more marketable.
William Shakespeare (1564–1616), *As You
Like It*, 1596–1600, act I, sc. II

6 No doubt Marketable.
William Shakespeare (1564–1616), *The
Tempest*, 1611, act V, sc. I

7 Let us, like merchants, show our foulest
                    wares,
And think perchance they'll sell; if not,
The lustre of the better shall exceed,
By showing the worst first.
William Shakespeare (1564–1616), *Troilus
and Cressida*, 1597–1602, act I, sc. III

8 Pan Am takes good care of you. Marks and
Spencer loves you. Securicor cares . . . At
Amstrad: 'We want your money'.
Alan Sugar, *Observer*, 'Sayings of the
Week', 3 May 1987

120 MARKETS
See also 119 MARKETING

1 The market, whether stock, bond, or super,
is a barometer of civilisation.
Jason Alexander, *Philosophy for Investors*,
1979, p. 54

2 The market is totally impartial.
Anonymous

3 Perhaps the Government needs to shoot a
few workers to get the message across to the
markets.
Anonymous, *Sydney Morning Herald*,
'Sayings of the Week', 14 September 1985

4 Fortune is like the market; where many
times, if you can stay a little, the price will
fall.
Francis Bacon (1561–1626), *Essays*, 1625,
'Of Delays'

5 In every market a dealer must conduct his
business according to the custom of the
market, or he will not be able to conduct it
at all.
Walter Bagehot (1826–1877), *Lombard
Street*, 1873, ch. 11

6 The belief of the money-market, which is
mainly composed of grave people, is as
imitative as any belief. You will find one day
everyone enterprising, enthusiastic,
vigorous, eager to buy, and eager to order:
in a week or so you will find almost the
whole society depressed, anxious, and
wanting to sell.
Walter Bagehot (1826–1877),
Physics and Politics, 1872, no. III,
'Nation-Making'

7 But the market is the best judge of value; for
by the concourse of buyers and sellers, the
quantity of wares, and the occasion for them
are best known. Things are just worth so
much, as they and be sold for, according to
the old rule *Valet Quantum Vendi Potest*.
Nicholas Barbon (? –1698), *A Discourse of
Trade*, 1690

8 A friend in the market is better than money in the chest.
Thomas Fuller (1654–1734), *Gnomologia*, 1732, no. 119

9 A man may come to market, though he don't buy oysters.
Thomas Fuller (1654–1734), *ibid.*, no. 293

10 A moneyless man goes fast through the market.
Thomas Fuller (1654–1734), *ibid.*, no. 330

11 Buy at a market, and sell at home.
Thomas Fuller, (1654–1734), *ibid.*, no. 1034

12 He that sits to work in the market-place, shall have many teachers.
Thomas Fuller (1654–1734), *ibid.*, no. 2303

13 He that cannot abide a bad market, deserves not a good one.
Thomas Fuller (1654–1734), *ibid.*, no. 2058

14 Send a fool to market, and a fool he'll return.
Thomas Fuller (1654–1734), *ibid.*, no. 4096

15 You may know by the market-folks, how the market goes.
Thomas Fuller (1654–1734), *ibid.*, no. 5952

16 Markets, generally, are both gender-blind and colour-blind.
L. Hannah, *Listener*, 21 August 1986

17 Three women make a market.
George Herbert (1593–1633), *Jacula Prudentum*, 1651

18 As soon goes the lambskin to the market as the old sheeps.
John Kelly, *Scottish Proverbs*, 1721, A, no. 36

19 A silverless man goes fast through the market.
James Kelly, *ibid.*, no. 56

20 As the market goes wares must sell.
James Kelly, *ibid.*, no. 335

21 The idea of the free market, with its stress on the sovereignty of the individual consumer, was diametrically opposed to all that Toryism stood for. To the Tory it was obvious that economic forces should be made to accommodate themselves to the established pattern of social relationships.
T.F. Lindsay and M. Harrington, *The Conservative Party, 1918–1970*, 1974, p. 4

22 Beware of the market; it is Capitalism's secret weapon! Comprehensive planning is the heart and core of genuine socialism. [With reference to Yugoslavia.]
Monthly Review, March 1964, editorial

23 Market forces, like the sea, are powerful, bountiful but dangerous. And, as with the seas, the wise man treats the free market with the utmost respect, interfering only at the margin and after much thought.
Graham Searjeant, *The Times*, 10 November 1986

24 I'll meet with you upon the mart.
William Shakespeare (1564–1616), *The Comedy of Errors*, 1592–3, act I, sc. II

25 Talk like the vulgar sort of market-men That come to gather money for their corn.
William Shakespeare (1564–1616), *Henry VI, Pt. I*, 1589–90, act III, sc. II

26 Poor market-folks that come to sell their corn.
William Shakespeare (1564–1616), *ibid.*

27 Enter, go in; the market-bell is rung.
William Shakespeare (1564–1616), *ibid.*

28 [Value] is adjusted . . . not by any accurate measure, but by the higgling and bargaining of the market, according to that sort of rough equality which, though not exact, is sufficient for carrying on the business of common life.
Adam Smith (1723–1790), *Wealth of Nations*, 1776, vol. I, bk. I, ch. V

29 Every individual . . . generally, indeed, neither intends to promote the public interest, nor knows how much he is promoting it. By preferring the support of domestic to that of foreign industry he intends only his own security; and by directing that industry in such a manner as its produce may be of the greatest value, he intends only his own gain, and he is in this, as in many other cases, led by an invisible hand to promote an end which was no part of his intention.
Adam Smith (1723–1790), *ibid.*, bk. IV, ch. II

30 Free markets cannot be invested with the

robe of moral virtue any more than they can be dismissed as evil, heartless or uncaring.
The Times, 16 January 1987

31 It is no use to throw a good thing away merely because the market isn't ripe yet.
Mark Twain (1835–1910), *A Connecticut Yankee in King Arthur's Court*, 1889, ch. 22

32 The one thing the market cannot measure is the satisfaction derived from its own use.
Barbara Wootton (1897–1988), *Lament for Economics*, 1938, p. 187

121 MARRIAGE

1 Th' June bride business wuz light this year, owin' t' th' good times we reckon.
Frank McKinney Hubbard (1868–1930), *New Sayings by Abe Martin*, 1917

2 [Marriage is] like signing a 356 page contract without knowing what's in it.
Mick Jagger, *Observer*, 'Sayings of the Week', 20 January 1985

3 Most English husbands are so busy making money or being with their friends that they're secretly relieved to have their wives kept happy by an expert.
John Pearson, *James Bond: The Authorised Biography of 007*, ch. 10

4 In olden times sacrifices were made at the altar — a custom which is still continued.
Helen Rowland (1876–1950) in B. House, *From Eve On*

5 It is a woman's business to get married as soon as possible, and a man's to keep unmarried as long as he can.
George Bernard Shaw (1856–1950), *Man and Superman*, 1903, act II

6 Marriage is a bribe to make a housekeeper think she's a householder.
Thornton Wilder (1897–1975), *The Matchmaker*, 1954, act I

122 MEDICINE
See also 93 HEALTH

1 A minor operation is one performed on someone else.
Anonymous

2 A specialist is a doctor who has discovered which of his talents will bring in the most money.
Anonymous

3 To add life to years, not just years to life.
Anonymous, motto of specialists in ageing

4 The first operation carried out in the private sector is a biopsy of the wallet.
Anonymous

5 You can always tell a Bart's man, but you can't tell him much.
Anonymous, *The Times Higher Education Supplement*, 23 May 1986

6 I do wish the more suspicious of our GPs would stop feeling nervously for their wallets every time I mention the word reform.
Kenneth Clarke, *Observer*, 'Sayings of the Week', 12 March 1989

7 The dental surgery is a hot-bed of emotions.
Dr Ruth Freeman, quoted in 'It's the Dentist that's the Pain', *The Times*, 17 September 1986

8 Commonly physicians, like beer, are best when they are old, and lawyers, like bread, when they are young and new.
Thomas Fuller (1608–1661), *The Holy State*, 1642, 'The Good Advocate'

9 The private patient pays to avoid waiting. The NHS [National Health Service] patient waits to avoid paying.
Richard Gordon, *Dr Gordon's Casebook*, 1982, '6 September'

10 Doctors think a lot of patients are cured who have simply quit in disgust.
Don Herold in Rudolf Flesch, *The Book of Unusual Quotations*, 1959

11 A dentist to be successful must be a surgeon, an artist, a sculptor and a mechanic.
Elbert Hubbard (1856–1915), *Notebook*, 1927, p. 173

12 There's another advantage of being poor — a doctor will cure you faster.
Frank McKinney Hubbard (1868–1930) in Rudolf Flesch, *The Book of Unusual Quotations*, 1959

13 I like dining with the medical profession, for it is agreeable to find out that mine is not the

only profession that does not always practise what it preaches.
William Randolph Inge (1860–1954), *Observer*, 'Sayings of the Week', 1 November 1925

14 If the doctor cures, the sun sees it, but if he kills, the earth hides it.
James Kelly, *Scottish Proverbs*, 1721, I, no. 62

15 Man dies too soon, beside his works
    half-planned.
   His days are counted and reprieve is
    vain:
Who shall entreat with Death to stay his
    hand,
   Or cloke the shameful nakedness of
    pain?

Send here the bold, the seekers of the way —
   The passionless, the unshakeable of soul,
Who serve the inmost mysteries of man's
    clay,
   And ask no more than leave to make
    them whole.
Rudyard Kipling (1865–1936), *Doctors*, 1923

16 Though rheumatology does not attract the fat incomes of some high-technology medical specialities . . . it is a profession on the march.
N.R. Kleinfield, 'The Arthritis Business: The Profitable Side of Pain', *International Herald Tribune*, 2 September 1985

17 The true aim of medicine is not to make men virtuous; it is to safeguard and rescue them from the consequences of their vices. The physician does not preach repentance; he offers absolution.
H.L. Mencken (1880–1956) in C. Bingham, *Wit and Wisdom*, 1982

18 I certify that the cause of death
Was something Latin and something long
And who is to say that the doctor's wrong?
Andrew Barton Paterson (1864–1941), 'The Hypnotist', 1890, in Clement Semmler, *The Banjo of the Bush*, 1966, ch. 6

19 It struck me as incomprehensible that I should be allowed to lead such a happy life when so many people were wrestling with care and suffering.
Albert Schweitzer (1875–1965) in James Beasley Simpson, *Best Quotes of '54, '55, '56*, 1957

20 Follow the practice of physicians, who when the usual remedies do not work try just the opposite.
Seneca (4 BC – AD 65), *De Clementia*, bk. I, ch. IX

21 It is a poor physician who doubts his ability to cure.
Seneca (4 BC – AD 65), *ibid.*, ch. XVII

22 I will not cast away my physic but on those that are sick.
William Shakespeare (1564–1616), *As You Like It*, 1596–1600, act III, sc. II

23 Kill thy physician, and the fee bestow Upon the foul disease.
William Shakespeare (1564–1616), *King Lear*, 1605–6, act I, sc. I

24 The patient dies while the physician sleeps.
William Shakespeare (1564–1616), *The Rape of Lucrece*, 1593–4, l. 934

25 Let no one suppose that the words doctor and patient can disguise from the parties the fact that they are employer and employee.
George Bernard Shaw (1856–1950), *The Doctor's Dilemma*, 1913

26 The patient who has been given up by the doctor does not necessarily die.
Rabindranath Tagore (1861–1941) in N.B. Sen, *Wit and Wisdom of India*, 1961

27 There is not a doctor in all the world who will bleed or purge you without a fee.
Voltaire (1694–1778), *Candide*, 1759, ch. IV

28 Choose your specialist and you choose your disease.
Westminster Gazette, 18 May 1906

123 MINING

1 A mine is a hole in the ground owned by a liar.
Anonymous

2 There are three groups that no British Prime Minister should provoke: the Vatican, the Treasury and the miners.
Stanley Baldwin (1867–1947), attributed

3 We shall have no coal industry if the miners are driven into the ground.
Claire Brooks, *Private Eye*, no. 602, 11 January 1985, 'Colemanballs'

4 [M]ining is the one-armed bandit of economic development: it is easy to pull the handle of the fruit-machine, but difficult to anticipate the consequences.
Donald Denoon, *Settler Capitalism*, 1983, ch. 5

5 The industrial customer burns coal to make money, not the other way round.
Sir Campbell Fraser, *Observer*, 'Sayings of the Week', 15 April 1984

6 The world is swimming in coal.
Ian MacGregor, *Observer*, 'Sayings of the Week', 15 January 1984

7 Who digs the mine, or quarry, digs with glee;
   No slave! — His option, and his gain are free.
Richard Savage (*c.*1697–1743), *Of Public Spirit* (first version), 1736

8 There is an old saying that nobody knows the reserves of an oilfield until the last barrel has been pumped out and the same is true of mines.
Trevor Sykes, *The Money Miners — The Great Australian Mining Boom*, 1979, p. 351

---

124 MONEY

See also 83 FINANCE, 90 GOLD, 213 WEALTH

---

1 The worth of money is not in its possession, but in its use.
Aesop (*fl. c.*550 BC), *Fables*, 'The Miser'

2 Money can't buy you friends; it can only rent them.
Anonymous

3 Money is the blood and soul of men and whosoever has none wanders dead among the living.
Anonymous

4 Where there's muck, there's brass.
Anonymous

5 Everything, then, must be assessed in money; for this enables men always to exchange their services, and so makes society possible.
Aristotle (384–322 BC), *Nicomachean Ethics*, bk. V, ch. 5

6 Money is like muck, not good except it be spread.
Francis Bacon (1561–1626), *Essays*, 1625, 'Of Seditions and Troubles'

7 Money is economical power.
Walter Bagehot (1826–1877), *Lombard Street*, 1873

8 Money is the measure of commerce.
Nicholas Barbon (? –1698), *Discourse Concerning Coining the New Money Lighter*, 1696

9 A man can no more make money suddenly and largely, and be unharmed by it, than one could suddenly grow from a child's stature to a man's without harm.
Henry Ward Beecher (1813–1887), *Proverbs from Plymouth Pulpit*, 1887

10 A feast is made for laughter, and wine maketh merry: but money answereth all things.
Bible, Authorized Version, Ecclesiastes 10: 19

11 For the love of money is the root of all evil.
Bible, Authorized Version, 1 Timothy 6:10

12 Money, *n.* A blessing that is of no advantage to us excepting when we part with it.
Ambrose Bierce (1842–1914?), *The Devil's Dictionary*, 1911

13 Money is the last enemy that shall never be subdued. While there is flesh there is money — or the want of money; but money is always on the brain so long as there is a brain in reasonable order.
Samuel Butler (1835–1902), *Note Books*, ed. Festing Jones, 1912, ch. II

14 It has been said that the love of money is the root of all evil. The want of money is so quite as truly.
Samuel Butler (1835–1902), *Erewhon*, 1872, ch. 10

15 In epochs when cash payment has become the sole nexus of man to man.
Thomas Carlyle (1795–1881), *Chartism*, 1839, ch. 2

16 In my experience, people who've lost a lot of money usually have a fair bit left.
Peter Corris, 'P.I. Blues', in *The Big Drop and Other Cliff Hardy Stories*, 1985

17 MONEY, Cash. *Money* comes from the Latin *moneta*, a surname of Juno, in whose temple at Rome money was coined. *Cash* from the French casse, a chest, signifies that which is put in a chest.
George Crabb (1778–1851), *Crabb's English Synonymes*, 1826

18 Every branch of knowledge has its fundamental discovery. In mechanics it is the wheel, in science fire, in politics the vote. Similarly, in economics, in the whole commercial side of man's social existence, money is the essential invention on which all the rest is based.
Sir Geoffrey Crowther (1907–1972), *An Outline of Money*, 1940, ch. 1

19 Money, it has been said, has two properties. It is flat so that it can be piled up. But it is also round so that it can circulate.
Sir Geoffrey Crowther (1907–1972), *ibid.*, ch. 2

20 My money doth make me full merry to be, And without my money none careth for me.
Thomas Deloney (1543?–1607?), *Jack of Newbury*, 1597, I

21 Money is money in whosoever's hands one finds it. It is the only power which one never disputes. Virtue, beauty, courage and genius are disputed but never money. There is no civilised being who, on getting up in the morning, does not recognise the sovereignty of money, without which he would have no roof to shelter him, no bed on which to sleep and no bread to eat.
A. Dumas, *fils* (1824–1895), *La Question d'Argent*, 1857, act 1, sc. 4

22 When a currency's only friends are central bankers, it is heading for a fall.
Economist, 5 December 1987

23 Money never bears interest except in the sense of creating convenience in the process of exchange.
Irving Fisher (1867–1947), *The Purchasing Power of Money*, 1920, ch. II, 1

24 Money is of no use to us until it is spent. The ultimate wages are not paid in terms of money but in the enjoyment it buys.
Irving Fisher (1867–1947), *The Theory of Interest*, 1930, ch. 1

25 The chief evil of an unstable dollar is uncertainty.
Irving Fisher (1867–1947), *Stabilizing the Dollar*, 1920, p. xxxv

26 Monetarism is a world wide disease.
Michael Foot, *Observer*, 'Sayings of the Week', 13 February 1983

27 A fool and his money are soon parted.
Thomas Fuller (1654–1734), *Gnomologia*, 1732, no. 98

28 A man without money, is a bow without an arrow.
Thomas Fuller (1654–1734), *ibid.*, no. 316

29 Be the business never so painful, you may have it done for money.
Thomas Fuller (1654–1734), *ibid.*, no. 857

30 But help me to money, and I'll help myself to friends.
Thomas Fuller (1654–1734), *ibid.*, no. 1030

31 He that is known to have no money, has no friends nor credit.
Thomas Fuller (1654–1734), *ibid.*, no. 2181

32 If thou wouldest reap money, sow money.
Thomas Fuller (1654–1734), *ibid.*, no. 2722

33 If you would know the value of a ducat, try to borrow one.
Thomas Fuller (1654–1734), *ibid.*, no. 2801

34 Love does much; but money does more.
Thomas Fuller (1654–1734), *ibid.*, no. 3286

35 Money is the best bait to fish for men with.
Thomas Fuller (1654–1734), *ibid.*, no. 3439

36 My money comes in at the door, and flies out at the window.
Thomas Fuller (1654–1734), *ibid.*, no. 3501

37 The study of money, above all fields in economics, is the one in which complexity is used to disguise truth or to evade truth, not to reveal it.
John Kenneth Galbraith, *Money*, 1975, ch. 1

38 Money talks, they say. All it ever said to me
was 'good-bye'.
Cary Grant in H. Haun, *The Movie Quote Book*

39 Bad money drives out good money.
['Gresham's Law'.]
Sir Thomas Gresham (1519–1579). The
phrase occurs in a Royal Proclamation of
1560, when Gresham was a leading
government adviser.

40 There's two languages, Squire, that's
univarsal: the language of love and the
language of money; the galls onderstand the
one, and the men onderstand the other, all
the world over, from Canton to Niagara.
Thomas Chandler Haliburton
(1796–1865), *The Attaché; or, Sam Slick in
England*, 1843, vol. I, ch. II

41 Would you know what money is, go borrow
some.
George Herbert (1593–1633), *Jacula
Prudentum*, 1651

42 Money is life to us wretched mortals.
Hesiod (*fl. c.*700 BC), *Works and Days*

43 Put not your trust in money, but put your
money in trust.
Oliver Wendell Holmes (1809–1894), *The
Autocrat of the Breakfast Table*, 1858, II

44 There is only one thing for a man to do who
is married to a woman who enjoys spending
money, and that is to enjoy earning it.
E.W. Howe (1853–1937), *Country Town
Sayings*, 1911

45 When a man says money can do anything,
that settles it: he hasn't any.
E.W. Howe (1853–1937), *Sinner Sermons*,
1926, p. 41

46 Money is the measure of power. Men do not
especially prize money for the sake of
money, but they prize it as a tangible
recognition of their ability.
Elbert Hubbard (1856–1915), *Notebook*,
1927, p. 134

47 It seems like hard earned money has th' best
wings.
Frank McKinney Hubbard (1868–1930),
New Sayings by Abe Martin, 1917

48 When a feller says, 'It hain't th' money but
th' principle o' th' thing,' it's th' money.
Frank McKinney Hubbard (1868–1930),
ibid.

49 The safest way to double your money is to
fold it over once and put it in your pocket.
Frank McKinney Hubbard (1868–1930) in
Esar and Bentley, *The Treasury of
Humorous Quotations*

50 Money having chiefly a fictitious value, the
greater or less plenty of it is of no
consequence.
David Hume (1711–1776), *Essays*,
1741–2, 'Of Interest'

51 The almighty dollar, that great object of
universal devotion throughout our land,
seems to have no genuine devotees in these
peculiar villages.
Washington Irving (1783–1859), 'The
Creole Village', *Knickerbocker Magazine*,
November 1836

52 A real woman has a special attitude toward
money. If she earns it, it is hers; if her
husband earns it, it is theirs.
Joyce Jillson, *Real Women Don't Pump Gas*,
1982, ch. 6

53 In civilized society, personal merit will not
serve you so much as money will. Sir, you
may make the experiment. Go into the
street, and give one man a lecture on
morality, and another a shilling, and see
which will respect you the most.
Samuel Johnson (1709–1784)
in Boswell's *Life of Johnson*,
20 July 1763

54 There are few ways in which a man can be
more innocently employed than in getting
money.
Samuel Johnson (1709–1784), *ibid.*, 27
March 1783

55 A full purse never wanted a friend.
James Kelly, *Scottish Proverbs*, 1721, A,
no. 352

56 Be it better, be it worse, be rul'd by him that
has the purse.
James Kelly, *ibid.*, B, no. 140

57 If you sell your purse to your wife, give your
breeks into the bargain.
James Kelly, *ibid.*, I, no. 140

58 He left his money in his other breeks.
James Kelly, *ibid.*, H, no. 90

59 He that has not silver in his purse, should
have silk on his tongue.
James Kelly, *ibid.*, no. 125

60 Money would be gotten, if there were
money to get it with.
James Kelly, *ibid.*, M, no. 54

61 If you want to make money, go where the
money is.
Joseph P. Kennedy (1888–1969) in A.M.
Schlesinger, *Robert Kennedy and his Times*

62 The importance of money essentially flows
from its being a link between the present
and the future.
John Maynard Keynes (1883–1946),
*The General Theory of Employment
Interest and Money*, 1936, bk. V,
ch. 21

63 Money is only important for what it will
procure.
John Maynard Keynes (1883–1946), *A
Tract on Monetary Reform*, 1924, ch.I

64 Come back next Thursday with a specimen
of your money.
Groucho Marx (1895–1977), *Groucho and
Me*, 1959

65 Money is the alienated essence of man's
work existence; this essence dominates him
and he worships it.
Karl Marx (1818–1883), 'On the Jewish
Question', 1843, *Early Writings*

66 Money is like a sixth sense without which
you cannnot make a complete use of the
other five.
W. Somerset Maugham (1874–1965), *Of
Human Bondage*, 1915, ch. 51

67 The chief value of money lies in the fact that
one lives in a world in which it is
overestimated.
H.L. Mencken (1880–1956) in E.C. Bursk,
D.T. Clark and R.W. Hidy, *The World of
Business*, 1962, vol. 2, 676

68 The demand for money . . . consists of all
the goods offered for sale. Every seller of
goods is a buyer of money, and the goods he
brings with him constitute his demand.
John Stuart Mill (1806–1873), *Principles of
Political Economy*, 1848, bk. III, ch. VIII

69 Money can't buy friends, but you can get a
better class of enemy.
Spike Milligan, attributed

70 Because it thus rationalises economic life
itself, the use of money lays the foundation
for a rational theory of that life. Money may
not be the root of *all* evil, but it is the root of
economic science.
Wesley Clair Mitchell (1874–1948), *The
Backward Art of Spending Money*, 1937,
p. 171

71 It must, however, never be forgotten that
this money system is only an elaborated
barter system.
A.F. Mummery (1855–1895) **and J.F.
Hobson** (1858–1940), *The Physiology of
Industry*, 1889, ch. VII

72 But it is pretty to see what money can do.
Samuel Pepys (1633–1703), *Diary*, 21
March 1667

73 Money is but the fat of the body politick,
whereof too much doth as often hinder its
agility, as too little makes it sick.
Sir William Petty (1623–1687), *Verbum
Sapienti*, in *The Economic Writings of Sir
William Petty*, ed. Hull, vol. I, p. 113

74 Having money is rather like being a blonde.
It is more fun but not vital.
Mary Quant, *Observer*, 'Sayings of the
Week', 2 November 1986

75 Money begets money.
John Ray (1627–1705), *English Proverbs*,
1670

76 In the use of money, every one is a trader.
David Ricardo (1772–1823), *Proposals for
an Economical and Secure Currency*, 1816,
sec. IV

77 Money makes a man laugh.
John Selden (1584–1654), *Table Talk*,
1689, 'Money'

78 Ready money.
William Shakespeare (1564–1616),
Measure for Measure, 1604–5, act IV, sc. III

79 They say if money go before, all ways do lie
open.
William Shakespeare (1564–1616), *The
Merry Wives of Windsor*, 1597–1601, act II,
sc. II

80 Money is a good soldier, sir, and will on.
William Shakespeare (1564–1616), *ibid.*

81 I will first make bold with your money.
William Shakespeare (1564–1616), *ibid.*

82 I like his money well.
William Shakespeare (1564–1616), *ibid.*,
act III, sc. V

83 Nothing comes amiss, so money comes
withal.
William Shakespeare (1564–1616), *The
Taming of the Shrew*, 1593–4, act I, sc. II

84 Money is worth nothing to the man who has
more than enough.
George Bernard Shaw (1856–1950),
Contemporary Review, February 1896

85 Money . . . enables us to get what we want
instead of what other people think we want.
George Bernard Shaw (1856–1950), *The
Intelligent Woman's Guide to Socialism*,
1928

86 Money is indeed the most important thing
in the world; and all sound and successful
personal and national morality should have
this fact for its basis.
George Bernard Shaw (1856–1950), *The
Irrational Knot*, 1905, preface

87 What is the use of money if you have to
work for it?
George Bernard Shaw (1856–1950), *Man
and Superman*, 1903, act IV

88 Money is the counter that enables life to be
distributed socially: it *is* life as truly as
sovereigns and banknotes are money.
George Bernard Shaw (1856–1950), *Major
Barbara*, 1907, preface

89 Money is the most important thing in the
world. It represents health, strength,
honour, generosity and beauty as
conspicuously and undeniably as the want
of it represents illness, weakness, disgrace,
meanness and ugliness.
George Bernard Shaw (1856–1950), *ibid.*

90 Money, by means of which the whole
revenue of the society is regularly distributed
among all its different members, makes itself
no part of that revenue. The great wheel of
circulation is altogether different from the
goods which are circulated by means of it.
Adam Smith (1723–1790), *Wealth of
Nations*, 1776, vol. I, bk. II, ch. II

91 That wealth consists in money, or in gold
and silver, is a popular notion, which
naturally arises from the double function of
money, as the instrument of commerce, and
as the measure of value.
Adam Smith (1723–1790), *ibid.*, bk. IV,
ch. I

92 Goods can serve many other purposes
besides purchasing money, but money can
serve no other purpose besides purchasing
goods . . . It is not for its own sake that men
desire money, but for the sake of what they
can purchase with it.
Adam Smith (1723–1790), *ibid.*

93 Money, as a physical medium of exchange
has made a diversified civilisation possible.
Sir Josiah Stamp (1880–1941), foreword to
Irving Fisher, *The Money Illusion*

94 Power, which according to the old maxim,
was used to follow land, is now gone over to
money.
Jonathan Swift (1667–1745), *The
Examiner*, no. 13, 2 November 1710

95 No man will take counsel, but every man
will take money: therefore money is better
than counsel.
Jonathan Swift (1667–1745), *Thoughts on
Various Subjects*, 1706

96 No one would have remembered the Good
Samaritan if he'd only had good intentions.
He had money as well.
Margaret Thatcher, *The Times*, 14 May
1987

97 Absolutely speaking, the more money, the
less virtue.
Henry D. Thoreau (1817–1862),
Resistance to Civil Government, 1849

98 'Your friend Rogers is a good fellow. It's a
pity his money is tainted.'
Mark Twain: 'It's twice tainted, tain't
yours, and tain't mine.'
Mark Twain (1835–1910), attributed

99 The prices of the produce or manufactures
of every nation will be higher or lower,
according as the quantity of cash circulating
in such nation is greater or less.
Jacob Vanderlint (? –1740), *Money
Answers All Things*, 1734, p. 3

100 Money should circulate like rainwater.
Thornton Wilder (1897–1975), *The
Matchmaker*, 1955

101 There is no-one quite as angry as someone
who has just lost a lot of money.
David Williamson, 'Writeous Indignation',
The Australian Listener, 12–18 November
1988, p. 7

102 We need to think more about earning
money and less about making it.
Harold Wilson, *Observer*, 'Sayings of the
Year', 1964

---

125 MONOPOLY
See also 33 CARTELS

---

1 Why is there only one Monopolies
Commission?
Anonymous

2 It may be preferable not to regulate
economic monopolies and to suffer their
bad effects, rather than to regulate them and
suffer the effects of political imperfections.
Gary S. Becker, 'Competition and
Democracy', *Journal of Law and
Economics*, 1958, p. 109

3 That life on earth as we know it will end if a
little competition arises is the monopolist's
stock defence. What they actually mean is
that they lack sufficient faith in their
product to let the public have a free choice.
Roger Eglin, *Sunday Times*, 15
September 1985

4 There is unfortunately no good solution for
technical monopoly. There is only a choice
among three evils: private unregulated
monopoly, private monopoly regulated by
the state, and government operation.
Milton Friedman, *Capitalism and Freedom*,
1962

5 Public monopoly is supported by the very
people whom it is savaging.
Jo Grimond in Institute of Economic
Affairs, *Could Do Better*, 1982

6 The best of all monopoly profits is a quiet
life.
J.R. Hicks, 'The Theory of Monopoly',
Econometrica, 1935, p. 8

7 Monopoly, in all its forms, is the taxation of
the industrious for the support of indolence,
if not plunder.
John Stuart Mill (1806–1873), *Principles of
Political Economy*, bk. IV, ch. VIII, 7

8 Like many businessmen of genius he learned
that free competition was wasteful,
monopoly efficient.
Mario Puzo, *The Godfather* (1969), bk. III,
ch. 14

9 We have much less reason to expect that
monopolists will . . . charge an equilibrium
price than we have in the case of perfect
competition; for competing producers *must*
charge it as a rule under penalty of economic
death, whilst monopolists, although having
a *motive* to charge the monopolistic
equilibrium price, are not forced to do so,
but may be prevented from doing so by
other motives.
J.A. Schumpeter (1883–1950), 'The
Instability of Capitalism', *The Economic
Journal*, September 1928, p. 371

10 Not only does the monopolist's secure
market position enable him to relax his
efforts of maximising profit, but his very
position may prevent his aiming at
maximising profit. He may regard his
immunity from competition as precarious or
be afraid of unfavourable publicity and
public censure.
Tibor Scitovsky, *Welfare and Competition*,
1951, p. 377

11 The monopolists, by keeping the market
constantly under-stocked, by never fully
supplying the effectual demand, sell their
commodities much above the natural price.
Adam Smith (1723–1790), *Wealth of
Nations*, 1776, vol. I, bk. I, ch. VII

12 The price of monopoly is upon every
occasion the highest which can be got.
Adam Smith (1723–1790), *ibid.*

13 Monopoly . . . is a great enemy to good
management.
Adam Smith (1723–1790), *ibid.*, ch. XI,
pt. I

14 The public have a right to every advantage
under permitted monopoly which they
would enjoy under free competition.
Sydney Smith (1771–1845), letter to the
Morning Chronicle, 21 May 1842

15 It is not enough to prove that a given
industry is not competitive. The crucial
question is: how far do conditions in the
industry depart from competition? In many
and perhaps most cases the answer is that
the departures are not large.
George Stigler, *The Theory of Price*, 1946,
pp. 215–16

16 All forms of personal excellence, superiority,
skill and distinguished attainment constitute
natural monopolies and find their reward

under applications of the monopoly principle.
William G. Sumner (1840–1910), *A Group of Natural Monopolies*, 1888

17 We can arrest and prevent monopoly.
Woodrow Wilson (1856–1924), speech, 7 August 1912

18 I dare not take the road that leads to regulated monopoly; because by regulating monopoly you adopt it, you render it permanent, you accept all the things by which it has been established.
Woodrow Wilson (1856–1924), speech, 18 September 1912

19 Private monopoly is absolutely indefensible and intolerable. If it is any monopoly, it must be a public monopoly and not a private monopoly.
Woodrow Wilson (1856–1924), speech, 18 October 1912

---

126 MORALITY
See also 94 HONESTY

---

1 If self-regulation worked, Moses would have come down from Mount Sinai with the ten guidelines.
Anonymous, P. Grabosky and J. Braithwaite, *Of Manners Gentle*, 1986, ch. 14

2 Merchants, who live upon confidence and credit, can ill afford to undermine the conscience of the community. Anything which weakens or paralyses this is taking beams from the foundations of the merchant's own warehouse.
Henry Ward Beecher (1813–1887), *Proverbs from Plymouth Pulpit*, 1887

3 Morality's not practical.
Robert Bolt, *A Man for All Seasons*, 1960

4 Increase of material comforts, it may generally be laid down, does not in any way whatsoever conduce to moral growth.
Mahatma Gandhi (1869–1948) in N.B. Sen, *Wit and Wisdom of India*, 1961

5 The bottom seems to have dropped out of morality.
Lord Hailsham, *Observer*, 'Sayings of the Week', 15 December 1985

6 Either the principle of industry is that of function, in which case slack work is only less immoral than no work at all; or it is that of grab, in which there is no morality in the matter. But it cannot be both.
R.H. Tawney (1880–1962), *The Acquisitive Society*, 1921, ch. 8

---

127 MOTOR VEHICLES
See also 14 AVIATION, 164 RAILWAYS, 207 TRANSPORT

---

1 We must not allow ourselves to be warped by any prejudice against motor cars, and so to strain the law against them.
Lord Chief Justice Alverstone (1842–1915), *Bastable* v. *Little*, 1907

2 When a man opens the car door for his wife, it's either a new car or a new wife.
Duke of Edinburgh, *Observer*, 'Sayings of the Week', 6 March 1988

3 I will build a motor car for the great multitudes.
Henry Ford (1863–1947), on the launch of the Model T in 1909

4 You can have any colour, as long as it's black.
Henry Ford (1863–1947), referring to the Model T Ford, attributed

5 Tell Binkley asked Mrs Tilford Moots what kind of an auto her uncle bought an' she said, 'It's a F.O.B., made in Detroit'.
Frank McKinney Hubbard (1868–1930), *New Sayings by Abe Martin*, 1917

6 The automobile changed our dress, manners, social customs, vacation habits, the shape of our cities, consumer purchasing patterns, common tastes and positions in intercourse.
John Keats, *The Insolent Chariots*, 1958, ch. 1

7 The car has become the carapace, the protective and aggressive shell, of urban and suburban man.
Marshall McLuhan (1911–1981), *Understanding Media*, 1964, ch. 22

8 We'll [Americans in 1932] hold the distinction of being the only nation in the history of the world that ever went to the

poor house in an automobile.
Will Rogers (1879–1935) in Clifton
Fadiman, *The American Treasury
1455–1955*, 1955

9 The great achievement of Mr Sloan of
General Motors was to structure this
gigantic firm in such a manner that it
became, in fact, a federation of fairly
reasonably sized firms.
E.F. Schumacher (1911–1977), *Small is
Beautiful*, 1973, pt. I, ch. 5

10 What is good for the country is good for
General Motors, and what's good for
General Motors is good for the country.
Charles E. Wilson (1890–1961), to the
Senate Armed Forces Committee, 1952

128 NATIONALIZATION
See also 92 GOVERNMENT,
146 PRIVATIZATION, 159 PUBLIC ENTERPRISE

1 If you want to show that crime doesn't pay,
put it in the hands of the government.
Anonymous, M.Z. Hepker, *A Modern
Approach to Tax Law*

2 Whatever may be thought as to be the
respective merits of private and public
ownership, it cannot be denied that private
enterprise does take more risk than any
government is likely to do except under
pressure of military necessities.
Sir George Gibb (1850–1925), *Railway
Nationalisation*, 1908, p. 9

3 There could be no greater triumph of hope
over experience than to advocate more
nationalisation. And I do not see how any
free society can make it a crime for
consenting adults to exchange money for
teaching or medical care, however
distasteful some of the social consequences
may be.
Bryan Magee, 'Why I Quit the Labour
Party', *Sunday Times*, 24 January 1982

129 NEGOTIATIONS
See also 40 COLLECTIVE BARGAINING

1 It's a well known proposition that you know
who's going to win a negotiation: it's he

who pauses the longest.
Robert Holmes à Court, *Sydney Morning
Herald*, 24 May 1986

2 Anybuddy'll agree with you if you've been
eatin' onions.
Frank McKinney Hubbard (1868–1930),
New Sayings by Abe Martin, 1917

3 Let us never negotiate out of fear, but let us
never fear to negotiate.
John F. Kennedy (1917–1963), Inaugural
Address, 20 January 1961

4 We cannot negotiate with those who say,
'What's mine is mine, what's yours is
negotiable.'
John F. Kennedy (1917–1963), attributed

130 NEWSPAPERS
See also 162 PUBLISHING, 163 RADIO,
199 TELEVISION

1 To a newspaperman a human being is an
item with the skin wrapped round it.
Fred Allen (1894–1956), attributed

2 The duty of a newspaper is to comfort the
afflicted and afflict the comfortable.
Anonymous

3. News is something someone, somewhere
doesn't want you to print — the rest is
advertising.
Anonymous, 'Old American Newspaper
Saw', *Sunday Times*, 2 November 1986

4 No news creates bad news.
Anonymous

5 The only things you can believe in a
newspaper are the date and the lighting up
times, and even these should be checked
against a diary.
Anonymous

6 To get the truth from a newspaper you have
to read between the lies.
Anonymous

7 The wages of sin are increased circulation.
Lord Ardwick, *Independent*, 'Quote
Unquote', 29 April 1989

8 If there is anything tougher than a sports
editor, I should not like to meet it.
Earl of Arran, House of Lords, 10 May
1962

9 From the American newspapers you'd think America was populated solely by naked women and cinema stars.
Nancy, Lady Astor (1879–1964) in James Beasley Simpson, *Best Quotes of '54, '55, '56*, 1957

10 Give somebody half a page in a newspaper and they think they own the world.
Jeffrey Barnard, *Observer*, 'Sayings of the Week', 1 June 1986

11 I suppose I will go on selling newspapers until at last will come the late night final.
Lord Beaverbrook (1879–1964) in James Beasley Simpson, *Best Quotes of '54, '55, '56*, 1957

12 Bax [Sir Beverley Baxter], I'm making you editor because you're the only man on the paper who knows less about journalism than I do.
Lord Beaverbrook (1879–1964), quoted by Lord Hartwell, House of Lords, 2 July 1984

13 The advertisements in a newspaper are more full of knowledge in respect to what is going on in a state or community than the editorial columns are.
Henry Ward Beecher (1813–1887), *Proverbs from Plymouth Pulpit*, 1887

14 I read the newspaper avidly. It is my one form of continuous fiction.
Aneurin Bevan (1897–1960), *Observer*, 'Sayings of the Week', 3 April 1960

15 Editor, *n*. A person who combines the judicial functions of Minos, Rhadamanthus and Aeacus, but is placable with an obolus; a severely virtuous censor, but so charitable withal that he tolerates the virtues of others and the vices of himself . . . Master of mysteries and lord of law, high-pinnacled upon the throne of thought, his face suffused with the dim splendors of the Transfiguration, his legs intertwisted and his tongue a-cheek, the editor spills his will along the paper and cuts it off in lengths to suit. And at intervals from behind the veil of the temple is heard the voice of the foreman demanding three inches of wit and six lines of religious meditation, or bidding him turn off the wisdom and whack up some pathos.
Ambrose Bierce (1842–1914?), *The Devil's Dictionary*, 1911

16 A convention of coloured editors have gravely resolved never to mention in their papers the name of the aspiring youth who shot President Garfield. Things have come to a pretty pass when a man can't keep his name out of the newspapers without shooting the chief magistrate of his beloved country.
Ambrose Bierce (1842–1914?) in Clifton Fadiman, *The American Treasury, 1455–1955*, 1955

17 My experience of the working press is that they are a very degenerate group. There is a terrible incidence of alcoholism and drug abuse.
Conrad Black, *The Times*, 14 December 1985

18 The lot of a financial journalist is not, totally, a happy one. The subject is inherently intractable. None of your colleagues want to read about it. Your audience of specialized business troglodytes usually know more than you do. They don't hesitate to say so.
Peter Brimelow, *The Times*, 31 October 1987

19 Writing good editorials is chiefly telling the people what they think, not what you think.
Arthur Brisbane (1864–1936) in Clifton Fadiman, *The American Treasury, 1455–1955*, 1955

20 Burke said that there were Three Estates in Parliament; but, in the Reporters' Gallery yonder, there sat a *Fourth Estate*, more important far than all.
Thomas Carlyle (1795–1881), *Heroes and Hero-Worship*, 1841

21 It is a seldom proffered argument as to the advantages of a free press that it has a major function in keeping the government itself informed as to what the government is doing.
Walter Cronkite in C. Bingham, *Wit and Wisdom*, 1982

22 *The Times* letters page . . . a handy enclosed area where top people can run amok without hurting anyone.
Peter Corrigan, *Observer*, 29 September 1985

23 When a dog bites a man that is not news, but when a man bites a dog that is news.
Charles A. Dana (1819–1897), attributed

24 We are not in business to be popular. We are in business to say unpopular things. Profits

must never distract us from our duties. Profits must never make newspapers fat cats without claws.
Lord (William) Deedes, *The Australian*, 7 December 1988

25 I've been in this business 25 years and whenever some MP is given a going-over in the Press, usually for all the right reasons, they start trying to get a privacy Bill.
Nigel Dempster, *Observer*, 'Sayings of the Week', 22 January 1989

26 Blame is safer than praise. I hate to be defended in a newspaper.
Ralph Waldo Emerson (1802–1882) in Clifton Fadiman, *The American Treasury, 1455–1955*, 1955

27 A newspaper expresses its own view which is an amalgam of the view of its proprietor, its editor and the tradition it represents.
Daily Express, *Observer*, 'Sayings of the Year', 2 January 1983

28 A newspaper consists of just the same number of words, whether there be any news in it or not.
Henry Fielding (1707–1754), *Tom Jones*, 1749, II

29 All Australian newspapermen have been hard men.
Jack Fingleton, *Battin From Memory*, 1981, ch. 7

30 Our press is absolutely free. In fact I feel sometimes it's even worse than your press.
Rajiv Gandhi (at the Washington Press Club), *Observer*, 'Sayings of the Week', 23 June 1985

31 I call 'journalism' everything that will be less interesting tomorrow than today.
André Gide (1869–1951) in C. Bingham, *Wit and Wisdom*, 1982

32 The press restrained! nefandous thought!
In vain our sires have nobly fought:
While free from force the press remains,
Virtue and Freedom cheer our plains.
Matthew Green (1696–1737), *The Spleen*, 1737

33 For the Press there is no such thing as too many scoundrels.
Alexander Haig, *Observer*, 'Sayings of the Week', 1 April 1984

34 The Labour Party is paranoid about the media. The simple reason we get such a bad Press is that we do such damned silly things.
David Hardy, *Observer*, 'Sayings of the Week', 3 October 1982

35 We [journalists] are not a profession, because anyone with aptitude can get in — and so nobody can be thrown out.
Lord Hartwell, House of Lords, 2 July 1984

36 Any man who can afford to buy a newspaper should not be allowed to own one.
Roy Hattersley in Tom Bower, *Maxwell, The Outsider*, 1988

37 In many newspaper offices the long way of telling an incident is regarded as editorial.
E.W. Howe (1853–1937), *Country Town Sayings*, 1911

38 Editor: . . . A person employed on a newspaper, whose business it is to separate the wheat from the chaff, and to see that the chaff is printed.
Frank McKinney Hubbard (1868–1930), *The Roycroft Dictionary*, 1923

39 Journalist: A newspaperman out of a job.
Frank McKinney Hubbard (1868–1930), *ibid.*

40 Newspaper Office: A figment factory.
Frank McKinney Hubbard (1868–1930), *ibid.*

41 The life of a newspaper editor resembles the discouraging eternity of those who, in hell, try to fill sieves with water.
Aldous Huxley (1894–1963), *Observer*, 'Sayings of the Week', 7 June 1925

42 The man who never looks into a newspaper is better informed than he who reads them, inasmuch as he who knows nothing is nearer to truth than he whose mind is filled with falsehoods and errors.
Thomas Jefferson (1743–1826), letter to John Norvell, 1807

43 I read but one newspaper and that . . . more for its advertisements than its news.
Thomas Jefferson (1743–1826), letter to Charles Pinckney, 1820

44 Advertisements . . . contain the only truths to be relied on in a newspaper.
Thomas Jefferson (1743–1826), letter to Daniel Macon, 12 January 1819

45 Do not pay any regard to the newspapers;
    you will only disturb yourself.
    Samuel Johnson (1709–1784), letter to
    Lucy Porter, 24 August 1779

46 I am accustomed to think little of
    newspapers.
    Samuel Johnson (1709–1784), letter, 15
    May 1782

47 The Soldier may forget his Sword,
        The Sailorman the sea,
    The Mason may forget the Word
        And the Priest his Litany:
    The Maid may forget both jewel and gem,
        And the bride her wedding-dress —
    But the Jew shall forget Jerusalem
        Ere we forget the Press!
    Rudyard Kipling (1865–1936), *The Press*

48 Newspapermen are nowadays frequently
    and unjustly maligned and insulted merely
    for doing the job they are paid to do.
    Sir Larry Lamb, *Observer*, 'Sayings of the
    Week', 1 May 1983

49 The Press should take a lesson from the
    under-tens — it might learn something.
    John McEnroe, *Observer*, 'Sayings of the
    Week', 24 June 1984

50 We have never had a free press in this
    country.
    Michael Meacher, *Observer*, 'Sayings of the
    Week', 3 October 1982

51 A good newspaper, I suppose, is a nation
    talking to itself.
    Arthur Miller, *Observer*, 'Sayings of the
    Week', 26 November 1961

52 British journalism will not suffer from a little
    less alcohol.
    Rupert Murdoch (on the shortage of pubs at
    the new presses at Wapping), *Sydney
    Morning Herald*, 'Sayings of the Week', 8
    February 1986

53 All the News That's Fit to Print.
    Adolph S. Ochs (1858–1935), motto of *The
    New York Times*

54 We live under a government of men and
    morning newspapers.
    Wendell Phillips (1811–1884), attributed

55 Journalists belong in the gutter because that
    is where the ruling classes throw their guilty
    secrets.
    Gerald Priestland, *Observer*, 'Sayings of the
    Week', 22 May 1988

56 Today's newspapers are tomorrow's fish and
    chip wrapping.
    Peter Roebuck, *Sunday Times*, 23
    November 1986

57 All I know is what I see in the papers.
    Will Rogers (1879–1935) in Clifton
    Fadiman, *The American Treasury,
    1455–1955*, 1955

58 Papers are about talent. When the talent
    goes, sales go.
    Viscount Rothermere, *Independent*, 15
    February 1989

59 No self-respecting dead fish would want to
    be wrapped in a Murdoch newspaper, let
    alone work for it.
    Mike Royko, *Observer*, 14 December 1986

60 The newspaper is of necessity something of
    a monopoly, and its first duty is to shun the
    temptations of monopoly. The primary
    office of a newspaper is the gathering of
    news. At the peril of its soul it must see that
    the supply is not tainted. Neither in what it
    gives, nor in what it does not give, nor in the
    mode of presentation, must the unclouded
    face of truth suffer wrong. Comment is free,
    but facts are sacred.
    Charles Prestwick Scott (1846–1932),
    Manchester Guardian, 6 May 1926 (the
    100th anniversary of the paper)

61 Newspapers should be news-carriers, not
    news-makers. — There is truth and
    entertainment enough to print, without
    fiction or falsehood, and to publish the latter
    is to betray the former.
    Charles Simmons (1798–1856) in Tryon
    Edwards, *The New Dictionary of Thoughts*

62 If your aim is to change the world,
    journalism is a more immediate short-term
    weapon.
    Tom Stoppard, *Observer*, 'Sayings of
    1988', 1 January 1989

63 Serious journalism is a high risk enterprise.
    Sunday Times, *Observer*, 'Sayings of the
    Week', 15 May 1983

64 The newspaper and magazine business is an
    intellectual brothel from which there is no
    escape.
    Count Leo Tolstoy (1828–1910) in C.
    Bingham, *Wit and Wisdom*, 1982

65 I made a most thoughtful, symmetrical and
    admirable argument. But a Michigan

newspaper editor answered, refuted it, utterly demolished it by saying I was in the constant habit of horsewhipping my great-grandmother.
Mark Twain (1835–1910), speech, 1879

66 There are only two forces that can carry light to all corners of the globe — only two — the sun in the heavens and the Associated Press down here.
Mark Twain (1835–1910), speech, 1906

67 There is so little dependence on newspaper publications, which take whatever complexion the editors please to give them, that persons at a distance, who have no other means of information, are oftentimes at a loss to form an opinion on the most important occurrences.
George Washington (1732–1799), letter to Oliver Wolcott, 15 May 1797

68 Journalists cannot afford to be too choosy about the newspapers they work for.
Auberon Waugh, *Private Eye*, no. 571, 4 November 1983, 'Auberon Waugh's Diary'

69 To the Savoy, for the centenary luncheon of the Parliamentary Press Lobby. It is attended by all the toadies and walking sausages whose job it is to repeat any lie told them by a politician without saying where it comes from.
Auberon Waugh, *ibid.*, no. 577, 27 January 1984

70 I don't know how to run a newspaper . . . I just try everything I can think of.
Orson Welles in *Citizen Kane*, in H. Haun, *The Movie Quote Book*

71 Newspapers have degenerated. They may now be absolutely relied on.
Oscar Wilde (1854–1900), *The Decay of Lying*, 1889

72 *Ernest*: But what is the difference between literature and journalism?
Gilbert: Oh! journalism is unreadable, and literature is not read.
Oscar Wilde (1854–1900), *The Critic As Artist*, 1891, pt. I

73 A lot of people think the hard noses of Fleet Street don't have a soft centre, but they do you know.
Gerald Williams, *Private Eye*, no. 619, 6 September 1985

74 Anybody who is rung up by more than one reporter thinks they're being hounded.
Sir Woodrow Wyatt, *Observer*, 'Sayings of the Year', 28 December 1986

131 THE OFFICE

1 How many work in your office?
About half.
Anonymous

2 If you've nothing nice to say about somebody — pull up a chair!
Anonymous

3 Next to the dog, the wastebasket is man's best friend.
Anonymous, James Beasley Simpson, *Best Quotes of '54, '55, '56*, 1957

4 A photocopier is a machine which can reproduce human error flawlessly.
Anonymous

5 The organisation of many offices is rather like a septic tank — the really big chunks rise to the top.
'Epson's Compleat Office Companion', *The Times*, 12 October 1987

6 Another drawback with office jobs is that the workers are generally in the same situation as a sledge-dog team — only the lead dog ever gets a change of scenery.
'Epson's Compleat Office Companion', *ibid.*

7 And the inventor of the xerox machine will, I am sure, find a special place reserved for him on one of the inner circles of Dante's Inferno.
Sir Nicholas Goodison in Ray Wild, *How to Manage*, 1982, p. 233

8 The office, we can safely conclude, is not the place for the more powerful manifestations of sex.
C. Northcote Parkinson, *In-Laws and Outlaws*, 1959, ch. 4

9 In the average office, S.O.B. stands for 'Son of Boss'.
Spencer Purinton in Jim Fisk and Robert Barron, *Great Business Quotations*, 1985

10 There is more truth in the bedroom than in the office or the boardroom.
François Truffaut, *Observer*, 'Sayings of the Week', 1 November 1981

11 Never resign, and never return to the office after a long lunch.
Cec Wallace, attributed

12 I yield to no one in my admiration for the office as a social centre, but it's no place actually to get any work done.
Katharine Whitehorn, *Sunday Best*

---

132 ORGANIZATION(S)

See also 24 BUREAUCRACY, 38 CIVIL SERVICE, 117 MANAGEMENT, 138 PERSONNEL MANAGEMENT

---

1 The individual and the organization are living organisms, each with its own strategy for survival and growth.
Chris Argyris, *Interpersonal Competence and Organizational Effectiveness*, 1962, introduction

2 Executive work is not that *of* the organization, but the specialized work of *maintaining* the organization in operation.
C.I. Barnard, *The Functions of the Executive*, 1938, ch. 15

3 What they could do with round here is a good war. What else can you expect with peace running wild all over the place? You know what the trouble with peace is? No organization.
Bertolt Brecht (1898–1956), *Mother Courage and Her Children*, 1941, act I

4 All organizations, nations, societies, and civilizations will prosper and advance only to the extent that they can encourage common men to perform uncommon deeds.
Courtney C. Brown, preface to Crawford H. Greenewalt, *The Uncommon Man*, 1959

5 I'm surprised that a government organization could do it that quickly. [Building the Great Pyramid in twenty years.]
Jimmy Carter, attributed

6 Large organization is loose organization. Nay, it would be almost as true to say that organization is always disorganization.
G.K. Chesterton (1874–1936), 'The Bluff of the Big Shops', *Outline of Sanity*, 1926

7 The question of centralization or decentralization is a simple question of proportion, it is a question of finding the optimum degree for the particular concern.
Henri Fayol (1841–1925), *General and Industrial Management*, 1916, ch. IV

8 It might seem more efficient to have the front half of the cow in the pasture grazing and the rear half in the barn being milked all of the time, but this organic division would fail.
Luther Gulick, 'Notes on the Theory of Organization', in Luther Gulick and Lyndall Urwick (eds.), *Papers on the Science of Administration*, 1937

9 The chief characteristic of all institutions is that if they have a purpose when they are started it is forgotten as they mature.
Robert M. Hutchins (1899–1977) in C. Bingham, *Wit and Wisdom*, 1982

10 The leadership and other processes of the organization must be such as to ensure a maximum probability that in all interactions and all relationships with the organization each member will, in the light of his background, values and expectations, view the experience as supportive and one which builds and maintains his sense of personal worth and importance.
R. Likert, *New Patterns of Management*, 1961, ch. 8

11 We have in fact passed beyond that stage of human organization in which effective communication and collaboration were secured by established routines of relationship.
Elton Mayo (1880–1949), *The Social Problems of an Industrial Civilization*, 1945, p. 13

12 It was just the day for Organizing Something, or for Writing a Notice signed Rabbit. . . . It was a Captainish sort of day, when everybody said 'Yes, Rabbit' and 'No, Rabbit' and waited until he had told them.
A.A. Milne (1882–1956), *The House at Pooh Corner*, 1928, ch. V

13 Subordinates obey not because the supervisor has the power to compel them to; rather, they follow reasonable instructions related to the control of their work behaviour because they expect that such directions will be given and followed.
J. Pfeffer, *Power in Organizations*, 1981, ch. 1

14 Of course, leadership is a necessary myth. It helps to legitimize the unequal distribution of power in hierarchies within an order which purports to hold all men equal.
D. Pym, 'Emancipation and Organization' in N. Nicholson and T.D. Wall, *The Theory and Practice of Organizational Psychology,* 1982, p. 222

15 Nobody really likes large-scale organization; nobody likes to take orders from a superior who takes orders from a superior who takes orders . . .
E.F. Schumacher (1911–1977), *Small is Beautiful,* 1973, pt. IV, ch. 2

16 The executive's job involves not only making decisions himself, but also seeing that the organization, or part of an organization, that he directs makes decisions effectively. The vast bulk of the decision-making activity for which he is responsible is not his personal activity, but the activity of his subordinates.
H.A. Simon, *The New Science of Management Decision,* 1960, pp. 4–5.

17 The question is not whether we shall decentralize, but how far we shall decentralize.
H.A. Simon, *ibid.,* p. 43

18 The most salient characteristic of modern industrial organization is that production is carried on under the general direction of business men, who do not themselves necessarily know anything of productive processes.
R.H. Tawney (1880–1962), *The Acquisitive Society,* 1921, ch. 10

19 This book is about the organization man. If the term is vague, it is because I can think of no other way to describe the people I am talking about. They are not the workers, nor are they the white-collar people in the usual, clerk sense of the word. These people only work for the Organization. The ones I am talking about *belong* to it as well.
William H. Whyte, *The Organization Man,* 1956, ch. 1

20 The criteria of the appropriateness of an organizational structure must be the extent to which it furthers the objectives of the firm not, as management teaching sometimes suggests, the degree to which it conforms to a prescribed pattern. There can be no best

way of organizing a business.
J. Woodward, *Management and Technology,* 1958

133 PARLIAMENT
See also 49 CONGRESS, 92 GOVERNMENT, 142 POLITICS

1 The House of Lords is like Heaven. Everyone wants to get there sometime but not just yet.
Anonymous, Lord Denning, *The Family Story,* 1981, p. 184

2 *Queen Elizabeth*: Now, Mr Speaker, what hath passed in the Lower House?
Mr Popham: If it please your Majesty, seven weeks.
Francis Bacon (1561–1626), *Apophthegms,* 1624

3 A Parliament is nothing less than a big meeting of more or less idle people.
Walter Bagehot (1826–1877), *The English Constitution,* 1867, ch. V

4 Parliamentary government is being asked to solve the problem which so far it has failed to solve: that is how to reconcile parliamentary popularity with sound economic planning.
Aneurin Bevan (1897–1960) quoted by Denis Healey, *The Times,* 17 April 1975

5 England is the mother of Parliaments.
John Bright (1811–1889), speech, Birmingham, 18 January 1865

6 The House of Lords is a model of how to care for the elderly.
Frank Field, *Observer,* 'Sayings of the Week', 24 May 1981

7 When in that House MPs divide, If they've a brain and a cerebellum too, They have to leave that brain outside, And vote just as their leaders tell 'em to.
W.S. Gilbert (1836–1911), *Iolanthe,* 1882, act II

8 When I am sitting [on the Woolsack in the House of Lords] I amuse myself by saying 'Bollocks!' *sotto voce* to the bishops.
Lord Hailsham, *Sunday Times,* 25 August 1985

9   Anybody who enjoys being in the House of Commons probably needs psychiatric care.
Ken Livingstone, *Observer*, 'Sayings of the Week', 7 February 1988

10   I believe, as a Conservative and as a businessman — at least I have spent my life running businesses and know how to read a balance sheet whereas the great majority of hon. Gentlemen opposite have not the qualifications to run a whelk store profitably — that every industrial investment, nationalized, state or otherwise, should turn in a profit.
Gerald Nabarro (1913–1973), House of Commons, 22 November 1966

11   Parliament itself would not exist in its present form had people not defied the law.
Arthur Scargill, *Observer*, 'Sayings of the Week', 6 April 1980

12   The House of Commons is terribly outdated, an old man's club with too much spare-time boozing.
Shirley Williams, *Observer*, 'Sayings of the Year', 3 January 1982

---

134 PARTNERSHIPS

1   The partner of my partner is not my partner. (*Socii mei socius, meus socius non est.*)
Legal Maxim

2   One of the most fruitful sources of ruin to men of the world is the recklessness or want of principle of partners, and it is one of the perils to which every man exposes himself who enters into partnership with another.
Sir R. Malins V.C. (1805–1882), *Mackay* v. *Douglas* (1872), 14 Eq. 106 at 118

---

135 PAYMENT

1   'Take what you want', said God, 'and pay for it'.
Anonymous, Arthur Seldon, *Charge*, 1977

2   Alas! how deeply painful is all payment!
Lord Byron (1788–1824), *Don Juan*, canto X, 1823, st. 79

3   He that pays last, never pays twice.
Thomas Fuller (1654–1734), *Gnomologia*, 1732, no. 2246

4   If you pay cash th' days won't roll by so fast.
Frank McKinney Hubbard (1868–1930), *New Sayings by Abe Martin*, 1917

5   It is an axiom as old as the hills that goods and services can be paid for only with goods and services.
Albert J. Nock (1837–1945), *Memoirs of a Superfluous Man*, III, ch. 3

6   He that paieth aforehand, hath neuer his worke well done.
Proverb, 16th century

7   He who pays the piper can call the tune.
John Ray (1628–1705), *English Proverbs*, 1670

8   For count of this, the count's a fool, I know it,
Who pays before, but not when he does owe it.
William Shakespeare (1564–1616), *All's Well That Ends Well*, 1602–4, act IV, sc. III.

9   Pay and yet pay still.
William Shakespeare (1564–1616), *Cymbeline*, 1609–10, act, I, sc. IV

10   Paid money that I borrowed — three or four times.
William Shakespeare (1564–1616), *Henry IV, Pt. I*, 1597–8, act III, sc. III

11   In cash most justly paid.
William Shakespeare (1564–1616), *Henry V*, 1598–9, act II, sc. I

12   Downright payment.
William Shakespeare (1564–1616), *Henry VI, Pt. III*, 1590–1, act I, sc. IV

13   He is well paid that is well satisfied.
William Shakespeare (1564–1616), *The Merchant of Venice*, 1596–7, act IV, sc. I

14   *Apothecary*: My poverty but not my will consents.
Romeo: I pay thy poverty and not thy will.
William Shakespeare (1564–1616), *Romeo and Juliet*, 1595–6, act V, sc. I

15   He humbly prays your speedy payment.
William Shakespeare (1564–1616), *Timon of Athens*, 1607–8, act II, sc. II

16   I'll pay thee bounteously.
William Shakespeare (1564–1616), *Twelfth Night*, 1599–1600, act I, sc. II

17 He pays you as surely as your feet hit the ground they step on.
William Shakespeare (1564–1616), *ibid.*, act III, sc. IV

18 There's money for thee; if you tarry longer I shall give you worse payment.
William Shakespeare (1564–1616), *ibid.*, act IV, sc. I

19 You pay a great deal too dear for what's given freely.
William Shakespeare (1564–1616), *The Winter's Tale*, 1610–11, act I, sc. I

---

136 PENSIONS
See also 170 RETIREMENT

---

1 I have considered the pension list of the republic a roll of honour.
Grover Cleveland (1837–1908), message to Congress, 3 July 1888

2 Pension never enriched young man.
George Herbert (1593–1633), *Jacula Prudentum*, 1651

3 *Pension*: An allowance made to anyone without an equivalent. In England it is generally understood to mean pay given to a state hireling for treason to his country.
Samuel Johnson (1709–1784), *Dictionary*, 1755

4 It ought to be quite as natural and straightforward a matter for a labourer to take his pension from his parish, because he has deserved well of his parish, as for a man in higher rank to take his pension from his country, because he has deserved well of his country.
John Ruskin (1819–1900), *Unto This Last*, 1862, preface

---

137 PEOPLE

---

1 People are a little bit like emus. They want to come and see everything. You know how to get a whole lot of emus to come to you? You've got to be unusual. Go out and lie on your back and kick your legs in the air and I

bet you every emu in sight comes over to have a look at you.
Sir Joh Bjelke-Petersen, *Sydney Morning Herald*, 'Sayings of the Week', 8 October 1988

2 Too bad all the people who know how to run the country are too busy driving taxi-cabs or cutting hair.
George Burns, *Punch*, 25 September 1985

3 The Busy Man's Creed: I believe in the stuff I am handing out, in the firm I am working for, and in my ability to get results.
Elbert Hubbard (1856–1915), *Notebook*, 1927, p. 21

4 There are three sorts of people in this world; those who make things happen, those who watch things happening, and those who don't know what is happening.
Sir David Nicholson in *Pass the Port Again*, 1981

5 There is something about the British character that equates service with being servile.
Lord Young, *Observer*, 'Sayings of the Week', 3 March 1985

---

138 PERSONNEL MANAGEMENT
See also 71 EMPLOYERS,
117 MANAGEMENT, 118 MANAGEMENT
CONSULTANCY

---

1 To err is human. To forgive is not company policy.
Anonymous sign to company executives

2 Management and personnel administration are one and the same. They should never be separated. Management *is* personnel administration.
Lawrence A. Appley in Mary Bosticco, *Modern Personnel Management*, 1964

3 As a personnel management trainee, I was told the perfect advertisement was the one which drew one reply and that was from the ideal candidate.
Len Peach, *The Times*, 29 August 1985

4 A personnel man with his arm around an employee is like a treasurer with his hand in the till.
Robert Townsend, *Up the Organization*, 1970

139 PIRACY

1   Piracy, *n.* Commerce without its
    folly-swaddles, just as God made it.
    Ambrose Bierce (1842–1914?), *The Devil's
    Dictionary*, 1911

2   He changes his flag, to conceal his being a
    pirate.
    Thomas Fuller (1654–1734), *Gnomologia*,
    1732, no. 1825

3   Charity and piracy are things of the past.
    They were always closely akin, for pirates
    were very charitable, and ever in their train
    were troops of sturdy beggars.
    Elbert Hubbard (1856–1915), *Notebook*,
    1927, p. 16

4   There be . . . water-thieves and land thieves;
    I mean pirates.
    William Shakespeare (1564–1616), *The
    Merchant of Venice*, 1596–7, act I, sc. III

5   Notable pirate! thou salt-water thief!
    William Shakespeare (1564–1616), *Twelfth
    Night*, 1599–1600, act V, sc. I

140 PLAIN ENGLISH

1   Gobbledygook is the methodology deployed
    by governmental bureaucracies, specifically
    designed to ensure that the simplest of
    instructions is encased in a plethora of
    treacherous sub-clauses, adverbial phrases
    and cross references with the result that the
    recipient is left baffled, bemused and
    confused.
    Martin Cutts and Chrissie Maher,
    Gobbledygook, 1984

2   It has been the custom in modern Europe to
    regulate, upon most occasions, the
    payments of the attorneys and clerks of
    courts according to the number of pages
    which they had occasion to write; the court,
    however, requiring, that each page should
    contain so many lines, and each line so
    many words. In order to increase their
    payment, the attorneys and clerks have
    contrived to multiply words beyond all
    necessity, to the corruption of the law
    language of, I believe, every court of justice
    in Europe.

Adam Smith (1723–1790), *Wealth of
Nations*, 1776, bk. V, ch. 1, pt. II, 'Of the
Expense of Justice'

3   The manufacture of a five-pronged
    implement for digging results in a fork even
    if the manufacturer, unfamiliar with the
    English language, insists that he intended to
    make and has made a spade.
    Lord Templeman, *Street* v. *Mountford*, 1985

4   It is no exaggeration to describe plain
    English as a fundamental tool of
    government.
    Margaret Thatcher, *Observer*, 'Sayings of
    the Week', 13 March 1988

5   The maxim 'for the lower orders one's
    language cannot be too plain' (that is, *clear*
    and *perspicuous*, so as to require no learning
    nor ingenuity to understand it).
    Richard Whateley (1787–1863), *Thoughts
    and Apophthegms*, 1856, pt. VI

141 PLANNING

1   He hath made a good progress in a business,
    that hath thought well of it before-hand.
    Thomas Fuller (1654–1734), *Gnomologia*,
    1732, no. 1891

2   Planning and competition can be combined
    only by planning for competition, but not by
    planning against competition.
    F.A. Hayek, *The Road to Serfdom*, 1944,
    ch. III

3   One of the most expensive things an
    economy can buy is economic trial, error
    and development.
    Jane Jacobs, *The Economy of Cities*, 1970,
    p. 228

4   Gresham's Law of Planning — that routine
    drives out nonprogrammed activity.
    H.A. Simon, *The New Science of
    Management Decision*, 1960, p. 39

5   The age of capitalism is . . . characterised
    precisely by the striking contrast between
    planning carried to the highest point in
    individual economies and a planlessness of
    the entire economy.
    Werner Sombart (1863–1941), *A New
    Social Philosophy*, 1937, trans. Geisher, pt.
    VI, ch. XVIII

142 POLITICS
See also 49 CONGRESS, 92 GOVERNMENT, 133 PARLIAMENT

1 Practical politics consists in ignoring facts.
Henry Adams (1838–1918), *The Education of Henry Adams*, 1907, ch. 22

2 Modern politics is a struggle not of men but of forces. The men become every year more and more creatures of force, massed about central power houses.
Henry Adams (1838–1918), *ibid.*, ch. 28

3 The divine science of politics is the science of social happiness.
John Adams (1735–1826), *Thoughts on Government*, 1776

4 The only remedy they [the Tories] have for every social problem is to enable private enterprise to suck at the teats of the state.
Aneurin Bevan (1897–1960) in V. Brome, *Aneurin Bevan*, ch. 12, p. 176

5 Arena, *n*. In politics, an imaginary rat-pit in which the statesman wrestles with his record.
Ambrose Bierce (1842–1914?), *The Devil's Dictionary*, 1911

6 Politics, *n*. The conduct of public affairs for private advantage.
Ambrose Bierce (1842–1914?), *ibid.*

7 The Left favours coercion in economic policy, and the Right coercion in everything else.
Samuel Brittan, *Daily Telegraph*, 22 September 1979

8 You scratch my back and I'll scratch yours.
Simon Cameron (1799–1889) in Clifton Fadiman, *The American Treasury, 1455–1955*, 1955

9 An honest politician is one who, when he is bought, will stay bought.
Simon Cameron (1799–1889), attributed

10 A mixed economy is essential to social democracy.
Anthony Crosland (1918–1977), *Daily Telegraph*, 25 January 1979

11 I cannot consent that the laws regulating the industry of a great nation should be made the shuttlecock of party strife.
Benjamin Disraeli (1804–1881), House of Commons, 11 February 1851

12 That fabulous animal formally called 'economic policy' and more familiarly called political interference.
G.A. Duncan, *Economic Journal*, December 1961, p. 811

13 There is a certain satisfaction in coming down to the lowest ground of politics, for we get rid of the cant and hypocrisy.
Ralph Waldo Emerson (1803–1882), *Representative Men*, 1850

14 Pouring ridicule on one's opponent is an approved method in 'civilized politics'.
Mahatma Gandhi (1869–1948) in N.B. Sen, *Wit and Wisdom of India*, 1961

15 Some comrades apparently find it hard to understand that democracy is just a slogan.
Mikhail Gorbachev, *Observer*, 'Sayings of the Week', 1 February 1987

16 The environment suffers very badly from the way it's become a party political football.
Nick Greiner, *Sydney Morning Herald*, 'Sayings of the Week', 21 January 1989

17 Most of our economic problems are political and arise from faith in our systems of politics, government and industrial relations.
Jo Grimond in Institute of Economic Affairs, *Could Do Better*, 1982, p. 20

18 Elections are like sex. The pleasure is momentary, the position is ridiculous and the result can be damnably expensive.
Keith Hampson, *The Times Higher Education Supplement*, 24 June 1983

19 *Will Rogers*: Do you want me to tell you the latest political jokes, Mr President?
President Harding: You don't have to Will, I know 'em already. I appointed most of them.
Warren G. Harding (1865–1923) in Donald Day, *Will Rogers: A Biography*, 1962, ch. 13

20 It is a good thing to follow the First Law of Holes; if you are in one, stop digging.
Denis Healey in Fred Metcalf, *The Penguin Dictionary of Modern Humorous Quotations*, 1986

21 I don't think that modesty is the outstanding characteristic of contemporary politics, do you?
Edward Heath, *Observer*, 'Sayings of the Week', 4 December 1988

22 Politicians an' actors never quit in time.
Frank McKinney Hubbard (1868–1930).
New Sayings by Abe Martin, 1917

23 Democracy: . . . A form of government by
popular ignorance.
Frank McKinney Hubbard (1868–1930),
The Roycroft Dictionary, 1923

24 Practical Politics: The glad hand, and a swift
kick in the pants.
Frank McKinney Hubbard (1868–1930),
ibid.

25 Politicians: . . . Men who volunteer the task
of governing us for a consideration.
Frank McKinney Hubbard (1868–1930),
ibid.

26 Politics is the clearing house of pressures.
That's what it is about, delivering.
Paul Keating, *Sydney Morning Herald*,
'Sayings of the Week', 17 May 1986

27 I sometimes think that given half a chance
politicians would like to give extra tax and
social security concessions to marginal
constituencies only.
William Keegan, *Observer*, 17 September
1978

28 The political problem of mankind is to
combine three things: economic efficiency,
social justice, and individual liberty.
John Maynard Keynes (1883–1946),
attributed

29 People in the larger corporate sector who get
in bed with the Labor Party, in my opinion,
will catch an incurable disease.
Michael Kreger, *Sydney Morning Herald*,
'Sayings of the Week', 19 November 1988

30 Politics: Who Gets What, When, How.
H.D. Laswell, title of book, 1936

31 Politics is a practical profession. If a criminal
has what you want, you do business with him.
Charles Laughton in H. Haun, *The Movie
Quote Book*

32 Political work is the life-blood of all
economic work.
Mao Tse-Tung (1893–1976), *Quotations
from Chairman Mao Tse-Tung*, 1976, p. 135

33 Bad officials are elected by good citizens
who do not vote.
George Jean Nathan (1882–1958) in
Clifton Fadiman, *The American Treasury,
1455–1955*, 1955

34 A politician is like quick-silver: if you try to
put your finger on him, you find nothing
under it.
Austin O'Malley (1858–1932) in Tryon
Edwards, *The New Dictionary of Thoughts*

35 People who suddenly get political power
without economic power are a time bomb
for revolution.
Frédéric de Plessis, *Observer*, 'Sayings of
1988', 1 January 1989

36 You don't lead people by following them,
but by saying what they want to follow.
Enoch Powell, *Observer*, 'Sayings of the
Week', 6 December 1970

37 The political practice of citing only
agreeable statistics can never settle
economic arguments.
James B. Ramsey, *Economic Forecasting —
Models or Markets?*, 1977, p. 77

38 The more you read and observe about
politics, you got to admit that each party is
worse than the other.
Will Rogers (1879–1935) in Donald Day,
Will Rogers: A Biography, 1962, ch. 13

39 'A priest should not talk politics in the
pulpit' . . . Yes. Only you must not taint
everything with politics; otherwise nothing
will be left to say.
Joseph Roux (1834–1905), *Meditations of
a Parish Priest*, trans. Hapgood, 1886, ch. II,
XXXIV

40 Get thee glass eyes;
And, like a scurvy politician, seem
To see the things thou dost not.
William Shakespeare (1564–1616), *King
Lear*, 1605–6, act IV, sc. VI

41 That insidious and crafty animal, vulgarly
called a statesman or politician, whose
councils are directed by the momentary
fluctuations of affairs.
Adam Smith (1723–1790), *Wealth of
Nations*, 1776, vol. I, bk. IV, ch. II

42 Who first reduced lying into an art, and
adapted it to politicks, is not so clear from
history; although I have made some diligent
enquiries.
Jonathan Swift (1667–1745), *The
Examiner*, no. 14, 9 November 1710

43 And he gave it for his opinion, that whoever
could make two ears of corn, or two blades
of grass, to grow upon a spot of ground

where only one grew before, would deserve better of mankind, and do more essential service to his country, than the whole race of politicians put together.
Jonathan Swift (1667–1745), *Gulliver's Travels*, 1726, 'Voyage to Brobdingnag', ch. 7

44 Politicks, as the word is commonly understood, are nothing but corruptions.
Jonathan Swift (1667–1745), *Thoughts on Various Subjects*, 1711

45 We're not in politics, but we have to be; it's the only way we can survive. Politics is today's method of power.
Vincent Teresa, *My Life in the Mafia*, 1974, ch. 7

46 In politics if you want anything said, ask a man. If you want anything done, ask a woman.
Margaret Thatcher, *Sydney Morning Herald*, 'Sayings of the Week', 14 September 1985

47 There is nothing more disgusting in British political life than the sight of a Conservative who thinks he has public opinion behind him.
Auberon Waugh, *Spectator*, 15 March 1986

48 A political prediction publicly uttered will often have had, or supposed to have had, a great share in bringing about its own fulfillment. He who gives out, for instance, that the people will certainly be dissatisfied with such and such a law, is, in this doing his utmost to *make* them dissatisfied.
Richard Whateley (1787–1863), *Thoughts and Apophthegms*, 1856, pt. VI

49 A friend of mine says that every man who takes office in Washington either grows or swells, and when I give a man an office, I watch him carefully to see whether he is swelling or growing.
Woodrow Wilson (1856–1924) in Rudolf Flesch, *The Book of Unusual Quotations*, 1959

143 PORNOGRAPHY

1 It'll be a sad day for sexual liberation when the pornography addict has to settle for the real thing.
Brendan Francis in E.F. Murphy, *The Macmillan Treasury of Relevant Quotations*

2 Porn is an ideal Thatcherite industry. It provides a service, demands dedication and requires little in the way of start-up capital. It would, in fact, be a prime candidate for the Business Expansion Scheme.
John Naughton, *Observer*, 26 June 1988

144 POVERTY

1 You cannot sift out the poor from the community. The poor are indispensable to the rich.
Henry Ward Beecher (1813–1887), *Proverbs from Plymouth Pulpit*, 1887

2 What mean ye that ye beat my people to pieces, and grind the faces of the poor? saith the Lord God of Hosts.
Bible, Authorized Version, Isaiah 3:15

3 He that loveth pleasure shall be a poor man: he that loveth wine and oil shall not be rich.
Bible, Authorized Version, Proverbs 21:17

4 For the needy shall not alway be forgotten: The expectation of the poor shall not perish for ever.
Bible, Authorized Version, Psalms 9:18

5 For ye have the poor always with you; but me ye have not always.
Bible, Authorized Version, Matthew 26:11

6 Beggar, *n*. One who has relied on the assistance of his friends.
Ambrose Bierce (1842–1914?), *The Devil's Dictionary*, 1911

7 How vainly shall we endeavour to repress crime by our barbarous punishment of the poorer class of criminals so long as children are reared in the brutalizing influences of poverty, so long as the bite of want drives men to crime.
Henry George (1839–1897), *Social Problems*, 1883, ch. IX

8 The best way to help the poor is not to become one of them.
Lang Hancock in Bill Wannan, *Great Aussie Quotes*, 1987

9 Beggars should be no choosers.
John Heywood (1506–1565), *Proverbs*, 1546, pt. I, ch. X

10 Miserie may be mother,
   Where one beggar is driven to beg of
                  another.
   John Heywood (1506–1565), *ibid.*, pt. II,
   ch. X

11 In theory, it is not respectable to be rich. In
   fact, poverty is a disgrace.
   E.W. Howe (1853–1937) in Clifton
   Fadiman, *The American Treasury
   1455–1955*, 1955

12 It's no disgrace to be poor, but it might as
   well be.
   Frank McKinney Hubbard (1868–1930) in
   Clifton Fadiman, *The American Treasury
   1455–1955*, 1955

13 All the arguments which are brought to
   represent poverty as no evil, shew it to be
   evidently a great evil. You never find people
   labouring to convince you that you may live
   very happily upon a plentiful fortune.
   Samuel Johnson (1709–1784) in Boswell's
   Life of Johnson, 20 July 1763

14 He will soon be a beggar, that cannot say
   nay.
   James Kelly, *Scottish Proverbs*, 1721, H, no.
   162

15 The poor man pays for all.
   James Kelly, *ibid.*, T, no. 170

16 The poor man's shilling is but a penny
   [because he must buy everything at the
   dearest rate].
   James Kelly, *ibid.*, no. 291

17 When poverty comes in at the door,
   friendship flees out at the window.
   James Kelly, *ibid.*, W, no. 54

18 If a free society cannot help the many who
   are poor, it cannot save the few who are
   rich.
   John F. Kennedy (1917–1963), Inaugural
   Address, 20 January 1961

19 If poverty is the mother of crime, stupidity is
   its father.
   Jean de La Bruyère (1645–1696),
   Characters, 1688, 'Of Man'

20 The greatest of our evils and the worst of
   our crimes is poverty, and . . . our first duty,
   to which every other consideration should
   be sacrificed, is not to be poor.
   George Bernard Shaw (1856–1950), *Major
   Barbara*, 1907, preface

21 Those who minister to poverty and disease
   are accomplices in the two worst of all
   crimes.
   George Bernard Shaw (1856–1950),
   Maxims for Revolutionists, 1903

22 What is the matter with the poor is Poverty:
   what is the matter with the rich is
   Uselessness.
   George Bernard Shaw (1856–1950), *ibid.*

23 Remember the poor — it costs nothing.
   Mark Twain (1835–1910), attributed

24 When the poor feel as poor as the rich do,
   there will be bloody revolution.
   Dame Rebecca West (1892–1983), *The
   Thinking Reed*, 1936

25 To recommend thrift to the poor is both
   grotesque and insulting. It is like advising a
   man who is starving to eat less.
   Oscar Wilde (1854–1900), *The Soul of Man
   Under Socialism*, 1895

---

145 PRICES
See also 100 INFLATION

---

1 Prices have work to do. Prices are to guide
  and direct the economic activities of the
  people. Prices are to tell them what to do.
  Prices must be free to tell the truth.
  Benjamin M. Anderson, *Economics and the
  Public Welfare*, 1949, p. 550

2 Our pricing policy: to charge like a
  wounded bull.
  Anonymous

3 Regulating the prices of goods in general
  would be an endless task, and no legislator
  has ever been weak enough to think of
  attempting it.
  Jeremy Bentham (1748–1832), *Defence of
  Usury*, 1787, letter V

4 Price, *n.* Value plus a reasonable sum for the
  wear and tear of conscience in demanding it.
  Ambrose Bierce (1842–1914?), *The Devil's
  Dictionary*, 1911

5 How extraordinary and contrary to reason
  is this ordinance for man to legislate about
  buying and selling or fix a definite price; for
  it is quite sure that the fertility or barrenness
  of the earth and all living things, yes, of

everything that multiplies, rests in the power of God alone.
Canon of Bridlington (1307–1377?) in Alan and Veronica Palmer, *Quotations in History*

6 Price in a market is not always the same thing as market price.
Thomas De Quincey (1785–1859), *Logic of Political Economy*, 1844, ch. II

7 One person's price is another person's income.
Walter W. Heller, 'What's Right With Economics?', *American Economic Review*, March 1975, p. 21

8 Natural price is only another name for cost of production.
David Ricardo (1772–1823), *Notes on Malthus*, in *Works*, ed. Sraffa, vol. II, pp. 46, 224

9 Poor fellow! never joyed since the price of oats rose; it was the death of him.
William Shakespeare (1564–1616), *Henry IV, Pt I*, 1597–8, act II, sc. I

10 At market-price have bought.
William Shakespeare (1564–1616), *All's Well That Ends Well*, 1602–4, act V, sc. III

11 If he overhold his price so much,
We'll none of him.
William Shakespeare (1564–1616), *Troilus and Cressida*, 1597–1602, act II, sc. III

12 The natural price . . . is as it were, the central price, to which the prices of all commodities are continually gravitating.
Adam Smith (1723–1790), *Wealth of Nations*, 1776, vol. I, bk. I, ch. VII

13 The price of commodities in the market is formed by means of a certain struggle which takes place between the buyers and the sellers.
Henry Thornton (1760–1815), *An Enquiry into the Nature and Effects of the Paper Credit of Great Britain*, 1802, ch. VIII, p. 193

14 The plenty or scarcity of any particular thing, is the sole cause whence any commodity or thing can become higher or lower in price; or, in other words, as the demand is greater or less in proportion to the quantity of any thing, so will such thing, whatsoever it is, be cheaper or dearer.
Jacob Vanderlint (? –1740), *Money Answers All Things*, 1734, p. 5

15 What is a cynic? . . . A man who knows the price of everything and the value of nothing . . . And a sentimentalist . . . is a man who sees an absurd value in everything, and doesn't know the market price of any single thing.
Oscar Wilde (1854–1900), *Lady Windermere's Fan*, 1892, act III

---

146 PRIVATIZATION
See also 128 NATIONALIZATION

---

1 It has taken long decades of empirical experience to discover that Government failure is often so much worse than so-called market failures.
Lord Harris, House of Lords, 4 February 1981

2 Privatisation is now starkly revealed as a massive plunder of public property.
Michael Meacher, *Independent*, 17 October 1988

3 Everything that is most beautiful in Britain has always been in private hands.
Malcom Rifkind, *Observer*, 'Sayings of the Week', 17 January 1988

---

147 PRODUCERS

---

1 Consumer's delusions result in producer's blunders.
John Bates Clark (1847–1938), introduction to K. Rodbertus, *Overproduction and Crises*, 1898

2 The diffuse and inchoate consumer interest has been no match for the sharply focussed, articulate and well-financed efforts of producer groups.
Walter W. Heller, 'What's Right With Economics?', *American Economic Review*, March 1975, p. 5

3 Sugar, then, is the most notable addiction in history that killed not the consumer but the producer.
Henry Hobhouse, *Seeds of Change*, 1985, p. 63

4   The supposed conflict of labour with capital
    is a delusion. The real conflict is between
    producers and consumers.
    W. Stanley Jevons (1835–1882), attributed

148 PRODUCTION

1   Man produces in order to consume.
    Frédéric Bastiat (1801–1850), *Sophismes
    Économiques*, 1846, ch. I, p. 8

2   To consult exclusively the immediate
    interest of production, is to consult an
    anti-social interest.
    Frédéric Bastiat (1801–1850), *ibid.*, p. 14

3   The principles of saving, pushed to excess,
    would destroy the motive to production. If
    every person were satisfied with the simplest
    food, the poorest clothing, and the meanest
    houses, it is certain that no other sort of
    food, clothing, and lodging would be in
    existence.
    Thomas Robert Malthus (1766–1834),
    Principles of Political Economy, 2nd ed.,
    introduction

4   Production not being the sole end of human
    existence, the term unproductive does not
    necessarily imply any stigma.
    John Stuart Mill (1806–1873), *Principles of
    Political Economy*, 1848, bk. I, ch. III, 1

149 PROFESSIONS

1   A professional is a person who tells you
    what you know already but in a way you
    cannot understand.
    Anonymous

2   I hold every man a debtor to his profession.
    Francis Bacon (1561–1626), *Maxims of the
    Law*, 1597, preface

3   Of the professions, it may be said that
    soldiers are becoming too popular, parsons
    too lazy, physicians too mercenary, and
    lawyers too powerful.
    C.C. Colton (1780–1832), *Lacon*, 1820

4   It is . . . entirely unreasonable that the
    closed solicitors' shop should remain closed
    when one considers that the bulk of legal
    advice is nowadays given outside that shop.
    Lord Donaldson, House of Lords, 5 July
    1984

5   The best augury of a man's success in his
    profession is that he thinks it the finest in
    the world.
    George Eliot (1819–1880), *Daniel
    Deronda*, 1876, II

6   Medicine is the only profession which has
    bestowed unquestionable benefits on
    mankind.
    Jo Grimond, *Daily Telegraph*, 31 March
    1986

7   Professionalization is thus an attempt to
    translate one order of scarce resources —
    special knowledge and skills — into another
    — social and economic rewards.
    M.S. Larson, *The Rise of Professionalism*,
    1977, introduction

8   The law, by any standards, is an
    extraordinary profession. Its practitioners
    are always anxious to voice the highest
    principles of fairness and impartiality in
    relation to everyone but themselves.
    Sir Robert Mark, *In the Office of Constable*,
    1978, ch. 22

9   Yet trades there are, though rather rare,
        Where men are not so jealous;
    Two lawyers know the coal to blow,
        Just like a pair of bellows.
    Lord Charles Neaves (1800–1876), *Songs
    and Verses*, 1868, 'A Song of Proverbs'

10 The restraining influence of the Law Society
    in a profession which once had a proverbial
    bad name is obvious.
    Gilbert Russell, *Nuntius: Advertising and
    Its Future*, 1926

11 The law is not a profession so easily
    acquired.
    Sir Walter Scott (1771–1832), *Journal*, 24
    March 1831

12 He was famous, sir, in his profession.
    William Shakespeare (1564–1616), *All's
    Well That Ends Well*, 1602–4, act I, sc. I

13 There is no ancient gentlemen but
    gardeners, ditchers and grave-makers: they
    hold up Adam's profession.
    William Shakespeare (1564–1616),
    Hamlet, 1599–1600, act V, sc. I

14 My profession's sacred from above.
William Shakespeare (1564–1616), *Henry VI, Pt. I*, 1589–90, act I, sc.II

15 There is boundless theft
In limited professions.
William Shakespeare (1564–1616), *Timon of Athens*, 1607–8, act IV, sc. III

16 All professions are conspiracies against the laity.
George Bernard Shaw (1856–1950), *The Doctor's Dilemma*, 1906, act I

17 A woman with a good jointure is a doosid deal easier a profession than the law, let me tell you.
William Makepeace Thackeray (1811–1863), *The History of Pendennis*, 1849, ch. XXVIII

---

150 PROFIT
See also 96 INCOME

---

1 What have I done for profits today?
Anonymous

2 If you mean to profit, learn to please.
Charles Churchill (1731–1764), *Gotham*, bk. II, 1, 8

3 It is a socialist idea that making profits is a vice; I consider the real vice is making losses.
Sir Winston Churchill (1874–1965), Esar and Bentley, *The Treasury of Humorous Quotations*

4 Civilization and profits go hand in hand.
Calvin Coolidge (1872–1933) in Clifton Fadiman, *The American Treasury 1455–1955*, 1955

5 Profits are not due to risks, but to superior skill in taking risks. They are not subtracted from the gains of labour but are earned, in the same sense in which the wages of skilled labour are earned.
Frank A. Fetter (1863–1949), *The Principles of Economics*, 1904, p. 291

6 All worldly profit, all pleasure is correspondent to a like measure of anxiety or wearisomness.
Thomas Fuller (1654–1734), *Gnomologia*, 1732, no. 571

7 Let him, that receives the profit, repair the inn.
Thomas Fuller (1654–1734), *ibid.*, no. 3, 186

8 We should re-define the word 'profits' to mean only the surplus available for distribution to shareholders after having allowed for that amount of investment necessary for a reasonable rate of growth.
Sir James Goldsmith in Geoffrey Wansell, *Sir James Goldsmith*, 1982, ch. 8

9 Men must have profits proportionable to their expense and hazard.
David Hume (1711–1776), *Essays*, 1741–2, 'Of Commerce'

10 Nothing dejects a trader like the interruption of his profits.
Samuel Johnson (1709–1784), *Taxation No Tyranny*, 1775

11 No great loss but some small profit.
James Kelly, *Scottish Proverbs*, 1721, N, no. 37

12 Quick returns make rich merchants.
James Kelly, *ibid.*, Q, no. 4

13 Net income . . . is shaped, as it were, by the interaction of the blades of a pair of shears — revenue as one, cost as the other. It is obvious that both blades are necessary to produce the result, but their action is not necessarily equal. One blade may rest passively on the table while the other blade moves actively up and down under the power of the operator's fingers. The passive blade represents revenue — the element under little direct managerial control; the active blade represents costs — the element under considerable managerial control in the process of producing net income.
A.C. Littleton, 'Business Profits as a Legal Basis for Dividends', *Harvard Business Review*, 1937, no. 1, p. 58

14 Profit in some cases, may be more properly said to be acquired than produced.
James Maitland (1759–1839), *An Inquiry Into the Nature and Origin of Public Wealth*, 1804, ch. II, p. 161

15 It is not the aim of this company [Marks & Spencer] to make more money than is prudent.
Lord Rayner, *Observer*, 'Sayings of the Week', 10 May 1987

16 Nothing contributes so much to the prosperity and happiness of a country as high profits.
David Ricardo (1772–1823), *On Protection to Agriculture*, 1822, sec. V

17 Normal profits are simply the supply price of entrepreneurship to a particular industry.
Joan Robinson (1903–1983), 'What is Perfect Competition?', *Quarterly Journal of Economics*, November 1934, p. 106

18 To apprehend thus
Draws us a profit from all things we see.
William Shakespeare (1564–1616), *Cymbeline*, 1609–10, act III, sc. III

19 Profits will accrue.
William Shakespeare (1564–1616), *Henry V*, 1598–9, act II, sc. I

20 For profit's sake.
William Shakespeare (1564–1616), *Henry VI, Pt. I*, 1589–90, act III, sc. III

21 Snail-slow in profit.
William Shakespeare (1564–1616), *The Merchant of Venice*, 1596–7, act II, sc. V

22 No profit grows where is no pleasure ta'en.
William Shakespeare (1564–1616), *The Taming of the Shrew*, 1593–4, act I, sc. I

23 The earnings of an entrepreneur sometimes represent nothing but the spoliation of the workmen. A profit is made not because the industry produces much more than it costs, but because it fails to give to the workman sufficient compensation for his toil.
Simonde de Sismondi (1773–1842) in Gide and Rist, *A History of Economic Doctrines*

24 In exchanging the complete manufacture . . . something must be given for the profits of the undertaker who hazards his stock in this adventure.
Adam Smith (1723–1790), *Wealth of Nations*, 1776, vol. I, bk. I, ch. VI

25 There is profit in other people's pleasure.
Margaret Thatcher, *Sunday Times*, 30 March 1986

151 PROFIT SHARING

1 The idea of making workers share in profits is a very attractive one and it would seem that it is from there that harmony as between Capital and Labour should come. But the practical formula for such sharing has not yet been found.
Henri Fayol (1841–1925), *General and Industrial Management*, 1916, ch. IV

152 PROGRESS

1 The Luddites were right.
Sir Arthur Bryant, *Illustrated London News*, 29 April 1944, p. 474

2 Compare society to a boat. Her progress through the water will not depend upon the exertion of her crew, but upon the exertion devoted to propelling her. This will be lessened by any expenditure of force in fighting among themselves, or in pulling in different directions.
Henry George (1839–1897), *Progress and Poverty*, 1879, bk. X, ch. III

3 It is hardly progress for a cannibal to use a knife and fork.
Sir Geoffrey Howe, *Independent*, 'Quote Unquote', 21 January 1989

4 Economic progress, in capitalist society, means turmoil.
Joseph A. Schumpeter (1883–1950), *Capitalism, Socialism and Democracy*, 1942, ch. III

5 Discontent is the first step in the progress of a man or a nation.
Oscar Wilde (1854–1900), *A Woman of No Importance*, 1893, act II

153 PROMOTION
See also 32 CAREERS, 77 EQUAL OPPORTUNITIES, 193 SUCCESS

1 To get on these days, it isn't what you know or even who you know that counts — it's usually what you know about who you know.
'Epson's Compleat Office Companion', *The Times*, 12 October 1987

2 He that waits for dead men's shoes, may go barefoot.
Thomas Fuller (1654–1734), *Gnomologia*, 1732, no. 2338

3 Who waite for dead men shoen shall goe long barefoote.
John Heywood (1506–1565), *Proverbs*, 1546, pt. I, ch. XI

4 I would not risk spoiling my chances for a large promotion by asking for a small one.
Elbert Hubbard (1856–1915), *Notebook*, 1927, p. 126

5 Progress in the Foreign Service is either vaginal or rectal. You marry the boss's daughter or you crawl up his bottom.
Nicholas Monsarrat (1910–1979), *Smith and Jones*, 1963, ch. 5

6 *The Peter Principle*; in a hierarchy every employee tends to rise to his level of incompetence.
Laurence J. Peter and Raymond Hull, *The Peter Principle*, 1969, ch. 1. See also the Paula Principle 77.12.

154 PROPERTY
See also 110 LAND

1 The right of property enables an industrious man to reap where he has sown.
Anonymous

2 Is it not lawful for me to do what I will with mine own?
Bible, Authorized Version, Matthew 20:15

3 Private property began the instant somebody had a mind of his own.
E.E. Cummings (1894–1962) in Clifton Fadiman, *The American Treasury 1455–1955*, 1955

4 Property has its duties as well as its rights.
Benjamin Disraeli (1804–1881), *Sybil*, 1845, bk. II, ch. XI

5 Property is necessary, but it is not necessary that it should remain forever in the same hands.
Rémy de Gourmont (1858–1915) in Esar and Bentley, *The Treasury of Humorous Quotations*

6 You do not need money to succeed in property; all you need is to know people with access to money.
Shirley Green, *Rachman*, 1979, ch. IV

7 'Th' accurate delimitation o' th' concept property would afford a theme especially apposite fer amplificative philosophical disquisition; however, you've chosen your path in life an' must take th' consequences,' said Justice Marsh Swallow, in sentencin' Stew Nugen this mornin'.
Frank McKinney Hubbard (1868–1930), *New Sayings by Abe Martin*, 1917

8 Property rights are of course human rights, i.e., rights which are possessed by human beings. The introduction of the wholly false distinction between property rights and human rights in many policy discussions is surely one of the all time great semantic flimflams.
Michael C. Jensen and William H. Meckling, 'Theory of the Firm,' *Journal of Financial Economics*, 1976, vol. 3, p. 307

9 *Where there is no property, there is no injustice* is a proposition as certain as any demonstration in Euclid: for the idea of property, being a right to any thing; and the idea to which the name injustice is given, being the invasion of violation of that right.
John Locke (1632–1704), *Essay Concerning Human Understanding*, 1690, bk. IV, ch. III, sec. 18

10 The right of property has not made poverty, but it has powerfully contributed to make wealth.
J.R. McCulloch (1789–1864), *Principles of Political Economy*, new ed., pt. I, ch. II

11 No one, I am sure, by the light of nature ever understood an English mortgage.
Lord Macnaghten (1830–1913), *Samuel* v. *Jarrah Timber & Wood Paving Corpn. Ltd.*, 1904.

12 [Property] A patent entitling one man to dispose of another man's labour.
Thomas Robert Malthus (1766–1834), attributed

13 The theory of the Communists may be summed up in the single sentence: Abolition of private property.
Karl Marx (1818–1883) **and Friedrich Engels** (1820–1895), *The Communist Manifesto*, 1848, ch. 2

14 The laws of property have never yet conformed to the principles on which the justification of private property rests. They have made property of things which never ought to be property, and absolute property

where only a qualified property ought to exist.
John Stuart Mill (1806–1873), *Principles of Political Economy*, 1848, bk. II, ch. I, 3

15 The institution of property, when limited to its essential elements, consists in the recognition, in each person, of a right to the exclusive disposal of what he or she have produced by their own exertions, or received either by gifts or fair agreement, without force or fraud, from those who produced it.
John Stuart Mill (1806–1873), *ibid.*, ch. II, 1

16 Property is theft.
Pierre-Joseph Proudhon (1809–1865), *What is Property?*, 1848, ch. I

17 Without the sense of security which property gives, the land would still be uncultivated.
François Quesnay (1694–1774) in Gide and Rist, *A History of Economic Doctrines*

18 It is clear that income from property is not the reward of waiting but the reward of employing a good stock broker.
Joan Robinson (1903–1983), 'The Second Crisis of Economic Theory', *American Economic Review*, May 1972, p. 9

19 Laws are always useful to those who have property, and harmful to those who have nothing.
Jean-Jacques Rousseau (1712–1778), *The Social Contract*, 1762, bk. I, ch. IX, note

20 Property assures what toil acquires.
Richard Savage (*c*.1697–1743), *Of Public Spirit*, 1736

21 Law in a free country is, or ought to be, the determination of the majority of those who have property in land.
Jonathan Swift (1667–1745), *Thoughts on Various Subjects*, 1711

22 It is foolish to maintain property rights for which no service is performed, for payment without service is waste.
R.H. Tawney (1880–1910), *The Acquisitive Society*, 1921, ch. VI

23 Property is the most ambiguous of categories. It covers a multitude of rights which have nothing in common except that they are exercised by persons and enforced by the state.
R.H. Tawney (1880–1962), *ibid.*, ch. V

24 That low, bestial instinct which men call the right of property.
Count Leo Tolstoy (1828–1910), *First Stories*, 'Story of a Horse'

25 If property had simple pleasures, we could stand it; but its duties make it unbearable. In the interest of the rich we must get rid of it.
Oscar Wilde (1854–1900), *The Soul of Man Under Socialism*, 1912, p. 9

26 Property is an instrument of humanity. Humanity is not an instrument of property.
Woodrow Wilson (1856–1924), speech, 18 September 1912

---

155 PROSPERITY

---

1 Can any body remember when the times were not hard, and money not scarce?
Ralph Waldo Emerson (1803–1882), *Society and Solitude*, 1870, 'Works and Days'

2 Prosperity has every thing cheap.
Thomas Fuller (1654–1734), *Gnomologia*, 1732, no. 3964

3 Let's be frank about it — most people have never had it so good.
Harold Macmillan, speech, 20 July 1957: from the American vernacular — 'You never had it so good'. Also used by the Democratic Party in the Presidential elections, 1952.

4 Too much prosperity makes men greedy and desires are never controlled sufficiently to stop at the point of attainment.
Seneca (4 BC–AD 65), *De Clementia*, bk. I, ch. I

5 Few of us can stand prosperity. Another man's I mean.
Mark Twain (1835–1910), 'Pudd'nhead Wilson's New Calendar', *Following the Equator*, 1897, vol. II, ch. IV

---

156 PROSTITUTION

---

1 Whether our reformers admit it or not, the economic and social inferiority of women is responsible for prostitution.
Emma Goldman (1869–1940), *Anarchism and Other Essays*, 1911

2 Prostitution gives her an opportunity to
meet people. It provides fresh air and
wholesome exercise, and it keeps her out of
trouble.
Joseph Heller, *Catch-22*, 1975, ch. 33

3 Prostitutes are a necessity. Without them
men would attack respectable women in the
streets.
Napoleon I (1769–1821), attributed

4 Prostitution is a labour-intensive activity
involving little in the way of intermediate
consumption.
OECD Economic Outlook, 'The hidden
economy', Occasional Studies, 1982

5 It is a silly question to ask a prostitute why
she does it . . . These are the highest paid
'professional' women in America.
Gail Sheehy, *Hustling*, ch. 4

6 Prostitutes believe in marriage. It provides
them with most of their trade.
'Suzie', *Knave*, 1975, vol. 7, no. 10

157 PROTECTIONISM
See also 195 TARIFFS

1 [Protectionism is] the sacrifice of the
consumer to the producer, — of the end to
the means.
Frédéric Bastiat (1801–1850), *Sophismes
Économiques*, 1846, ch. XVII, p. 126

2 There never has been an infant industry that
has been weaned.
Michael Cobb, *Sydney Morning Herald*, 26
June 1982

3 The protectionists are fond of flashing to the
public eye the glittering delusion of great
money-results from manufacturing, mines,
artificial exports . . . But the really
important point of all is, *into whose pockets
does this plunder really go?*
Walt Whitman (1819–1892), 'Notes Left
Over', *Democratic Vistas*, 1881

158 THE PUBLIC

1 Gold is not found in quartz alone; its richest
lodes are in the eyes and ears of the public,
but these are harder to work and to prospect
than any quartz vein.
Samuel Butler (1835–1902), *Note Books*,
ed. Festing Jones, 1912, ch. XIV

2 There is not a more mean, stupid, dastardly,
pitiful, selfish, spiteful, envious, ungrateful
animal than the public.
William Hazlitt (1778–1830), *Table Talk*,
1821–2, 'On Living to One's-Self'

3 There are three things which the public will
always clamour for, sooner or later: namely,
Novelty, novelty, novelty.
Thomas Hood (1799–1845),
announcement of *Comic Annual*, 1836

4 No public interest is anything other or
nobler than a massed accumulation of
private interests.
Mark Twain (1835–1910), speech, 1906

5 The public have an insatiable curiosity to
know everything, except what is worth
knowing.
Oscar Wilde (1854–1900), *The Soul of Man
Under Socialism*, 1891

159 PUBLIC ENTERPRISE
See also 128 NATIONALIZATION

1 A public utility thrives only as it is backed
up by the best people in the town.
Elbert Hubbard (1856–1915), *Notebook*,
1927, p. 133

2 The common remark that public business is
worse managed than all other business, is
not altogether unfounded.
Herbert Spencer (1820–1903), *Social
Statics*, 1870, pt. III, ch. XXII, sec. 6

160 PUBLIC EXPENDITURE
See also 92 GOVERNMENT

1 The King's exchequer was like the spleen;
for when that did swell, the whole body did
pine.
Francis Bacon (1561–1626), *Apophthegms*,
1624

2 We urgently need a government equivalent
of Weight Watchers.
Sir Rod Carnegie, *Sydney Morning News*,
'Sayings of 1985', 28 December 1985

3 It is exasperating, even though inevitable, that although it is the taxpayers' money that is being spent those who advocate any such expenditure are regarded as warm-hearted, forward-looking and generous and those who oppose it are thought of and described as mean.
Leslie Chapman *Your Disobedient Servant*, 1978, ch. 6

4 The inherent tendency will always be for public services to fall behind public production.
John Kenneth Galbraith, *The Affluent Society*, 1958, ch. 18, III

5 Thrift should be the guiding principle in our government expenditure.
Mao Tse-Tung (1893–1976), *Quotations from Chairman Mao Tse-Tung*, 1976, p. 189

6 Great nations are never impoverished by private, though they sometimes are by public prodigality and misconduct. The whole, or almost the whole public revenue is employed in maintaining unproductive hands.
Adam Smith (1723–1790), *Wealth of Nations*, 1776, vol. I, bk. I, ch. III

161 PUBLIC RELATIONS

1 Public Relations is the management function which evaluates public attitudes, identifies the policies and procedures of an individual or an organization with the public interest, and executes a program of action to earn public understanding and acceptance.
Anonymous, James Beasley Simpson, *Best Quotes of '54, '55, '56*, 1957

2 PR is like Christianity. If you don't believe in it, it won't work.
Alan Crompton-Batt, *Independent*, 23 July 1988

3 Facts influence. They are revered by people who cannot contradict them. Like statistics, they are extremely dangerous. They must be controlled and only revealed where essential.
Michael Shea, *Independent*, 'Quote Unquote', 24 September 1988

162 PUBLISHING
See also 130 NEWSPAPERS

1 I really think that this assault was carried to a very inconsiderate length, and that if an author is to go and give a beating to a publisher who has offended him, two or three blows with a horse-whip ought to be quite enough to satisfy his irritated feelings.
Lord Abinger (1767–1844), *Fraser* v. *Berkeley*, 1836

2 Of making many books there is no end; and much study is a weariness of the flesh.
Bible, Authorized Version, Ecclesiastes 12: 12

3 Publish, *v.* In literary affairs, to become the fundamental element in a cone of critics.
Ambrose Bierce (1842–1914?), *The Devil's Dictionary*, 1911

4 Barabbas was a publisher.
Thomas Campbell (1777–1844), attributed, and also attributed to Byron. See also Hubbard below.

5 The best time for planning a book is while you're doing the dishes.
Agatha Christie (1891–1976) in James Beasley Simpson, *Best Quotes of '54, '55, '56*, 1957

6 A publisher is a man who cannot be persuaded to publish a book. He doesn't think it worth printing and reduces writers to despair — then he makes a fortune out of them. Some publishers are honest and never rob their clients of more than 200 per cent.
Miles Franklin (1879–1954) in A.W. Barker, *The End of My Career*, 1902 (unpublished), *Dear Robertson, Letters to an Australian Publisher*, 1982, p. 35

7 Publish everything. We need a pluralism of opinion.
Mikhail Gorbachev, *Independent*, 'Quote Unquote', 1 October 1988

8 Publisher: 1. An emunctory business, first functioned by Barabbas. 2. One of a band of panders which sprang into existence soon after the death of Gutenberg and which now overruns the world. 3. The patron saint of the mediocre.
Frank McKinney Hubbard (1868–1930), *The Roycroft Dictionary*, 1923. See also Campbell above.

9 The assets of a publishing house are people
— editors, the authors they attract, sales
and publicity; all assets that are possessed of
two feet and can walk away.
Hammond Innes, *Sydney Morning Herald,*
7 January 1989

10 No man but a blockhead ever wrote except
for money.
Samuel Johnson (1709–1784) in Boswell's
Life of Johnson, 5 April 1776

11 The best part of every author is in general to
be found in his book.
Samuel Johnson (1709–1984), *Johnsonian
Miscellanies,* 1897, vol. II, p. 310

12 Authors are easy enough to get on with — if
you are fond of children.
Michael Joseph, *Observer,* 'Sayings of the
Week', 29 May 1949

13 The road that leads to publishers' counting
houses is paved with the bones of artists and
writers starved on the track.
Norman Lindsay (1879–1969) in A.W.
Barker, *Dear Robertson, Letters to an
Australian Publisher,* 1982, p. 64

14 As Dante said when they asked him what he
was doing rowing through the inferno, 'Just
gathering material for a book'.
Peter Luck, *Sydney Morning Herald,* 16
January 1989

15 [Bookselling] is, like prostitution, a trade in
which the amateurs think they are better
than the professionals.
Roger Page, *Australian Bookselling,* 1970,
ch. 2

16 I object to publishers; the one service they
have done me is to teach me to do without
them. They combine commercial rascality
with artistic touchiness and pettishness,
without being either good business men or
fine judges of literature.
George Bernard Shaw (1856–1950), letter
to Frederick H. Evans, 14 August 1895

17 Literature is like any other trade; you will
never sell anything unless you go to the right
shop.
George Bernard Shaw (1856–1950) in
James Beasley Simpson, *Best Quotes of '54,
'55, '56,* 1957

18 Publish and be damned.
Duke of Wellington (1769–1852),
attributed

163 RADIO
See also 130 NEWSPAPERS, 199 TELEVISION

1 The sixty-four dollar question.
Anonymous, first used on 21 April 1940 on
Take It or Leave It, a CBS programme.
Clifton Fadiman, *The American Treasury,
1455–1955,* 1955

2 The greatest thing that could happen to the
state and nation [Australia] is when we get
rid of the media. Then we would live in
peace and tranquillity and no one would
know anything. I think if we could put you
[the media] out of existence that could be
the best thing to happen to anything.
Sir Joh Bjelke-Petersen, *Australian Financial
Review,* 18 April 1986

3 Politicians have finally realised that
television gives them exposure, not
exposition. Radio does that.
Sir Robin Day, *Sunday Times,* 29
September 1985

4 It's a one-to-one dialogue. You open your
mouth and you're talking to six million
people.
Derek Jameson on BBC Radio 4, *Private
Eye,* no. 662, 1 May 1987

5 The ideal voice for radio may be defined as
having no substance, no sex, no owner, and
a message of importance for every
housewife.
Harry V. Wade in Clifton Fadiman, *The
American Treasury, 1455–1955,* 1955

164 RAILWAYS
See also 14 AVIATION, 44 COMMUTERS,
127 MOTOR VEHICLES, 182 SHIPPING,
207 TRANSPORT

1 No one — not even a railway manager —
gives away money as a business transaction.
The manager who reduces a rate on coal, or
a third-class fare, does so hoping that traffic
will be so stimulated that there will be a
greater net profit on the larger traffic at the
lower rate than there was on the smaller
traffic at the higher rate . . . whatever
railway critics may say, the Irish
applewoman's principle, that you can afford

to sell each apple at a loss if you only sell enough, is not universally true.
W.M. Acworth, *The Elements of Railway Economics*, 1905, ch. VII

2 All that the traffic will bear.
Anonymous: common saying about railroad freight rates, *c.*1900, Clifton Fadiman, *The American Treasury 1455–1955*, 1955

3 Dirty train stations cause terminal illness.
Anonymous graffito, New York subway, R. Reisner and L. Wechsler, *Encyclopaedia of Graffiti*

4 Trains Running Late Are Likely to Make Up Time.
Anonymous, railway sign at Sirpur, quoted by Paul Theroux, *The Great Railway Bazaar*, 1975

5 On the whole, a great railway is, I think, less liable to unforeseen accidents than the strange Empire of India.
Walter Bagehot (1826–1877), *Lombard Street*, 1873, ch. 7

6 If they want to get rid of me, they'll get rid of me through British Rail sandwiches.
Tony Benn, *Observer*, 'Sayings of the Week', 30 September 1984

7 If hell is other people, purgatory, some would say, is perpetual train travel in the company of other people.
Rosemary Burton, *Punch*, 25 September 1985

8 Travelling by rails is like being stowed away in a parcel in the boot, you can't see nothing nor hear nothing.
Thomas Chandler Haliburton (1786–1865), *The Letter Bag of the Great Western*, 1840, 'Letter from a Coachman on the Railroad Line'.

9 If Doctor Goodrich had invented the rubber tire before Stephenson utilized the steel rail, the railroads would never have been built.
Elbert Hubbard (1856–1915), *Notebook*, 1927, p. 107

10 Fast train: One that has no diner.
Frank McKinney Hubbard (1868–1930), *The Roycroft Dictionary*, 1923

11 Is there any other business that runs through more marginal constituencies than we do?
Sir Peter Parker, *Observer*, 'Sayings of the Week', 3 April 1983

12 Nothing pleases the British public more than to see British Rail making a loss.
Sir Robert Reid, attributed

13 No railroad will be safe until they have made a Bishop *in partibus*.
Sydney Smith (1771–1845) in W. Jerrold, *Bon-Mots of Sydney Smith and R. Brinsley Sheridan*, p. 108

14 We have been, up to this point, very careless of our railway regulations. The first person of rank who is killed will put everything in order, and produce a code of the most careful rules.
Sydney Smith (1771–1845), letter to the *Morning Chronicle*, 7 June 1842

15 Second-class carriages, though fairly full, are always reasonably quiet; first-class carriages are excessively noisy with their occupants all on expense accounts, boasting of their commercial ingenuity.
A.J.P. Taylor, *A Personal History*, 1983, ch. 19

16 Everyone loves trains. No one loves British Rail.
Sue Thomas, *Sunday Times*, 27 November 1988

17 We do not ride on the railroad; it rides upon us.
Henry David Thoreau (1817–1862), *Walden*, 1845, ch. 2

18 The Caledonian Railway Company, the work neither of lawyers, nor of old women, not spendthrifts, but of shrewd middle-aged mercantile men, is just such a tangle as one might dream of after supping on lobster salad and champagne.
The Times, 30 September 1850

19 The railway power, we know well, will not admit of being materially counteracted by sentiment.
William Wordsworth (1770–1850), *Two Letters Re-printed from the Morning Post*, 1844, I

165 REFERENCES

1 'As to being a reference,' said Pancks, 'you know in a general way, what being a reference means. It's all your eye, that is!

Look at your tenants down the yard here.
They'd all be references for one another, if
you'd let 'em. What would be the good of
letting 'em? It's no satisfaction to be done by
two men instead of one. One's enough. A
person who can't pay, gets another person
who can't pay, to guarantee that he can
pay.'
Charles Dickens (1812–1870), *Little
Dorrit*, 1857, ch. XXIII

166 RENT

1   Rent is an economical result as certain and
as inevitable as the harvest is a natural result
after the seed-time.
Benjamin Disraeli (1804–1881), House of
Commons, 11 February 1851

2   Compensation for improvements will not
benefit the tenant so much as is generally
supposed, because the privilege itself will
have a pecuniary value; that is to say, a
landlord will demand, and the tenant can
afford to give, a higher rent in proportion.
J. Shield Nicholson (1850–1927), *Principles
of Political Economy*, 2nd ed., 1902, vol. I,
bk. II, ch. IX, p. 322

3   Who is entitled to the rent of land? The
producer of land, without doubt. Who made
the land? God. Then, proprietor, retire!
Pierre-Joseph Proudhon (1809–1865),
What is Property?, 1848, ch. III

4   Rent is a symptom, but it is never a cause of
wealth.
David Ricardo (1772–1823), *Principles of
Political Economy and Taxation*, 1821,
ch. II

5   The interest of the landlord is always
opposed to that of the consumer and
manufacturer.
David Ricardo (1772–1823), *ibid.*,
ch. XXIV

6   Economic rent, arising as it does from
variation of fertility or advantages of
situation, must always be held as common
or social wealth, and used, as the revenues
raised by taxation are now used, for public
purposes.
George Bernard Shaw (1856–1950), 'The
Economic Basis of Socialism', *Fabian
Essays*, 1889

7   As soon as the land of any country has all
become private property, the landlords, like
all other men, love to reap where they never
sowed, and demand a rent even for its
natural produce.
Adam Smith (1723–1790), *Wealth of
Nations*, 1776, vol. I, bk. I, ch. VI

167 REPUTATION

1   A reputation for good judgment, for fair
dealing, for truth, and for rectitude, is itself
a fortune.
Henry Ward Beecher (1813–1887),
Proverbs from Plymouth Pulpit, 1887

2   Reputation, reputation, reputation! O, I
have lost my reputation! I have lost the
immortal part of myself, and what remains
is bestial.
William Shakespeare (1564–1616),
Othello, 1604–5, act II, sc. III

3   The purest treasure mortal times afford
Is spotless reputation; that away,
Men are but gilded loam or painted clay.
William Shakespeare (1564–1616), *Richard
III*, 1592–3, act I, sc. I

4   There was worlds of reputation in it, but no
money.
Mark Twain (1835–1910), *A Connecticut
Yankee in the Court of King Arthur*, 1889,
ch. 9

168 RESIGNATION

1   Among other little things that'll allus remain
a myster t' th' average layman is how a feller
kin resign a ten thousand dollar job.
Frank McKinney Hubbard (1868–1930),
New Sayings by Abe Martin, 1917

2   It seems like nothin' ever gits t' goin' good
till ther's a few resignations.
Frank McKinney Hubbard (1868–1930),
ibid.

3   The son of a bitch [General MacArthur]
isn't going to resign on me. I want him fired.
Harry S. Truman (1884–1972), attributed

169 RETAILING
See also 179 SELLING

1 Shopping has become a vital means of
expression during a time of
authoritarianism.
Neville Brody and Jon Wozencroft,
Independent, 'Quote Unquote', 3 December
1988

2 A small shop may have a good trade.
Thomas Fuller (1654–1734), *Gnomologia,*
1732, no. 411

3 Keep your shop and your shop will keep
you.
Thomas Fuller (1654–1734), *ibid.,*
no. 3122

4 But who is worse shod than the shoemakers
wife,
With shops full of new shooes all her life?
John Heywood (1506–1565), *Proverbs,*
1546, pt. I, ch. XI

5 If th' butcher would jest leave th' meat on
th' scales long enough t' see what it weighed
we wouldn' feel so stung.
Frank McKinney Hubbard (1868–1930),
New Sayings by Abe Martin, 1917

6 A unit trust which falls in value might
detract from customers' confidence in the
underwear, that intangible asset from which
all the riches have flowed.
Robert Peston (on the projected launch of
unit trusts by Marks & Spencer), 'The
Counter Revolution', *Spectator,* 23 July
1988

170 RETIREMENT
See also 136 PENSIONS

1 O blest retirement, friend to life's decline,
Retreats from care, that never must be mine,
How blest is he who crowns in shades like
these,
A youth of labour with an age of ease.
Oliver Goldsmith (1730–1774), *The
Deserted Village,* 1770

2 The man who retires from business will
shortly be retired by death.
Elbert Hubbard (1856–1915), *Notebook,*
1927, p. 143

3 The love of retirement has, in all ages,
adhered closely to those minds which have
been most enlarged by knowledge, or
elevated by genius.
Samuel Johnson (1709–1784), *The
Rambler,* 10 April 1750

4 You can't put off being young until you
retire.
Philip Larkin (1922–1985), *Money*

5 Two weeks ago I went into retirement. Am I
glad that's over! I just didn't like it. Took all
the fun out of Saturdays.
Ronald Reagan, *Independent,* 'Quote
Unquote', 18 February 1989

171 RISK
See also 186 SPECULATION

1 Prudent business men in their dealings incur
risk.
Vice-Chancellor Bacon (1798–1895), Re
Godfrey, 1883

2 Risk varies inversely with knowledge.
Irving Fisher (1867–1947), *The Theory of
Interest,* 1930, ch. IX, p. 221

3 The ultimate risk is not taking a risk.
Sir James Goldsmith, *Independent,* 'Quote
Unquote', 15 July 1989

4 Take calculated risks. That is quite different
from being rash.
George Smith Patton (1885–1966), letter, 6
June 1944

5 Behold, the fool saith, 'Put not all thine eggs
in the one basket', — which is but a manner
of saying, 'Scatter your money and your
attention', but the wise man saith, 'Put all
your eggs in the one basket and — WATCH
THAT BASKET.'
Mark Twain (1835–1910), *Pudd'nhead
Wilson,* 1894, ch. 15

172 SALES
See also 6 ADVERTISING, 119 MARKETING,
179 SELLING

1 Sales resistance is the triumph of mind over
patter.
Anonymous

2 The smoothest thing about a second-hand
   car is the salesman.
   Anonymous

3 A salesman with bad breath is dear at any
   price.
   Elbert Hubbard (1856–1915), *Notebook*,
   1927, p. 19

4 Go, make my coarse commodities look sleek
   With subtle art beguile the honest eye.
   Thomas Middleton (1570?–1627),
   Michaelmas Term, 1606, I, i

5 Base sale of chapmen's tongues.
   William Shakespeare (1564–1616), *Love's
   Labour's Lost* 1594–5, act II, sc. I

6 The salesman knows nothing of what he is
   selling save that he is charging a great deal
   too much for it.
   Oscar Wilde (1854–1900), lecture, 11 May
   1882

173 SAVING

1 The last dime that is earned is the first one
   that is saved.
   John Bates Clark (1847–1938),
   'Distribution as Determined by a Law of
   Rent', *Quarterly Journal of Economics*,
   April 1891, p. 297

2 Whenever you save five shillings, you put a
   man out of work for a day.
   John Maynard Keynes (1883–1946),
   'Inflation and Deflation', in *Essays in
   Persuasion*, 1933, pt. II, p. 152

3 The power to save depends on excess of
   income over necessary expenditure.
   Alfred Marshall (1842–1924), *Principles of
   Economics*, 8th ed., 1920, bk. IV, ch. VII, 7

4 The person who saves his income is no less a
   consumer than he who spends it: he
   consumes it in a different way; it supplies
   food and clothing to be consumed, tools and
   materials to be used, by productive
   labourers.
   John Stuart Mill (1806–1873), *Essays on
   Some Unsettled Questions of Political
   Economy*, 1844, p. 48

5 Unequal distribution of income is an
   excessively uneconomic method of getting
   the necessary saving done.
   Joan Robinson (1903–1983), *An Essay on
   Marxian Economics*, 1947, ch. VIII

6 Practically all business savings which, in
   turn, constitute the greater part of total
   saving — is done with a specific investment
   purpose in view.
   Joseph A. Schumpeter (1883–1950),
   Capitalism, Socialism and Democracy,
   1942, ch. XXVIII

174 SCIENCE
See also 175 SCIENTISTS, 198 TECHNOLOGY

1 If science has taught us anything, it is that
   the environment is full of uncertainties. It
   makes no sense to test it to destruction.
   While we wait for the doctor's diagnosis, the
   patient may easily die.
   Prince Charles, speech, November 1987

2 Professors in every branch of the sciences
   prefer their own theories to truth: the reason
   is that their theories are private property,
   but the truth is common stock.
   C.C. Colton (1780–1832), *Lacon*, 1820

3 The sciences are beneficent; they prevent
   man from thinking.
   Anatole France (1844–1942) in Rudolf
   Flesch, *The Book of Unusual Quotations*,
   1959

4 Science frees us in many ways . . . from the
   bodily terror which the savage feels. But she
   replaces that, in the minds of many, by a
   moral terror which is far more
   overwhelming.
   Charles Kingsley (1819–1875), sermon, 26
   November 1866

5 It is not necessary for politicians and other
   leaders to be professional scientists, but it is
   necessary for them to understand what
   science is; to know that it is one of the
   contributions to world civilisation at which
   this country [UK] excelled until a decade
   ago; to know that it is the basis of all
   technology and, hence, of future industry;
   and to know that it can only be carried out
   by dedicated and committed people in ways
   which do not respond well to political
   directives.
   Sir George Porter, *Guardian*, 2 December
   1986

6 Science is not an absolute to which all things
   have to be subordinated.
   Cardinal Joseph Ratzinger, *Observer*,
   'Sayings of the Week', 15 March 1987

7 Science is for those who learn; poetry, for
   those who know.
   Joseph Roux (1834–1905), *Meditations of
   a Parish Priest*, trans. Hapgood, 1886, ch. I,
   LXXI

8 A great deal of science goes for little without
   an eloquent tongue.
   Joseph Roux (1834–1905), *ibid.*, ch. II,
   XXVIII

9 Life based upon mere science is attractive to
   some men, because it has all the
   characteristics of sport; it feigns seriousness,
   but is not profound.
   Rabindranath Tagore (1861–1941) in N.B.
   Sen, *Wit and Wisdom of India*, 1961

175 SCIENTISTS
See also 174 SCIENCE

1 You mustn't think scientists are stupid.
   Sir Monty Finniston, *Observer*, 'Sayings of
   the Week', 16 January 1983

2 The businessman is our only scientist, and
   to him we must look for a Science of
   Economics that will eradicate poverty,
   disease, superstition — all that dissipates
   and destroys. The day is dawning.
   Elbert Hubbard (1856–1915), *Notebook*,
   1927, p. 197

3 If a scientist cannot explain to the woman
   scrubbing the lab-floor what he is doing, he
   does not know what he is doing.
   Lord Rutherford (1871–1937) in C.
   Bingham, *Wit and Wisdom*, 1982

176 SECRETARIES
See also 131 THE OFFICE

1 If you want to get something done, give it to
   a busy man so he can get his secretary to do
   it.
   Anonymous

2 A good secretary can save her boss more
   time in a year than a business jet plane can.
   Malcolm Baldridge in Michèle Brown and
   Ann O'Connor, *Woman Talk*, vol. I

3 Never screw the editor's secretary. I did
   once and she had a nervous breakdown and
   told all.
   Jeffrey Bernard, *Spectator*, 29 March 1986

4 Secretaries may be specially prized, and the
   top secretaries exceptionally well paid,
   because they give men who can afford to
   pay well the subservient, watchful and
   admiring attention that Victorian wives
   used to give their husbands.
   Caroline Bird, *Born Female*, 1968, ch. 4

5 Reliable office staff come in the shape of
   mature married women working from 9.30
   to 3.30 (inside school hours) during which
   they will do more than the 9–5ers.
   Chris Brasher in Ray Wild, *How to Manage*,
   1982, p. 212

6 The corporation man sometimes emerges as
   much less than heroic to the one person in a
   real position to know — his secretary, on
   whom he often becomes markedly dependent.
   Myron Brenton, *The American Male*, 1967

7 Most secretaries can do their bosses' jobs,
   but their skills are generally not recognised.
   M'lissa Dunn, *Sydney Morning Herald*, 10
   May 1986

8 You can run the office without a boss, but
   you can't run an office without secretaries.
   Jane Fonda, *Observer*, 'Sayings of the Year',
   3 January 1982

9 Different secretaries go different ways: some
   get laid and married, others old and harried.
   Arthur Hailey, *In High Places*, 1962, ch. 4

10 The boss's secretary can wield great power,
   like the king's mistress, without any
   authority at all.
   Antony Jay in Michèle Brown and Ann
   O'Connor, *Woman Talk*, vol. I

11 Millionaires are marrying very often their
   secretaries because they're so busy making
   money they haven't time to see other girls.
   Doris Lilly in James Beasley Simpson, *Best
   Quotes of '54, '55, '56*, 1957

177 SECURITY

1 The *borrower* is a slave to the *lender*; the
   security to *both*.
   Benjamin Franklin (1706–1790), *Poor
   Richard's Almanac*, 1757

178 SELF-INTEREST

1 The world will always be governed by self-interest. We should not try to stop this, we should try to make the self-interest of cads a little more coincident with that of decent people.
Samuel Butler (1835–1902), *Note Books*, ed. Festing Jones, 1912

2 To feather one's own nest.
Thomas Fuller (1654–1734), *Gnomologia*, 1732, no. 5164

3 It is not from the benevolence of the butcher, the brewer, or the baker, that we expect our dinner, but from their regard to their own interest. We address ourselves, not to their humanity but to their self-love, and never talk to them of our necessities but of their advantages.
Adam Smith (1723–1790), *Wealth of Nations*, 1776, vol. I, bk. I, ch. II

179 SELLING
See also 6 ADVERTISING, 119 MARKETING, 172 SALES

1 Pile it high and sell it cheap.
Sir John Cohen, *Observer*, 13 April 1986

2 A wool-seller knows a wool-buyer.
Thomas Fuller (1654–1734), *Gnomologia*, 1732, no. 484

3 He that sells wares for words, must live by the loss.
James Kelly, *Scottish Proverbs*, 1721, H, no. 359

4 To sell no matter what, no matter how, to no matter whom; behold in three words the whole diplomacy of the peasant at the fair.
Joseph Roux (1834–1905), *Meditations of a Parish Priest*, trans. Hapgood, ch. VIII, LVI

5 Sell when you can; you are not for all markets.
William Shakespeare (1564–1616), *As You Like It*, 1596–1600, act III, sc. IV

6 To things of sale a seller's praise belongs.
William Shakespeare (1564–1616), *Love's Labour's Lost*, 1594–5, act IV, sc. III

7 Fair Diomed, you do as chapmen do, Dispraise the thing that you desire to buy: But we in silence hold this virtue well, — We'll not commend what we intend to sell.
William Shakespeare (1564–1616), *Troilus and Cressida*, 1597–1602, act IV, sc. I

8 Every one lives by selling something.
Robert Louis Stevenson (1850–1894), *Across the Plains*, 1892, 'Beggars'

180 SERVICE INDUSTRIES

1 It is rare to find anywhere in the world a city of pleasure without an economically vital hinterland that supports and sustains the fun and games.
Henry Hobhouse, *Seeds of Change*, 1985, p. 161

2 They also serve who only stand and wait.
John Milton (1608–1674), Sonnet: 'On his Blindness', 1652

3 Calvin Coolidge notwithstanding, the business of America today is service.
Time, 2 September 1985. See 25.20

181 SHAREHOLDERS
See also 186 SPECULATION, 191 STOCK MARKETS

1 The shares are a penny, and ever so many
  are taken by
    Rothschild and Baring.
And just as a few are allotted to you, you
  awake with a
    shudder despairing.
W.S. Gilbert (1836–1911), *Iolanthe*, 1882, act II

2 The Annual Report was originally a dull, if respectable publication . . . For the modern stockholder the Company must provide, and does provide, a brightly coloured, smartly illustrated brochure, printed on art paper and bound in imitation vellum. . . . The general effect is festive, innocent and gay, well suited to the more junior groups at kindergarten.
C. Northcote Parkinson, *In-Laws and Outlaws*, 1959, ch. 7

3 The typical entrepreneur is no longer the bold and tireless business man of Marshall, or the sly rapacious Moneybags of Marx, but a mass of inert shareholders, indistinguishable from *rentiers*, who employ salaried managers to run their concerns.
Joan Robinson (1903–1983), *An Essay on Marxian Economics*, 1947, ch. III

4 Now it was a little astounding, and one could not help wondering, whether those who managed big companies did not forget sometimes that the body of directors of the company were the agents of the shareholders, that they owed them full information subject to proper commercial and reasonable necessities, and it was the shareholders' interests they had to study. They were not to regard shareholders as sheep who might look up if they were not fed.
Mr Justice Wright, *The Accountant*, 8 August 1931, p. 237

182 SHIPPING
See also 14 AVIATION, 164 RAILWAYS, 207 TRANSPORT

1 A shipbuilding industry is crucial to a shipping industry.
Lord Molloy, House of Lords, 21 February 1985

2 In all the ancient states and empires those who had the shipping had the wealth.
William Petty (1623–1687), *Political Arithmetic*, 1677, I

3 Ships are but boards, sailors but men.
William Shakespeare (1564–1616), *The Merchant of Venice*, 1596–7, act I, sc. III

4 Life's like a shipping business you know; take a calculated risk with a stout heart and it almost always pays off.
Warren Tute, *The Golden Greek*, 1960, ch. 2

183 SHOW BUSINESS

1 If it's a good script, I'll do it. And if it's a bad script, and they pay me enough, I'll do it.
George Burns, *Observer*, 'Sayings of the Week', 13 November 1988

2 A lot of people have made a lot of money out of me, and I've decided that I'm going to be one of them.
Joan Collins, *Observer*, 6 October 1985

3 Film was and is still a romantic business, just as life is romantic.
Katharine Hepburn, *Observer*, 'Sayings of the Week', 4 October 1987

4 That's what show business is — sincere insincerity.
Benny Hill, *Observer*, 'Sayings of the Week', 12 June 1977

5 Movie actors don't have t' work — they jest go thro' the motions.
Frank McKinney Hubbard (1868–1930), *New Sayings by Abe Martin*, 1917

6 I'm a businessman, I'm interested in the movie making money. I'm not hung up on being an actor's actor or doing what they call artistic movies.
Arnold Schwarzenegger, *Time*, 28 October 1985

7 Once you've been a comedian nobody takes you seriously any more.
Eric Sykes, *Observer*, 'Sayings of the Week', 24 August 1986

8 Success in show business depends on your ability to make and keep friends.
Sophie Tucker (1884–1960), attributed

9 The play was a great success, but the audience was a disaster.
Oscar Wilde (1854–1900), attributed

184 SOCIALISM
See also 43 COMMUNISM

1 Levelling takes away all creativity. People just don't work if they are just going to end up on the same level as everyone else.
Anatoli Adamischin (Soviet Deputy Foreign Minister), *Sydney Morning Herald*, 'Sayings of the Week', 2 August 1986

2 Under capitalism man exploits man, under socialism, it's just the opposite.
Anonymous

3 Socialists make the mistake of confusing individual worth with success. They believe

you cannot allow people to succeed in case
those who fail feel worthless.
Kenneth Baker, *Observer*, 'Sayings of the
Week', 13 July 1986

4 The language of priorities is the religion of
Socialism.
Aneurin Bevan (1897–1960) in V. Brome,
Aneurin Bevan, ch. 1

5 Grapeshot, *n*. An argument which the future
is preparing to answer to the demands of
American Socialism.
Ambrose Bierce (1842–1914?), *The Devil's
Dictionary*, 1911

6 You can't eat socialism.
Deng Xiaoping, *Sydney Morning Herald*,
'Sayings of the Week', 24 May 1986

7 The ideal of Socialism is grand and noble;
and it is, I am convinced, possible of
realization; but such a state of society
cannot be manufactured — it must grow.
Society is an organism, not a machine.
Henry George (1839–1897), *Progress and
Poverty*, 1879, VI

8 Socialism: . . . A sincere, sentimental,
beneficent theory, which has but one
objection, and that is, it will not work.
Frank McKinney Hubbard (1868–1930),
The Roycroft Dictionary, 1923

9 Socialist: 1. A person easily peeved. 2. In
economics, a school of thought founded by
Cain.
Frank McKinney Hubbard (1868–1930),
ibid.

10 The masses have a potentially inexhaustible
passion for socialism.
Mao Tse-Tung (1893–1976), *Quotations
from Chairman Mao Tse-Tung*, 1976,
p. 121

11 How can you be a millionaire and a
socialist? That's a silly question because
what it implies is that a socialist cannot be
an efficient manager.
Robert Maxwell, *Observer*, 'Sayings of the
Year', 30 December 1984

12 The cry of equality pulls everyone down.
Iris Murdoch, *Observer*, 'Sayings of the
Week', 13 September 1987

13 Because of evolution, God cannot be a
socialist. Evolution meant getting rid of the
dinosaurs and replacing them with more
efficient animals. Any socialist would have

been dedicated to protecting the dinosaurs
in the name of compassion or conservation
or something.
Norman Tebbitt, *Sydney Morning Herald*,
'Sayings of the Week', 7 June 1986

14 Socialism is about giving people what
socialists think is good for them.
Brian Walden, *Sydney Morning Herald*,
'Sayings of the Week', 10 May 1986

185 SOCIETY
See also 39 CLASS

1 Name a society whose economic advance
delights its statisticians and you name one in
which the good qualities of its earlier life are
decaying and in which no new civilization
has emerged.
D.M. Bensusan-Butt, *On Economic
Growth*, 1960, p. 213

2 Society is a joint stock company, in which
the members agree, for the better securing of
his bread to each shareholder, to surrender
the liberty and culture of the eater.
Ralph Waldo Emerson (1803–1882),
Essays, First Series, 1841, 'Self-Reliance'

3 Society is like the air, necessary to breathe,
but insufficient to live on.
George Santayana (1863–1952), *Little
Essays*, 1920

4 As long as men are men, a poor society
cannot be too poor to find a right order of
life, nor a rich society too rich to have need
to seek it.
R.H. Tawney (1880–1962), *The
Acquisitive Society*, 1921

5 There is no such thing as society: there are
only individual men and women, and there
are families.
Margaret Thatcher, *Woman's Own*, 31
October 1987

186 SPECULATION
See also 88 GAMBLING,
181 SHAREHOLDERS, 191 STOCK MARKETS

1 If a man but knew what would be dear,
He need be a merchant, but only one year.
Thomas Fuller (1654–1734), *Gnomologia*,
1732, no. 6077

2 Every transaction in which an individual buys produce in order to sell it again is, in fact, a speculation.
J.R. McCulloch (1789–1864), *Principles of Political Economy*, new ed., pt II, ch. III

3 October. This is one of the peculiarly dangerous months to speculate in stocks in. The others are July, January, September, April, November, May, March, June, December, August, and February.
Mark Twain (1835–1910), *Pudd'nhead Wilson*, 1894, ch. 13

4 There are two times in a man's life when he should not speculate: when he can't afford it, and when he can.
Mark Twain (1835–1910), 'Pudd'nhead Wilson's New Calendar', *Following the Equator*, 1897, vol. 2, ch. 20

187 SPENDING

1 If it were not for holes in the pocket, we should all be rich. A pocket is like a cistern, a small leak at the bottom is worse than a large pump at the top.
Henry Ward Beecher (1813–1887), *Proverbs from Plymouth Pulpit*, 1887

2 Know when to spend, and when to spare,
And you need not be busy, and you'll never be bare.
James Kelly, *Scottish Proverbs*, 1721, K, no. 5

3 With a will to spend there is a way.
A. Wildavsky, 'A Budget for all Seasons? Why the Traditional Budget Lasts', *Public Administration*, Nov/Dec 1978

4 Getting and spending, we lay waste our powers.
William Wordsworth (1770–1850), Sonnet: 'The World is Too Much With Us', 1807

188 SPORT

1 There is no business like show business — except sports business.
William J. Baker, *Sports in the Western World*, 1982, ch. 19

2 Just as businessmen get ulcers through business, so sportsmen must expect to suffer the strain of their work in sport.
Ken Barrington, *Playing It Straight*, 1968, ch. 13

3 The average Australian business man is intensely fond of sport, but no ordinary mercantile concern could afford to carry a cricketer who was incessantly absent from his employment.
Jack Fingleton, *Cricket Crisis*, 1946, pt. I, ch. 11

4 Football is business. And business is business.
Rinus Michels in Jonathan Green, *A Dictionary of Contemporary Quotations*

5 Businesses are not philanthropic; they expect a return for their sponsorship.
Geoffrey Nicholson, *Observer*, 8 September 1985, p. 34

6 Those who have the money to purchase first-class horses cannot ride them, and those who can ride them have not the money.
Andrew Barton Paterson (1864–1941), article on Polo in *Australian Magazine*, 6 July 1899, in Clement Semmler, *The Banjo of the Bush*, 1966, ch. 6

7 Cricket is now a business . . . [but] . . . I know of only a handful of administrators who run cricket in a businesslike manner.
Mike Procter, *Mike Procter and Cricket*, 1981, ch. 12

8 When I was a director of Sheffield United for six months, the chairman told me normal business standards didn't apply in football. It was the most stupid advice I ever had.
Mike Watterson, *Observer*, 'Quotes of the Year', 19 December 1982

9 I am working very hard on this relaxation business.
Graeme Wood, *Sydney Morning Herald*, 'Sayings of the Week', 13 July 1985

189 STATISTICS

1 Any figure that looks interesting is probably wrong.
Anonymous

2 Statistics are no substitute for judgement.
Henry Clay (1777–1852) in Tryon
Edwards, *The New Dictionary of Thoughts*

3 There are three kinds of lies: lies, damned
lies and statistics.
Benjamin Disraeli (1804–1881), attributed
by Mark Twain, *Autobiography*, vol. 1,
p. 246, also attributed to others.

4 Figures won't lie, but liars will figure.
Charles H. Grosvenor (1833–1917),
attributed

5 Statistics are like a bikini. What they reveal
is suggestive, but what they conceal is vital.
Aaron Levenstein in Michael Becket,
Quarterly Account, no. 30, 1985

---

190 STEEL

1 Steel is Prince or Pauper.
Andrew Carnegie (1837–1919) in Burton J.
Hendrick, *Life of Andrew Carnegie*, 1933

2 He found an America of wood and iron, and
turned it into steel.
Burton J. Hendrick, *Life of Andrew
Carnegie*, 1933

---

191 STOCK MARKETS
See also 181 SHAREHOLDERS,
186 SPECULATION

---

1 Long-term investments are usually
short-term investments which have gone
wrong.
Anonymous

2 Sell in May and go away.
Anonymous stock market maxim

3 The Stock Market, old boy? It's a hot-bed of
cold feet!
Anonymous, *Financial Times*, 21 October
1981

4 No one was ever ruined by taking a profit.
Anonymous stock exchange maxim

5 Wall Street, *n*. A symbol of sin for every
devil to rebuke. That Wall Street is a den of
thieves is a belief that serves every

unsuccessful thief in place of a hope in
Heaven.
Ambrose Bierce (1842–1914?), *The Devil's
Dictionary*, 1911

6 Since when was the stock market an
accurate barometer of anything?
Arthur Hailey, *The Money Changers*, 1976,
pt. 2, ch. 6

7 The freedom to make a fortune on the Stock
Exchange has been made to sound more
alluring than freedom of speech.
John Mortimer, *Independent*, 'Quote
Unquote', 29 October 1988

8 There is no moral difference between
gambling at cards or in lotteries or on the
race track and gambling in the
stock-market. One method is just as
pernicious to the body politic as the other
kind, and in degree the evil worked is far
greater.
Theodore Roosevelt (1858–1919), Message
to Congress, 31 January 1908

---

192 STRIKES
See also 40 COLLECTIVE BARGAINING,
206 TRADE UNIONS

---

1 Strikes are probably the easiest way of
measuring labour relations.
Anonymous, 'Political and Economic
Planning', *Attitudes in British Management*,
1966, ch. 5

2 The general strike has taught the working
classes more in four days than years of
talking could have done.
A.J. Balfour (1848–1930), *Observer*,
'Sayings of the Week', 14 November 1926

3 A strike has to reach a climax before it gets
better, just like a boil.
Sir Joh Bjelke-Petersen, *Sydney Morning
Herald*, 'Sayings of the Week', 7 September
1985

4 There is no right to strike against the public
safety by anybody, anywhere, anytime.
Calvin Coolidge (1872–1933), telegram
relating to the police strike at Boston,
Mass., 14 September 1919

5 If industrial workers are taking industrial
action when they are not working, one

wonders what they are doing when they are working.
Duke of Edinburgh, *Observer*, 'Sayings of the Week', 16 September 1984

6 The most successful strike is a defeat.
Elbert Hubbard (1856–1915), *Notebook*, 1927, p. 126

7 One of the main things that distinguishes democracies from dictatorships is the right to go on strike.
Len Murray, *Observer*, 'Sayings of the Week', 6 March 1983

8 There is no virtue in being on strike. The virtue lies in winning.
Jimmy Reid, *Observer*, 'Sayings of the Week', 20 January 1985

9 There is no such thing as a no-strike agreement.
Peter Wickens, *Observer*, 'Sayings of the Week', 28 April 1985

---

193 SUCCESS
See also 32 CAREERS, 77 EQUAL OPPORTUNITIES, 153 PROMOTION

---

1 Many a man owes his success to his first wife, and his second wife to his success.
Jim Backus in J. Green, *A Dictionary of Contemporary Quotations*

2 Always make yourself essential, that's been my golden rule.
Sir Joh Bjelke-Petersen, *Sydney Morning Herald*, 'Sayings of the Week', 10 May 1986

3 Be awful nice to 'em goin' up, because you're gonna meet 'em all comin' down.
Jimmy Durante (1893–1980) in Jim Fisk and Robert Barron, *Great Business Quotations*, 1985

4 Success is never blamed.
Thomas Fuller (1654–1734), *Gnomologia*, 1732, no. 4273

5 The line between failure and success is so fine that we scarcely know when we pass it . . . In business, sometimes, prospects may seem darkest when really they are on the turn. A little more persistence, a little more effort, and what seemed hopeless failure may turn to glorious success.
Elbert Hubbard (1856–1915), *Notebook*, 1927, p. 13

6 There is no such thing as success in a bad business.
Elbert Hubbard (1856–1915), *ibid.*, p. 21

7 The fool is not the man who merely does foolish things. The fool is the man who does not know enough to cash in on his foolishness.
Elbert Hubbard (1856–1915), *ibid.*, p. 36

8 The success of a business turns on its esprit de corps.
Elbert Hubbard (1856–1915), *ibid.*, p. 63

9 The measure of a man's success in business is his ability to organise.
Elbert Hubbard (1856–1915), *ibid.*, p. 84

10 Success: . . . The thing that spoils many a good failure.
Frank McKinney Hubbard (1868–1930), *The Roycroft Dictionary*, 1923

11 I cannot bear successful people who are miserable.
Elton John, *Sydney Morning Herald*, 'Sayings of the Week', 4 January 1986

12 *Paul Keating*: This is the great coming of age of Australia. This is the golden age of economic change.
Q: How much credit do you take?
Keating: Oh, a very large part.
Paul Keating, Channel 9, Australia, 18 September 1987

13 The worse fault of the working classes is telling their children they're not going to succeed, saying, 'There is a life, but it's not for you.'
John Mortimer, *Observer*, 'Sayings of 1988', 1 January 1989

14 Keep looking tanned, live in an elegant building (even if you're in the cellar) be seen in smart restaurants (even if you nurse one drink) and if you borrow, borrow big.
Aristotle Onassis (1906–1975), *The Times*, 15 August 1986

15 We are members of a strange species that devotes its energies to climbing the ladder of success in order to make money to buy things we don't need to impress people we don't like.
Lawrence Peter, *Sydney Morning Herald*, 'Sayings of the Week', 28 June 1986

16 Success causes us to be more praised than known.
Joseph Roux (1834–1905), *Meditations of a Parish Priest*, trans. Hopgood, 1886, ch. IV, XLVI

17 It is a very rare thing for a man of talent to succeed by his talent.
Joseph Roux (1834–1905), *ibid.*, LXXXVIII

18 The great fault all over the world in business is that people over-complicate and forget that the main ingredients for success are commonsense and simplicity. I use lawyers and accountants as little as possible.
Peter de Savary, *Sunday Telegraph Magazine*, 8 September 1985

19 Well we cannot greatly condemn our success.
William Shakespeare (1564–1616), *All's Well That Ends Well*, 1602–4, act III, sc. VI

20 Behind every successful man you'll find a woman who has nothing to wear.
James Stewart, attributed

21 It is not so easy to see the face of success in this world.
Rabindranath Tagore (1861–1941) in N.B. Sen, *Wit and Wisdom of India*, 1961

22 There is no disinfectant like success.
Elizabeth Taylor, *Sydney Morning Herald*, 'Sayings of the Week', 5 July 1986

23 Big companies are small companies that succeeded.
Robert Townsend, *Up the Organization*, 1970

24 She's the kind of girl who climbed the ladder of success, wrong by wrong.
Mae West (1892–1980), *I'm No Angel*, 1933

194 TAKEOVERS

1 Takeovers are for the public good, but that's not why I do it. I do it to make money.
Sir James Goldsmith, *Sunday Times*, 8 September 1985

2 You cannot buy a company merely by buying its shares.
Sir James Goldsmith, in Geoffrey Wansell, *Sir James Goldsmith*, 1982, ch. 11

195 TARIFFS
See also 157 PROTECTIONISM, 196 TAXATION

1 For other countries to tax our exports to them is an injury to us and an obstacle to trade. For us to tax their exports to us is not a correction of that injury; it is just a separate additional obstacle to trade.
Sir William Beveridge (1879–1963) *et al.*, *Tariffs: The Case Examined*, 1931, p. 110

2 Tariff, *n.* A scale of taxes on imports, designed to protect the domestic producer against the greed of his consumer.
Ambrose Bierce (1842–1914?), *The Devil's Dictionary*, 1911

3 A protecting duty can never be a cause of gain, but always and necessarily a loss, to the country imposing it, just so far as it is efficacious to its end.
John Stuart Mill (1806–1873), *Essays on some Unsettled Questions of Political Economy*, 1844

4 We've got so much taxation. I don't know of a single foreign product that enters this country untaxed except the answer to prayer.
Mark Twain (1835–1910), speech, 1906

196 TAXATION
See also 195 TARIFFS

1 He's spending a year dead for tax reasons.
Douglas Adams, *The Restaurant at the End of the Universe*, 1980, p. 89

2 I have to refer to the attached form. I regret so grave I am unable to complete the form as I do not know what is meant by filling this form. However, I am not interested in this income service. Could you please cancel my name in your books, as this system has upset my mind and I do not know who registered me as one of your customers.
Anonymous: reply sent by a newly independent Zimbabwean to the Commissioner of Income Tax in Salisbury, now Harare.

3 Taxes on wealth are capital punishment.
Anonymous

4 Whoever said, 'Better late than never', obviously never went through a tax audit.
Anonymous, *Globe and Mail*, Toronto, Canada, 11 September 1986

5 *Lord Aylestone*: Is it possible to be registered for VAT [Value Added Tax] if one is carrying out something that is completely illegal . . . Would the Customs and Excise register, for example, a burglar, a prostitute, or a brothel?
Noble Lords: Yes!
Lord Aylestone, House of Lords, 14 January 1985

6 The ambassadors of Asia Minor came to Antonius, after he had imposed a double tax, and said plainly to him, 'That if he would have two tributes in one year, he must give them two seed-times and two harvests.'
Francis Bacon (1561–1626), *Apophthegms*, 1624

7 Neither will it be, that a people overlaid with taxes should ever become valiant and martial.
Francis Bacon (1561–1626), *Essays*, 1625, 'Of the True Greatness of Kingdoms and Estates'

8 And Joseph made it a law over the land of Egypt unto this day, that Pharaoh should have the fifth part.
Bible, Authorized Version, Genesis 47:26

9 And Jehoiakim gave the silver and the gold to Pharaoh; but he taxed the land to give the money according to the commandment of Pharaoh: he exacted the silver and the gold of the people of the land, of every one according to his taxation.
Bible, Authorized Version, II Kings 23:35

10 Render therefore unto Caesar the things which are Caesar's.
Bible, Authorized Version, Matthew 22:21

11 And it came to pass in those days, that there went out a decree from Caesar Augustus, that all the world should be taxed.
Bible, Authorized Version, Luke 2:1

12 It is better to tax 25 per cent of something rather than 60 per cent of nothing.
Sir Joh Bjelke-Petersen, *Sydney Morning Herald*, 'Sayings of the Week', 6 July 1985

13 Oh what a tangled web we weave when we practise to relieve.
Sir Hermann Black, *Sydney Morning Herald*, 'Sayings of the Week', 6 July 1985

14 An economy breathes through its tax loopholes.
Barry Bracewell-Milnes, 'Tax Avoidance can be Good News for the Tax Collector', *Daily Telegraph*, 16 July 1979

15 The Tax Office misses the sharks while netting the minnows.
John Braithwaite, *Sydney Morning Herald*, 'Sayings of the Week', 6 July 1985

16 To tax and to please, no more than to love and be wise, is not given to men.
Edmund Burke (1729–1797), *Speech on American Taxation*, 19 April 1774

17 Would twenty shillings have ruined Mr Hampden's fortune? No! but the payment of half twenty shillings, on the principle that it was demanded, would have made him a slave.
Edmund Burke (1729–1797), *ibid.*

18 Taxing is an easy business. Any projector can contrive new compositions; any bungler can add to the old.
Edmund Burke (1729–1797), House of Commons, 11 February 1780

19 That a great reluctance to pay taxes existed in all the colonies, there can be no doubt. It was one of the marked characteristics of the American People long after their separation from England.
G.S. Callender (1865–1915), *Selections from the Economic History of the United States 1765–1860*, 1909, p. 123

20 There is no such thing as a good tax.
Winston Churchill (1874–1965), *Observer*, 'Sayings of the Week', 6 June 1937

21 No man in this country is under the smallest obligation, moral or other, so to arrange his legal relations of his business or to his property as to enable the Inland Revenue to put the largest possible shovel into his stores.
Lord Clyde (1863–1944), *Ayrshire Pullman Motor Services and D.M. Ritchie v. The Commissioners of Inland Revenue*, 1929

22 The Inland Revenue is not slow — and quite rightly — to take every advantage which is open to it under the taxing statutes for the

purpose of depleting the taxpayer's pocket.
Lord Clyde (1863–1944), *ibid.*

23 The art of taxation consists in so plucking the goose as to obtain the largest amount of feathers with the smallest possible amount of hissing.
Jean Baptiste Colbert (1619–1683), attributed

24 The most 'equitable' tax is the one someone else pays.
Robert P. Crum, 'Value Added Taxation', *Accounting Historians' Journal*, Fall 1982

25 The avoidance of tax may be lawful, but it is not yet a virtue.
Lord Denning, Re *Weston's Settlements*, 1969

26 'It was as true,' said Mr Barkis, 'as taxes is. And nothing's truer than them.'
Charles Dickens (1812–1870), *David Copperfield*, 1850, ch. 21

27 There are few greater stimuli to human ingenuity than the prospect of avoiding fiscal liability. Experience shows that under this stimulus human ingenuity outreaches Parliamentary prescience.
Lord Diplock (1907–1985), *Commissioners of Customs and Excise* v. *Top Ten Promotions Ltd.*, 1969

28 The long-perverted question of local taxation.
Benjamin Disraeli (1804–1881), House of Commons, 11 February 1851

29 An Englishman's home is his tax haven.
The Economist, 17 November 1979

30 The science of taxation comprises two subjects to which the character of pure theory may be ascribed: the laws of incidence, and the principle of equal sacrifice.
F.Y. Edgeworth (1845–1926), *Papers Relating to Political Economy*, 1925, vol. II, p. 64

31 That taxation upon the profits of a monopolist cannot be shifted is universally acknowledged.
F.Y. Edgeworth (1845–1926), *ibid.*, p. 97

32 Of all debts, men are least willing to pay the taxes.
Ralph Waldo Emerson (1803–1882), *Essays*, Second Series, 1844, 'Politics'

33 In this world nothing can be said to be certain, except death and taxes.
Benjamin Franklin (1706–1790), letter to Jean Baptiste Le Roy, 13 November 1789

34 There should be no taxation without comprehension.
John Gummer, *The Times*, 24 October 1988

35 Any one may so arrange his affairs that his taxes shall be as low as possible; he is not bound to choose that pattern which will best pay the Treasury; there is not even a patriotic duty to increase one's taxes.
Learned Hand (1872–1961), *Helvering* v. *Gregory*, 1934

36 There can be no taxation without misrepresentation.
J.B. Handelsman in Y. Barzel, *Journal of Political Economy*, 1976, p. 1177

37 Now it is notorious — and is, indeed, a long-standing injustice — that the scale of the taxpayer's allowance under Schedule E are on an altogether more niggardly and restricted scale than under Schedule D. Indeed, it has been said that the pleasure of life depends nowadays upon the schedule under which a man lives.
Lord Justice Harman (1894–1970) in Gwyneth McGreggor, *Employees' Deductions under the Income Tax*

38 It is barbarous to tax musical and dramatic art like a bottle of whisky.
A.P. Herbert (1890–1971) in C. Bingham, *Wit and Wisdom*, 1982

39 It is the small owner who offers the only really profitable and reliable material for taxation . . . He is made for taxation . . . He swarms; he is far more tied to his place and his calling than the big owner; he has less skill, and ingenuity as regards escape; and he still has a large supply of 'ignorant patience of taxation'.
Auberon Herbert (1836–1906) in F. Coffield, *A Popular History of Taxation*

40 To Equall Justice, appertaineth also the Equall imposition of Taxes . . . Which considered, the Equality of Imposition, consisteth rather in the Equality of that which is consumed, than of the riches of the persons that consume the same. For what reason is there, that he which laboureth much, and sparing the fruits of his labour, consumeth little, should be more charged,

than he that living idley, getteth little, and spendeth all he gets; seeing that one hath no more protection from the Common-wealth, than the other? But when the Impositions, are layd upon those things which men consume, every man payeth Equally for what he useth: Nor is the Common-wealth defrauded by the luxurious waste of private men.
Thomas Hobbes (1588–1679), *Leviathan*, 1651, ch. XXX

41 One-half of the world don't know how th' other half dodges taxes.
Frank McKinney Hubbard (1868–1930), *New Sayings by Abe Martin*, 1917

42 There is a prevailing maxim among some reasoners, *That every new tax creates a new ability in the subject to bear it, and that each increase of public burdens increases proportionably the industry of the people.*
David Hume (1711–1776), *Essays*, 1741–2, 'Of Taxes'

43 The wisdom of man never yet contrived a system of taxation that would operate with perfect equality.
Andrew Jackson (1767–1845), speech, 1832

44 Excise: A hateful tax levied upon commodities, and adjudged not by the common judges of property, but wretches hired by those to whom the excise is paid.
Samuel Johnson (1709–1784), *Dictionary of the English Language*, 1755

45 To render an increase of taxation productive of greater exertion, economy, and invention, it should be slowly and gradually brought about; and it should never be carried to such a height as to incapacitate individuals from meeting the sacrifices it imposes, by such an increase in their industry and economy as it may be in their power to make without requiring any very violent change of their habits.
J.R. McCulloch (1789–1864), *Principles of Political Economy*, New ed., pt. 1, ch. II, p. 112

46 What an increase of rent is to the farmers, an increase of taxation is to the public . . . so long as it is confined within moderate limits, it acts as a powerful stimulus to industry and economy, and most commonly occasions the production of more wealth than it abstracts.
J.R. McCulloch (1789–1864), *ibid.*, p. 114

47 You must never let the tax tail wag the commercial dog.
R.M.S. McLellan, attributed

48 Income tax, if I may be pardoned for saying so, is a tax on income.
Lord Macnaghten (1830–1913), *L.C.C. v. A.G.*, 1901

49 'I pay my taxes', says somebody, as if that were an act of virtue instead of one of compulsion.
Sir Robert Menzies, *The Wit of Sir Robert Menzies*, 1966

50 Experience has shown that a large proportion of the results of labour and abstinence may be taken away by fixed taxation, without impairing, and sometimes even with the effect of stimulating, the qualities from which a great production and an abundant capital rise.
John Stuart Mill (1806–1873), *Principles of Political Economy*, 1871, bk. IV, ch. 1

51 The proper mode of assessing an income tax would be to tax only the part of income devoted to expenditure, exempting that which is saved. For when saved and invested . . . it thenceforth pays income tax on the interest or profit which it brings, notwithstanding that it has already been taxed on the principal. Unless, therefore, savings are exempted from income tax, the contributors are twice taxed on what they save, and only once on what they spend.
John Stuart Mill (1806–1873), *ibid.*, bk. V, ch. II

52 A direct tax is one which is demanded from the very persons who, it is intended or desired, should pay it. Indirect taxes are those which are demanded from one person in the expectation and intention that he shall indemnify himself at the expense of another.
John Stuart Mill (1806–1873), *ibid.*, ch. III

53 The very reason which makes direct taxation disagreeable, makes it preferable . . . If all taxes were direct, taxation would be much more perceived than at present; and there would be a security which now there is not, for economy in the public expenditure.
John Stuart Mill (1806–1873), *ibid.*, ch. VI

54 Taxation is a most flexible and effective but also a dangerous instrument of social

reform. One has to know precisely what one is doing lest the results diverge greatly from one's intentions.
Gunnar Myrdal, *The Political Element in the Development of Economic Theory*, 1953, p. 188

55 Taxation without representation is tyranny.
James Otis (1725–1783), attributed

56 That which angers men most is to be taxed above their neighbours.
Sir William Petty (1623–1687), *A Treatise of Taxes and Contributions*, 1662

57 Everyone owes tax, don't they?
Lester Piggott (on being prosecuted for tax evasion), *The Times*, 1 January 1987

58 Our tax system is an outstanding example of complexity built upon complexity. I can't describe it as a house of cards because the damn thing certainly won't fall down.
E.E. Ray, speech at Swansea, 4 February 1983

59 A taxed commodity will not rise in proportion to the tax, if the demand for it diminish, and if the quantity cannot be reduced.
David Ricardo (1772–1823), *Principles of Political Economy and Taxation*, 1821, ch. XVI

60 Taxation can never be so equally applied, as to operate in the same proportion on the value of all commodities, and still to preserve them at the same relative value. It frequently operates very differently from the intention of the legislature by its indirect effects.
David Ricardo (1772–1823), *ibid.*

61 Almost all taxes on production fall finally on the consumer.
David Ricardo (1772–1823), *On Protection to Agriculture*, 1822, sec. IX

62 The income tax has made more Liars out of the American people than Golf has.
Will Rogers (1879–1935) in Donald Day, *Will Rogers: A Biography*, 1962, ch. 13

63 Taxes are paid in the sweat of every man that labours.
Franklin D. Roosevelt (1882–1945), speech, 19 October 1932

64 Taxes, after all, are the dues that we pay for the privileges of membership in an organised society.
Franklin D. Roosevelt (1882–1945), speech, 21 October 1936

65 No real advantage could possibly result from the introduction of a general definition that had to cover so multifarious a subject as taxable income.
Royal Commission on the Taxation of Profits and Income, *Final Report*, 1955, ch. 1, para. 28

66 You'll be whipp'd for taxation one of these days.
William Shakespeare (1564–1616), *As You Like It*, 1596–1600, act I, sc. II

67 Levy great sums of money through the realm.
William Shakespeare (1564–1616), *Henry VI, Pt. II*, 1590–1, act III, sc. I

68 Daily new exactions are devis'd.
William Shakespeare (1564–1616), *Richard III*, 1595–6, act II, sc. I

69 All is fair in love, war and tax evasion.
Tom Sharpe, *The Throwback*, 1978, ch. 19

70 Tomorrow, lad, we will consider some aspects of Income Tax Evasion as a Path to Damnation.
Robert Sheckley, 'The Accountant', in *Citizen in Space*, 1955

71 The nation should have a tax system which looks like someone designed it on purpose.
William E. Simon, US Treasury, *Blueprints for Basic Tax Reform*, 1977

72 The subjects of every state ought to contribute towards the support of government, as nearly as possible, in proportion to their respective abilities; that is, in proportion to the revenue which they respectively enjoy under the protection of the state.
Adam Smith (1723–1790), *Wealth of Nations*, 1776, vol. II, bk. V, ch. II, pt. II

73 Every tax ought to be so contrived as both to take out and to keep out of the pockets of the people as little as possible, over and above what it brings into the public treasury of the state.
Adam Smith (1723–1790), *ibid.*

74 It is not very unreasonable that the rich should contribute to the public expense, not only in proportion to their revenue, but something more than in that proportion.
Adam Smith (1723–1790), *ibid.*

75 The schoolboy whips his taxed top; the beardless youth manages his taxed horse, with a taxed bridle, on a taxed road; and the dying Englishman, pouring his medicine, which has paid seven per cent, into a spoon that has paid fifteen per cent — flings himself back upon his chintz bed, which has paid twenty-two per cent — and expires in the arms of an apothecary who has paid a licence of a hundred pounds for the privilege of putting him to death.
Sydney Smith (1771–1845), *Words*, 1859, vol. I, 'Review of Seybert's Statistical Annals of the United States'

76 To produce an income tax return that has any depth to it, any feeling, one must have Lived — and Suffered.
Frank Sullivan in Rudolf Flesch, *The Book of Unusual Quotations*, 1959

77 The women were proposed to be taxed according to their beauty and skill in dressing; wherein they had the same privilege with the men, to be determined by their own judgement. But constancy, chastity, good sense and good nature were not rated, because they would not bear the cost of collecting.
Jonathan Swift (1667–1745), *Gulliver's Travels*, 1726, 'Voyage to Laputa' ch. VI

78 Like old ships' hulls the tax codes of the western nations are barnacled with exemptions, reliefs and concessions.
The Times, 14 December 1985

79 The power to tax . . . is not only the power to destroy but also the power to keep alive.
United States Supreme Court in P.A. Samuelson, *Economics*, 8th ed.

80 WARD'S LAW: Pay nothing in tax today that you can argue about tomorrow.
Christopher Ward, *How to Complain*, 1976, p. 221

81 In such experience as I have had with taxation — and it has been considerable — there is only one tax that is popular, and that is the tax that is on the other fellow.
Sir Thomas White (1866–1955), debate in the Canadian Parliament, 1917

82 It would be strange if taxation by interest groups should not result in taxation according to interest.
Knut Wicksell (1851–1926) in R.A. Musgrave, *Theory of Public Finance*, 1959

197 TEA

1 The occupation of tea lady cannot by any stretch of the imagination be described as hazardous.
Mr Justice Comyn, *Observer*, 'Sayings of the Week', 31 October 1982

2 Retired to tea and scandal, according to their ancient custom.
William Congreve (1670–1729), *The Double Dealer*, 1649, act I, sc. 1

3 While there's tea there's hope.
Sir Arthur Pinero (1855–1934), attributed

198 TECHNOLOGY
See also 47 COMPUTERS, 174 SCIENCE

1 Any sufficiently advanced technology is indistinguishable from magic.
Arthur C. Clarke, attributed

2 The imperatives of technology and organization, not the images of ideology, are what determine the shape of economic society.
John Kenneth Galbraith, *The New Industrial State*, 1967, ch. 1

3 The reality is that many of the changes in science and technology are complex because of the complexity of them.
Barry Jones, *Sydney Morning Herald*, 'Sayings of the Week', 12 July 1986

4 For tribal man space was the uncontrollable mystery. For technological man it is time that occupies the same role.
Marshall McLuhan (1911–1981), *The Mechanical Bride*, 1967

5 The technology of *mass production* is inherently violent, ecologically damaging, self-defeating in terms of non-renewable resources, and stultifying for the human person.
E.F. Schumacher (1911–1977), *Small is Beautiful*, 1973, pt. II, ch. 5

6 Technology makes possible what good management knew but was formerly unable to achieve.
W. Wriston, *Listener*, 28 August 1986

199 TELEVISION
See also 130 NEWSPAPERS, 163 RADIO, 183 SHOW BUSINESS

1 Since we got the video recorder, we find we don't watch much television.
Anonymous, *Financial Times*, 7 February 1989

2 I don't like television, it's for dedicated non-thinkers.
Billy Connolly, *Independent*, 'Quote Unquote', 11 February 1989

3 Television is for appearing on, not looking at.
Noël Coward (1899–1973), attributed

4 Why should people go out and pay money to see bad films when they can stay at home and see bad television for nothing?
Samuel Goldwyn (1882–1974), *Observer*, 'Sayings of the Week', 9 September 1956

5 In this country we take a paternalistic view of television — hence the great 'Auntie BBC'.
Michael Grade, *Private Eye*, no. 709, 17 February 1989

6 Television? The word is half Latin and half Greek. No good can come of it.
C.P. Scott (1846–1932), attributed

7 A stake in commercial television is the equivalent of having a licence to print money.
Lord Thomson of Fleet (1894–1977), attributed

8 Television is now so desperately hungry for material that they're scraping the top of the barrel.
Gore Vidal in James Beasley Simpson, *Best Quotes of '54, '55, '56*, 1957

9 I hate television. I hate it as much as peanuts. But I can't stop eating peanuts.
Orson Welles in James Beasley Simpson, *Best Quotes of '54, '55, '56*, 1957

200 THEFT
See also 54 CORRUPTION, 85 FRAUD

1 Old thieves never die, they just steal away.
Anonymous

2 Thou shalt not steal.
Bible, Authorized Version, Exodus 20:15

3 Kill a man's family, and he may brook it, But keep your hands out of his breeches' pocket.
Lord Byron (1788–1824), *Don Juan*, canto X, 1823–4, st. LXXIV

4 In a very plain sense the proverb says, call one a thief, and he will steal.
Thomas Carlyle (1795–1881), *Sartor Resartus*, 1836, bk. II, ch. I

5 Thou shalt not steal; an empty feat, When it's so lucrative to cheat.
Arthur Hugh Clough (1819–1861), *The Latest Decalogue*, 1862

6 It's much safer to steal from your employer than the tax man.
Dick Francis, *Risk*, 1977, ch. 10

7 It is easy to rob an orchard, when none keep it.
Thomas Fuller (1654–1734), *Gnomologia*, 1732, no. 2925

8 Pick-pockets are sure traders; for they take ready money.
Thomas Fuller (1654–1734), *ibid.*, no. 3872

9 A thief believes everybody steals.
E.W. Howe (1853–1937), *Country Town Sayings*, 1911

201 TIME
See also 202 TIMING

1 To choose time is to save time.
Francis Bacon (1561–1626), *Essays*, 1625, 'Of Dispatch'

2 Can ye not discern the signs of the times?
Bible, Authorized Version, Matthew 16:3

3   We are the kind of people who know the value of time, and you are the kind of people who don't know the value of time.
Charles Dickens (1812–1870), *Hard Times*, 1854, bk. I, ch. VI

4   Remember that time is money.
Benjamin Franklin (1706–1790), *Advice to Young Tradesmen*, 1748

5   Time is a merciless enemy, as it is also a merciless friend and healer.
Mahatma Gandhi (1869–1948) in N.B. Sen, *Wit and Wisdom of India*, 1961

6   Rome was not built in one day.
John Heywood (1506–1565), *Proverbs*, 1546, pt. I, ch. XI

7   That old bald cheater, Time.
Ben Jonson (1574–1637), *The Poetaster*, 1601, act I, sc. V. See also 201.13 below.

8   Time that devours all things.
Ovid (42 BC–AD 18), *Metamorphoses*, XV

9   Time conquers all, and we must time obey.
Alexander Pope (1688–1744), *Pastorals* (1709), 'Winter', l. 88

10   Time travels in divers paces with divers persons. I will tell you who time ambles withal, who time trots withal, who time gallops withal, and who he stands still withal.
William Shakespeare (1546–1616), *As You Like It*, 1596–1600, act III, sc. II

11   Time is the old justice that examines all such offenders, and let time try.
William Shakespeare (1564–1616), *ibid.*, act IV, sc. I

12   There's a time for all things.
William Shakespeare (1564–1616), *The Comedy of Errors*, 1592–3, act II, sc. II

13   Time himself is bald.
William Shakespeare (1564–1616), *ibid.* See also 201.7 above.

14   Come what come may,
Time and the hour runs through the roughest day.
William Shakespeare (1564–1616), *Macbeth*, 1606–7, act I, sc. III

15   Time itself is Play. Its only object is Pas-time.
Rabindranath Tagore (1861–1941) in N.B. Sen, *Wit and Wisdom of India*, 1961

16   We don't waste Time . . . it wastes us.
Miles Tripp, *The Once a Year Man*, 1977, ch. 13

17   Time is of more importance than is generally imagined.
George Washington (1732–1799), letter to James Anderson, 10 December 1799

---

202 TIMING
See also 201 TIME

---

1   And one good lesson to this purpose I pike
From the Smith's forge, when th' iron is hot, strike.
John Heywood (1506–1567), *Proverbs*, 1546, pt. I, ch. III

2   Timing is the greatest single factor you're dealing with in art, people, or business.
Warren Tute, *The Golden Greek*, 1960, ch. 3

---

203 TOURISM

---

1   Protecting people's lives is far more important than having a lot of crocodiles as a tourist attraction.
Sir Joh Bjelke-Petersen, *Sydney Morning Herald*, 'Sayings of the Week', 4 January 1986

2   Tourists want more than pie and peas and a Windsor sausage salad, which is being offered at one Queensland island resort.
David Jull, *Sydney Morning Herald*, 'Sayings of the Week', 5 December 1981

3   Of all noxious animals, too, the most noxious is a tourist.
Francis Kilvert (1840–1879), *Diary*, 5 April 1870

4   In the middle ages people were tourists because of their religion, whereas now they are tourists because tourism is their religion.
Dr Robert Runcie, *Observer*, 'Sayings of the Week', 11 December 1988

5   Tourism, with obvious exceptions, is largely a low-paid, poorly represented and lowly skilled enterprise with increasing tendency towards part-time workers.
Michael Smith, *Guardian*, 7 September 1985

6 With twenty seaside resorts planning to open up nude and topless beaches this summer, I really do not see that we have any need to keep the Elgin Marbles in Bloomsbury any longer.
Auberon Waugh, *Private Eye*, no. 560, 3 June 1983, 'Auberon Waugh's Diary'

204 TRADE

See also 25 BUSINESS, 41 COMMERCE, 120 MARKETS

1 The great source of the flourishing state of this kingdom is its trade, and commerce, and paper currency, guarded by proper regulations and restrictions, is the life of commerce.
Judge Ashhurst (1725–1807), *Jordaine v. Lashbrooke*, 1798

2 Go to now, ye that say, To day or to morrow we will go into such a city, and continue there a year, and buy and sell, and get gain.
Bible, Authorized Version, James 4:13

3 Being a Trade Minister is the nearest thing you can get to being War Minister in peacetime. It is not for nothing that world trade is expressed daily in adversarial terms of rivalry and defeats.
Alan Clark, *Sydney Morning Herald*, 'Sayings of the Week', 31 May 1986

4 Trade is in its nature free, finds its own channel, and best directeth its own course: and all laws to give it rules and directions, and to limit and circumscribe it, may serve the particular ends of private men, but are seldom advantageous to the public.
Charles D'Avenant (1656–1714), *An Essay on the East India Trade*, 1697

5 Trade must, I say, be work'd at, not play'd with: he that trades in jest, will certainly break in earnest.
Daniel Defoe (*c.*1660–1731), *The Complete Tradesman*, 2nd ed., 1727, vol. I, letter V

6 Over-trading is among tradesmen as over-lifting is among strong men; such people vain of their strength, and their pride prompting them to put it to the utmost trial, at last lift at something too heavy for them, over-strain their sinews, break some of nature's bands, and are cripples ever after.
Daniel Defoe (*c.*1660–1731), *ibid.*, letter VI

7 Trade is not a Ball, where people appear in Masque, and act a part to make sport.
Daniel Defoe (*c.*1660–1731), *ibid.*, letter X

8 Trade is a plant which grows wherever there is peace, as soon as there is peace, and as long as there is peace.
Ralph Waldo Emerson (1803–1882), *The Young American*, 1844

9 Buy and sell, and live by the loss.
Thomas Fuller (1654–1734), *Gnomologia*, 1732, no. 1033

10 Buying and selling is but winning and losing.
Thomas Fuller (1654–1734), *ibid.*, no. 1036

11 He who hath a trade, hath a share everywhere.
Thomas Fuller (1654–1732), *ibid.*, no. 2386

12 Jack of all trades, is of no trade.
Thomas Fuller (1654–1734), *ibid.*, no. 3051

13 There is nothing Japan really wants to buy from foreign countries except, possibly, neckties with unusual designs.
Yoshihiro Inayama, *Sydney Morning Herald*, 'Sayings of the Week', 3 August 1985

14 A merchant may, perhaps, be a man of an enlarged mind, but there is nothing in trade connected with an enlarged mind.
Samuel Johnson (1709–1784), in Boswell's *Journal of a Tour to the Hebrides*, 18 October 1773

15 A man who has never been engaged in trade himself may undoubtedly write well upon trade, and there is nothing which requires more to be illustrated by philosophy than trade does.
Samuel Johnson (1709–1784) in Boswell's *Life of Johnson*, 16 March 1776

16 A handful of trade is worth a handful of gold.
James Kelly, *Scottish Proverbs*, 1721, A, no. 72

17 It is sometimes said that traders do not produce: that while the cabinet-maker produces furniture, the furniture-dealer merely sells what is already produced. But there is no scientific foundation for this distinction. They both produce utilities.
Alfred Marshall (1842–1924), *Principles of Economics*, 8th ed., 1920, bk. II, ch. III, 1

18 Trade is a social act.
John Stuart Mill (1806–1873), *On Liberty*, 1859, ch. 5

19 An honest man is not accountable for the vice and folly of his trade, and therefore ought not to refuse the exercise of it. It is the custom of his country, and there is profit in it. We must live by the world, and such as we find it, so make use of it.
Michel de Montaigne (1533–1592), *Essays*, 1588

20 A nation should never prevent another nation from trading with it, except for very great reasons.
Charles de Secondat, Baron de Montesquieu (1689–1755), *The Spirit of the Laws*, 1748, bk. XX, 9

21 There can be no trade unprofitable to the public; for if any prove so, men leave it off; and whenever the traders thrive, the public, of which they are a part, thrives also.
Sir Dudley North (1641–1691), *Discourses upon Trade*, 1691, preface

22 If there be not a conscience to be used in every trade we shall never prosper.
William Shakespeare (1564–1616), *Pericles*, 1608–9, act IV, sc. II

23 It is extraordinary how little barrier an unknown language makes between a willing buyer and a willing seller.
Nevil Shute (1899–1960), *A Town Like Alice*, 1950, ch. 3

24 After all the maxims and systems of trade and commerce, a stander-by would think the affairs of the world were most ridiculously contrived.
Jonathan Swift (1667–1745), *Thoughts on Various Subjects*, 1711

25 Every time we buy a foreign car we put someone out of work.
Woodrow Wyatt, *The Times*, 4 October 1986

205 TRADERS
See also 27 BUSINESSMEN

1 It is the privilege of a trader in a free country, in all matters not contrary to the law, to regulate his own mode of carrying it on according to his own discretion and choice.
Baron Alderson (1787–1857), *Hilton* v. *Eckersley*, 1855

2 The kingdom of heaven is like unto a merchant man, seeking goodly pearls: who, when he had found one pearl of great price, went and sold all that he had, and bought it.
Bible, Authorized Version, Matthew 13:45–6

3 Manufacturers and merchants as a rule seem only to desire riches that they may be enabled to prostrate themselves at the feet of feudalism.
Richard Cobden (1804–1865) in John Morley, *Life of Richard Cobden*, 1881, vol. II, pp. 481–2

4 What are today's aristos but yesterday's merchants?
Peter Conrad, *Observer*, 30 October 1983

5 A merchant's happiness hangs upon chance, winds and waves.
Thomas Fuller (1654–1734), *Gnomologia*, 1732, no. 323

6 Two of a trade seldom agree.
Thomas Fuller (1654–1734), *ibid.*, no. 5332

7 Our tradesmen singing in their shops, and going
About their functions friendly.
William Shakespeare (1564–1616), *Coriolanus*, 1607–8, act IV, sc. VI

8 Ye tradefull merchants, that with weary toyle,
Do seeke most pretious things to make your gain;
And both the Indias of their treasures spoile,
What needeth you to seek so farre in vaine?
Edmund Spenser (1552?–1599), *Amoretti*, 1595, XV

9 Who but a fool would have faith in a tradesman's ware or his word?
Alfred, Lord Tennyson (1809–1892), *Maud*, 1855, pt. I, sec. I, st. VII

10 Priests pray for blessings; merchants pour
    them down.
    Edward Young (1683–1765), 'Imperium
    Pelagi. A Naval Lyric', 1729

206 TRADE UNIONS
See also 40 COLLECTIVE BARGAINING,
129 NEGOTIATIONS, 192 STRIKES

1 Had the employers of past generations dealt
  fairly with men, there would have been no
  trade unions.
  Stanley Baldwin (1867–1947), *Observer*,
  'Sayings of the Week', 18 January 1931

2 He has been a union official since he was
  18, which is the best advertisement for
  limited tenure of trade union officials I have
  ever seen.
  Meredith Burgmann (on Norman
  Gallagher, Builders' Labourers' Federation),
  Sydney Morning Herald, 'Sayings of the
  Week', 15 May 1982

3 Trade unionists and the courts should be
  kept far apart.
  Winston Churchill (1874–1965), attributed

4 The methods by which a trade union can
  alone act, are necessarily destructive; its
  organization is necessarily tryannical.
  Henry George (1839–1897), *Progress and
  Poverty*, 1879, bk. VI, ch. I

5 All classes of society are trades unionists at
  heart, and differ chiefly in the boldness,
  ability, and secrecy with which they pursue
  their respective interests.
  W. Stanley Jevons (1835–1882), *The State
  in Relation to Labour*, 1882, p. vi

6 I don't know if the cause be wrong,
    Or if the cause be right —
  I've had my day and sung my song,
    And fought the bitter fight.
  To tell the truth, I don't know what
    The boys are driving at,
  But I've been Union twenty years,
    And I'm too old to 'rat'.
  Henry Lawson (1867–1922), *The Old
  Unionist*

7 The only real power this country's union
  leaders have is the power to keep their
  members poor.
  Bernard Levin, *The Times*, 19 June 1986

8 Capacity to labour is to the poor man what
  stock is to the capitalist. But you would not
  prevent a hundred or a thousand capitalists
  from forming themselves into a company, or
  combination who should . . . dispose of
  their property as they might, in their
  collective capacity judge most advantageous
  for their interests: so why then should not a
  hundred or a thousand labourers be allowed
  to do the same thing by *their stock*.
  J.R. McCulloch (1789–1864), *Treatise on
  the Succession to Property Vacant by Death*,
  1848

9 If the kamikaze pilots were to form their
  own union, Arthur Scargill would be an
  ideal choice for leader.
  Jimmy Reid, *Observer*, 'Sayings of the
  Week', 17 January 1988

10 It is one of the characteristics of a free and
   democratic modern nation that it have free
   and independent labor unions.
   Franklin D. Roosevelt (1882–1945),
   speech, September 1940

11 Trade Unionism is not Socialism: it is the
   Capitalism of the Proletariat.
   George Bernard Shaw (1856–1950),
   attributed

12 The organized trade unionists have not only
   outstripped the well-to-do middle class, they
   have become the principal exploiters of the
   poor and the humble. Like all aristocrats
   they cling to their privileges at the expense
   of everyone else.
   A.J.P. Taylor, *A Personal History*, 1983,
   ch. 18

207 TRANSPORT
See also 14 AVIATION, 127 MOTOR
VEHICLES, 164 RAILWAYS, 182 SHIPPING

1 Why should we make the assumption that
  bureaucrats or even politicians should have
  some God-given right to decide what kind
  of roads we need and where? Why should
  not private enterprise now play a larger
  part?
  Paul Channon, *Independent*, 'Quote
  Unquote', 15 October 1988

2   A fertile country is worth nothing without
    fine roads.
    Joseph Roux (1834–1905), *Meditations of
    a Parish Priest*, trans. Hapgood, 1886, ch. II,
    XXVIII

3   Considering the tax we pay for turnpikes,
    the roads of this country constitute a most
    intolerable grievance.
    Tobias Smollett (1721–1771), *The
    Expedition of Humphry Clinker*, 1771,
    vol. I

4   Transport may rank very low on the
    political totem pole, but like the sewerage
    system it can generate a lot of trouble once it
    starts going seriously wrong.
    Sunday Times, 28 August 1988

---

208 UNEMPLOYMENT

---

1   He was fired with enthusiasm because he
    wasn't fired with enthusiasm.
    Anonymous, Fred Metcalf, *The Penguin
    Dictionary of Modern Humorous
    Quotations*, 1986

2   I was unemployed with debts of £400,000. I
    know what unemployment is like and a lot
    of it is getting off your backside and finding
    a job.
    Jeffrey Archer, *Observer*, 'Sayings of the
    Week', 13 October 1985

3   A man willing to work, and unable to find
    work, is perhaps the saddest sight that
    Fortune's inequality exhibits under this sun.
    Thomas Carlyle (1795–1881), *Chartism*,
    1839, ch. IV

4   Men and women denied the right to work
    will turn to violence.
    Michael Foot, *Observer*, 'Sayings of the
    Week', 27 September 1981

5   There must be something wrong with a
    system where it pays to be sacked.
    Jo Grimond, *Observer*, 'Sayings of the
    Week', 1 May 1983

6   We believe that if men have the talent to
    invent new machines that put men out of
    work, they have the talent to put those men
    back to work.
    John F. Kennedy (1917–1963), speech,
    1962

7   If we just sit tight there will be still more
    than a million men unemployed six months
    or a year hence. That is why I feel that a
    radical policy of some kind is worth trying,
    even if there are risks about it.
    John Maynard Keynes (1883–1946), radio
    broadcast, 1930, quoted by Elizabeth
    Johnson, *Journal of Political Economy*,
    1974, p. 101

8   I don't think full employment is necessary or
    desirable.
    Len Murray, *Observer*, 'Sayings of the
    Week', 28 August 1983

9   Unemployment is a reproach to a
    democratic government.
    Joan Robinson (1903–1983), 'What has
    become of the Keynesian Revolution?', in
    Milo Keynes, *Essays on John Maynard
    Keynes*, 1975, p. 130

10 I don't think people are free if they are
    unemployed.
    Peter Shore, *Observer*, 'Sayings of the
    Week', 3 April 1983

11 I foresee that in 10 or 15 years' time we shall
    never use the word 'unemployment'. We
    shall refer to the proper use of leisure and
    how to deploy it.
    Earl of Stockton (Harold Macmillan)
    (1894–1986), House of Lords, 13
    November 1984

12 It's a recession when your neighbour loses
    his job: it's a depression when you lose
    yours.
    Harry S. Truman (1884–1972), *Observer*,
    'Sayings of the Week', 13 April 1958

---

209 USED CARS
See also 127 MOTOR VEHICLES, 172 SALES

1   Would you ever buy a used car from me?
    John De Lorean, *Observer*, 'Sayings of the
    Week', 30 December 1984

2   My greatest asset is that people would buy a
    used car from me.
    Helmut Kohl, *Observer*, 'Sayings of the
    Week', 13 March 1983

210 VACATION

1 When some fellers take a vacation
ever'buddy gits a rest.
Frank McKinney Hubbard (1868–1930),
New Sayings by Abe Martin, 1917

2 The red-letter days, now become, to all
intents and purposes, dead-letter days.
Charles Lamb (1775–1834), *Essays of Elia*,
1823, 'Oxford in the Vacation'

3 I find that a change of nuisances is as good
as a vacation.
David Lloyd George (1863–1945),
attributed

4 If all the year were playing holidays,
To sport would be as tedious as to work;
But when they seldom come, they wish'd-for
come.
William Shakespeare (1564–1616), *Henry
IV, Pt. I*, 1597–8, act I, sc. II

5 Being holiday, the beggar's shop is shut.
William Shakespeare (1564–1616), *Romeo
and Juliet*, 1595–6, act V, sc. I

211 VALUE
See also 145 PRICES

1 The value of all wares arise from their use;
things of no use have no value, as the
English phrase it, *they are good for nothing*.
Nicholas Barbon (?–1698), *A Discourse of
Trade*, 1690, p. 13

2 For what is worth in anything,
But so much money as 'twill bring.
Samuel Butler (1612–1680), *Hudibras*, pt.
I, 1663, canto I, l. 465

3 Value is the most invisible and impalpable
of ghosts, and comes and goes unthought of
while the visible and dense matter remains
as it was.
W. Stanley Jevons (1835–1882),
Investigations in Currency and Finance,
1884, II, ch. IV, p. 80

4 Value depends entirely on utility.
W. Stanley Jevons (1835–1882), *Theory of
Political Economy*, 1911, ch. I

5 The value which a commodity will bring in
any market is no other than the value which,

in that market, gives a demand just
sufficient to carry off the existing supply.
John Stuart Mill (1806–1873), *Principles of
Political Economy*, 1871, bk. III, ch. II, 4

6 What is aught but as 'tis valued?
William Shakespeare (1564–1616), *Troilus
and Cressida*, 1597–1602, act II, sc. II

7 The word VALUE . . . has two different
meanings, and sometimes expresses the
utility of some particular object, and
sometimes the power of purchasing other
goods which the possession of that object
conveys. The one may be called 'value in
use'; the other, 'value in exchange'.
Adam Smith (1723–1790), *Wealth of
Nations*, 1776, vol. I, bk. I, ch. IV

212 WAGES

1 The labourer is worthy of his hire.
Bible, Authorized Version, Luke 10:7

2 Jay Gould, the 'financier', got more 'pay'
and held more wealth than Gladstone, and
Carlyle, and Darwin, and Koch, and
Galileo, and Columbus, and Cromwell, and
Caxton, and Stephenson, and Washington,
and Raphael, and Mozart, and Shakespeare,
and Socrates, and Jesus Christ ever got
amongst them. So perfect is the present
system of pay!
Robert Blatchford (1851–1943), *Merrie
England*, 1894

3 A good servant must have good wages.
Thomas Fuller (1654–1734), *Gnomologia*,
1732, no. 176

4 Men work but slowly, that have poor
wages.
Thomas Fuller (1654–1734), *ibid.*,
no. 3407

5 He that serves well, need not be afraid to
ask his wages.
Thomas Fuller (1654–1734), *ibid.*,
no. 2296

6 It is but a truism that labour is most
productive where its wages are largest.
Poorly paid labour is inefficient labour, the
world over.
Henry George (1839–1897), *Progress and
Poverty*, 1879, bk. IX, ch. II

7 In the not-too-distant future the notion of the annual pay increase must become as exceptional as it was novel a generation ago.
Sir Geoffrey Howe, *Observer*, 'Sayings of the Week', 24 October 1982

8 All wages are based primarily on productive power. Anything else would be charity.
Elbert Hubbard (1856–1915), *Notebook*, 1927, p. 33

9 *Wages* are determined by the bitter struggle between capitalist and worker.
Karl Marx (1818–1883), 'First Manuscript' in *Early Writings*, ed. Bottomore

10 It is known that the bad workmen who form the majority of the operatives in many branches of industry are decidedly of opinion that bad workmen ought to receive the same wages as good, and that no one ought to be allowed, through piecework or otherwise, to earn by superior skill or industry more than others can without it.
John Stuart Mill (1806–1873), *On Liberty*, 1859, ch. 4

11 The price of ability does not depend on merit, but on supply and demand.
George Bernard Shaw (1856–1950), 'Socialism and Superior Brains', *Fortnightly Review*, April 1894

12 In this world, the salary or reward is always in inverse ratio of the duties performed.
Sydney Smith (1771–1845) in W. Jerrold, *Bon-Mots of Sydney Smith and R. Brinsley Sheridan*, p. 45

13 One man's wage rise is another man's price increase.
Sir Harold Wilson, *Observer*, 'Sayings of the Week', 11 January 1970

---

213 WEALTH
See also 124 MONEY

---

1 A rich man's pocket ought to be like an old fashioned well with two buckets — one constantly coming up full, the other constantly going down to get full.
Henry Ward Beecher (1813–1887), *Proverbs from Plymouth Pulpit*, 1887

2 He becometh poor that dealeth with a slack hand:
But the hand of the diligent maketh rich.
Bible, Authorized Version, Proverbs 10:4

3 Wealth gotten by vanity shall be diminished:
But he that gathereth by labour shall increase.
Bible, Authorized Version, *ibid.*, 13:11

4 The poor is hated even of his own neighbour:
But the rich hath many friends.
Bible, Authorized Version, *ibid.*, 14:20

5 Labour not to be rich:
Cease from thine own wisdom.
Wilt though set thine eyes upon that which is not?
For riches certainly make themselves wings;
They fly away as an eagle toward heaven.
Bible, Authorized Version, *ibid.*, 24:4–5

6 There is but one right mode of using enormous fortunes — namely, that the possessors from time to time during their own lives should so administer these as to promote the permanent good of the communities from which they were gathered.
Andrew Carnegie (1835–1919), 'The Administration of Wealth', in *The Gospel of Wealth and Other Timely Essays*, 1862, p. 30

7 The wealth of all nations arises from the labour and industry of the people.
Charles D'Avenant (1656–1714), *Discourses on the Public Revenues and on the Trade of England*, 1698

8 The art of getting rich consists not in industry, much less in saving, but in a better order, in timeliness, in being at the right spot.
Ralph Waldo Emerson (1830–1882), *The Conduct of Life*, 1860, 'Wealth'

9 He that hordeth up money, taketh pains for other men.
Thomas Fuller (1654–1734), *Gnomologia*, 1732, no. 2165

10 He is not fit for riches, who is afraid to use them.
Thomas Fuller (1654–1734), *ibid.*, no. 1934

11 Riches rather enlarge than satisfy appetites.
Thomas Fuller (1654–1734), *ibid.*,
no. 4048

12 Rich men long to be richer.
Thomas Fuller (1654–1734), *ibid.*,
no. 4038

13 Wealth, in even the most improbable cases,
manages to convey the aspect of
intelligence.
John Kenneth Galbraith, *Sydney Morning
Herald*, 22 May, 1982, p. 28

14 If you can actually count your money, then
you are not really a rich man.
John Paul Getty (1892–1976), *Observer*,
'Sayings of the Week', 3 November 1957

15 I find all this money a considerable burden.
John Paul Getty II, *Observer*, 'Sayings of the
Week', 15 December 1985

16 It is not difficult for a millionaire to make
money, except in times of deepest economic
crisis.
Frank Hardy, *Power Without Glory*, 1975,
ch. 12

17 Riches bring oft harme and ever feare.
John Heywood (1506–1565), *Proverbs*,
1546, pt. I, ch. XII

18 If th' rich spent as much as those who run in
debt we couldn' take care o' th' business.
Frank McKinney Hubbard (1868–1930),
New Sayings by Abe Martin, 1917

19 It is wonderful to think how men of very
large estates not only spend their yearly
income, but are often actually in want of
money.
Samuel Johnson (1709–1784) in Boswell's
Life of Johnson, 10 April 1778

20 It is better that a man should tyrannise over
his bank balance than over his fellow-
citizens.
John Maynard Keynes (1883–1946), *The
General Theory of Employment Interest and
Money*, 1936, bk. VI, ch. 24

21 Affluence means influence.
Jack London (1876–1916), attributed

22 Men do not desire to be *rich*, but to be richer
than other men.
John Stuart Mill (1806–1873), Posthumous
Essay on Social Freedom, *Oxford and
Cambridge Review*, January 1907

23 People do not grow rich by keeping their
money unused . . . they must be willing to
spend in order to gain.
John Stuart Mill (1806–1873), *Principles of
Political Economy*, 1848, 'Preliminary
Remarks'

24 When excessive wealth destroys the spirit of
commerce, then it is that the inconveniences
of inequality begin to be felt.
**Charles de Secondat, Baron de
Montesquieu** (1689–1755), *The Spirit of the
Laws*, 1748, bk. V, 6

25 I am a Millionaire. That is my religion.
George Bernard Shaw (1856–1950), *Major
Barbara*, 1907, act II

26 Who made your millions for you? Me and
my like. What's kep us poor? Keepin you
rich.
George Bernard Shaw (1856–1950), *ibid.*

27 Such are the rich,
That have abundance, and enjoy it not.
William Shakespeare (1564–1616), *Henry
IV, Pt. II*, 1597–8, act IV, sc. IV

28 Who would not wish to be from wealth
                              exempt
Since riches point to misery and contempt.
William Shakespeare (1564–1616), *Timon
of Athens*, 1607–8, act IV, sc. II

29 Nobody is so poor and so distressed as men
of very large fortunes.
Sydney Smith (1771–1845), *Game Laws*

30 Those who own much have much to fear.
Rabindranath Tagore (1861–1941) in N.B.
Sen, *Wit and Wisdom of India*, 1961

31 Wealth is that, and that only, whereby a
man may be benefited.
Xenophon (*c.*440–*c.*355 BC), *Economist*,
trans. Dakyns, ch. I

---

214 WORK
See also 108 LABOUR

---

1 Hard work never killed anybody, but
worrying about it did.
Anonymous

2 Most people are too busy earning a living to make any money.
Anonymous

3 The only person who had his work done by Friday was Robinson Crusoe.
Anonymous

4 Work is a dull way to get rich.
Neal Ascherson, *Observer*, 20 October 1985

5 It was the Chinese who invented the wok ethic.
Julian Barnes, *Observer*, 4 November 1984, p. 28

6 It is a good sign where a man is proud of his work or his calling.
Henry Ward Beecher (1813–1887), *Proverbs from Plymouth Pulpit*, 1887

7 Work is not the curse, but drudgery is.
Henry Ward Beecher (1813–1887), *ibid.*

8 Abolish work tomorrow and the mental hospitals would be full in a month.
Guy Bellamy, *The Secret Lemonade Drinker*, 1977, ch. 4

9 In the sweat of thy face shalt thou eat bread, till thou return unto the ground; for out of it wast thou taken: for dust thou art, and unto dust shalt thou return.
Bible, Authorized Version, Genesis 3:19

10 Man goeth forth unto his work
And to his labour until the evening.
Bible, Authorized Version, Psalms 104:23

11 If any would not work, neither should he eat.
Bible, Authorized Version, 2 Thessalonians 3:10

12 Oh, of course, I'd do it again [the Great Train Robbery] because it has given me the lifestyle I'd always dreamt of. There's a certain drudgery in working hard.
Ronnie Biggs, *Independent*, 'Quote Unquote', 29 October 1988

13 The increase of the 'black' economy shows that people do not, once they are freed of their companies, their unions and, to a certain extent, their Government, shirk the idea of work.
Prince Charles, *Observer*, 'Sayings of the Week', 22 November 1981

14 He looked as if he'd worked hard at something every day of his life and was puzzled by people who didn't.
Peter Corris, *The Greenwich Apartments*, 1986, ch. 5

15 There is no substitute for hard work.
Thomas Edison (1847–1931), *Life*, 1932, ch. 24

16 At the end of the work, you may judge the workman.
Thomas Fuller (1654–1734), *Gnomologia*, 1732, no. 827

17 It is working, that makes a workman.
Thomas Fuller (1654–1734), *ibid.*, no. 3034

18 Many hands make light work.
John Heywood (1506–1565), *Proverbs*, 1546, pt. II, ch. V

19 The nobility of manual toil, that mid-Victorian concept much promoted by Ruskin, did not appeal to those who knew what work was.
Henry Hobhouse, *Seeds of Change*, 1985, p. 170

20 The vintage of wisdom is to know that rest is rust and that real life is in love, laughter and work.
Elbert Hubbard (1856–1915), *Notebook*, 1927, p. 17

21 The best preparation for tomorrow's work is to do your work as well as you can today.
Elbert Hubbard (1856–1915), *ibid.*, p. 23

22 If you want work well done, select a busy man, the other kind has no time.
Elbert Hubbard (1856–1915), *ibid.*, p. 48

23 Work: . . . That which keeps us out of trouble.
Frank McKinney Hubbard (1868–1930), *The Roycroft Dictionary*, 1923

24 Nobody works as hard for his money as the man who marries it.
Frank McKinney Hubbard (1868–1930) in Esar and Bentley, *The Treasury of Humorous Quotations*

25 I like work: it fascinates me. I can sit and look at it for hours. I love to keep it by me: the idea of getting rid of it nearly breaks my heart.
Jerome K. Jerome (1859–1927), *Three Men in a Boat*, 1889, ch. 15

26 It is not always possible to graduate work to the worker's liking; in some businesses a

man who insisted on working only a few hours a day would soon have no work to do
W. Stanley Jevons (1835–1882), *Theory of Political Economy*, 4th ed., 1911, ch. V, p. 180

27 Better play for nought, than work for nought.
James Kelly, *Scottish Proverbs*, 1721, B, no. 30

28 Work bears witness who well does.
James Kelly, *ibid.*, W, no. 73

29 Women's work is never done.
James Kelly, *ibid.*, no. 131

30 It's all in the day's work, as the huntsman said when the lion ate him.
Charles Kingsley (1819–1875), *Westward Ho!*, 1855, IV

31 For many wage earners *work is perceived as a form of punishment* which is the price to be paid for various kinds of satisfactions away from the job.
D. McGregor, *The Human Side of Enterprise*, 1960, ch. 3

32 Work is a drug that dull people take to avoid the pangs of unmitigated boredom.
W. Somerset Maugham (1874–1966), *The Explorer*, 1907, ch. 3

33 There is nothing laudable in work for work's sake.
John Stuart Mill (1806–1873), 'The Negro Question', *Fraser's Magazine*, January 1850

34 Work expands so as to fill the time available for its completion.
C. Northcote Parkinson, *Parkinson's Law*, 1971, ch. 1

35 If you don't work, you can't play.
J.B. Priestley (1894–1984), *Out of Town*, 1968, pt. 2, ch. 4

36 To work is not necessarily to produce anything.
Pierre-Joseph Proudhon (1809–1865), attributed

37 When you see what some girls marry, you realise how they must hate to work for a living.
Helen Rowland (1876–1950), *Reflections of a Bachelor Girl*, 1909

38 Work is of two kinds: first, altering the position of matter at or near the earth's surface relatively to other matter; second,

telling other people to do so. The first kind is unpleasant and ill paid, the second is pleasant and highly paid.
Bertrand Russell (1872–1970), *In Praise of Idleness*, 1932

39 It was Christmas Day in the workhouse.
George Robert Sims (1847–1922), *Christmas Day in the Workhouse*

40 The law of work does seem utterly unfair — but there it is: the higher the pay in enjoyment the worker gets out of it, the higher shall be his pay in cash, also.
Mark Twain (1835–1910), *A Connecticut Yankee in King Arthur's Court*, 1889, ch. 28

41 As I never tire of explaining, the English don't really like working and are not much good at it anyway.
Auberon Waugh, *Private Eye*, no. 597, 2 November 1984

42 When a man says he wants to work, what he means is that he wants wages.
Richard Whateley (1787–1863) in Henry Sidgwick, *Principles of Political Economy*

215 WORKERS
See also 108 LABOUR

1 The quality of the workers who leave the factory doors every evening is an even more important thing than the quality of the products which it delivers to the customers.
Samuel Courtauld (1876–1947), *Ideals and Industry*, 1949, p. 26

2 A bad workman never gets a good tool.
Thomas Fuller (1654–1734), *Gnomologia*, 1732, no. 5

3 All ill workmen quarrel with their tools.
Thomas Fuller (1654–1734), *ibid.*, no. 521

4 As is the workman, so is the work.
Thomas Fuller (1654–1734), *ibid.*, no. 702

5 No good workman without good tools.
Thomas Fuller (1654–1734), *ibid.*, no. 3579

6 Not to oversee workmen, is to leave them your purse open.
Thomas Fuller (1654–1734), *ibid.*, no. 3685

7 What is a workman without tools?
  Thomas Fuller (1654–1734), *ibid.,*
  no. 5494

8 What is a workman without his tools?
  John Heywood (1506–1565), *Proverbs,*
  1546, pt. II, ch. IX

9 The possibilities for mobilising the
  experience, imaginations and intelligence of
  workers, both employed and unemployed
  are limitless.
  Emlyn Williams, *Observer,* 'Sayings of the
  Week', 16 January 1983

INDEX OF AUTHORS AND SOURCES

In this index the entries refer to individual quotations rather than pages. Each entry contains two numbers, the first of which indicates the number of the topic and the second the actual quotation. For example, under Allen, the first reference is 117.1. This refers to the first quotation appearing under the 117th topic, which is 'Management'. The numbers and titles of the topics appear at the top of the pages.

Where an author is quoted frequently it did not seem very helpful to provide each reference. Therefore, to save space, where the number of quotations from a single author exceeds 50 the name is simply marked with an asterisk.

INDEX OF KEY WORDS

This index is arranged alphabetically, both for the key words and for the entries following each key word. If the key word sought is the same as a topic title (shown in bold print), the topic title should be consulted first as this index does not usually repeat words appearing under the same topic.

For entries other than topic titles, the reference consists of two numbers, the first of which indicates the topic and the second the quotation itself. For example, an entry under 'Advertisements' reads 'A. . . . only truths . . . in a newspaper. 130.44'. This refers to the 44th quotation appearing under the 130th topic, which is 'Newspapers'.

book-keepers: women might make excellent b. 3.4
bookkeeping: advantages . . . from double entry b. 1.7
    Capital is simply a b. term 29.1
    system of b. by double entry 1.6
books: A Tradesman's b. 1.2
    b. being so essential to his trade 1.3
    Of making many b. there is no end 162.2
bookselling: B. . . . is like prostitution 162.15
borrow: Better buy than b. 28.2, 28.9
    if you b., b. big 193.14
    know what money is, go b. some. 124.41
borrowed: Paid money that I b. 135.10
borrower: b. is a slave to the lender 177.1
    Neither a b. nor a lender be 20.11
Borrowing: Topic 20
    b. dulls the edge of husbandry 20.11
    must be b. and lending 104.2
boss: b.'s secretary can wield great power 176.10
    can run the office without a b. 176.8
    good secretary can save her b. 176.2
    marry the b.'s daughter 153.5
    S.O.B. stands for Son of B. 131.9
Bosses: Topic 21
    Most secretaries can do their b.'s job 176.7
bottom: b. seems to have dropped out of morality. 126.5
    crawl up his b. 153.5
bottomless: Law is a b. pit. 112.2
bottoms: we clap on Dutch b. 41.9
bought: At market-price have b. 145.10
    where he nearly b. something 28.8
bounteously: I'll pay thee b. 135.16
bourgeoisie: b. . . . class of modern capitalists 31.2
boxes: Of Empty Economic B. 65.3
boys: Women managers are not viewed as one of the b. 117.18
brandy: drink cold b. and water. 64.22
    hero must drink b. 64.15
brass: Where there's muck, there's b. 124.4
bread: in the sweat of thy face shalt thou eat b. 214.9
    no b. to eat. 124.21
    that b. should be so dear 108.7
break: Men of business must not b. their word twice 27.18
breakfast: No business before b. 25.80
breath: salesman with bad b. 172.3
breeks: give your b. 124.57
    left his money in his other b. 124.58
brewer: benevolence of the butcher, the b., or the baker 178.3
brewers: b. would be out of business. 64.35
    When successful b. join the aristocracy 64.6
brewery: sale of Thrale's b. 64.16
bribe: Marriage . . . b. to make a housekeeper 121.5
bride: like a b. undrest 1.3
bridges: poor to sleep under the b. 39.2
British: to foul up the B. economy 38.2
British Rail: B. sandwiches. 164.6
    B. making a loss 164.12
    makes B. look like Concorde. 24.2
    No one loves B. 164.16
Brokers: Topic 22
brothel: magazine business is an intellectual b. 130.64
brotherhood: one common b. 41.13
brow: shall not press down upon the b. of labor 90.1
brutality: industry without art is b. 99.14
bucket: advertising . . . stick inside a swill b. 6.44
Budgets: Topic 23
bullshit: professional b. artist. 118.5
bum: the boss's b. is more important 21.3
bureaucracies: Gobbledygook . . . deployed by . . . b. 140.1
Bureaucracy: Topic 24
bus'ness: Men, some to b., some to pleasure take 27.31
Bush: I found out where George B. is today. 66.2
Business: Topic 25
    A b. with an income at its heels 96.4
    accounts are a snapshot of a b. 1.12
    B. as usual 25.16

b. of the wine merchant and banker 64.32
be the b. never so painful 124.29
best assurance of a healthy b. 46.12
brewers would be out of b. 64.35
can't run a b. like a communist cell 117.25
carrying on the b. of common life. 120.28
Corruption . . . b. without scruples. 54.1
cosmetics b. 55.1
Credit in b. 57.2
Cricket is now a b. 188.7
Cultivate courtesy as a b. asset 11.2
days when b. was pillage 53.6
dinner lubricates b. 75.3
dividing one's team . . . sin against the b. 117.10
gambling known as b. 88.1
hath made a good progress in a b. 141.1
hereditary b. of great magnitude 101.1
In b. one way to obtain credit 57.34
large b. may be managed tolerably 117.4
let people manage their own b. 112.32
manager of a theatre is a man of b. 10.17
managing a b. requires 117.8
mankind in the ordinary b. of life. 65.8
never believed that the b. of government 92.22
no best way of organizing a b. 132.20
no such thing a success in a bad b. 193.6
not the b. of economists 66.13
Organised b. is a thing of law 112.6
public b. is worse managed 159.2
science of b. 65.1
sons who have no aptitude for b. 68.21
sports b. 188.1
success of a b. turns on its esprit de corps. 193.8
the b. of America 25.20
the b. of America today is service. 180.3
the true b. precept 18.4
who retires from b. 170.2
wisdom of b. 68.4
Wise b. management 117.33
working very hard on this relaxation b. 188.9
Business Cycle: Topic 26
Business Expansion Scheme: Porn . . . candidate for the B. 143.2
business men: artists or authors making fun of b. 10.3
business men: general direction of b. 132.18
    Prudent b. 171.1
business savings: Practically all b. 173.6
business studies: professor of b. 68.5
businesses: I am awful at managing b. 105.14
businessman: b. is our only scientist. 175.2
    good thing for a b. 88.2
Businessmen: Topic 27
    Like many b. of genius 125.8
bust: That kind of entrepreneur usually ends up b. 76.1
busted: many a man has b. in business 25.49
busy: select a b. man 214.22
butcher: b. would jest leave th' meat 169.5
    not from the benevolence of the b. 178.3
buy: If we will not b., we cannot sell. 86.5
    make people b. 6.61
    to b. in the cheapest market 86.2
buyers: struggle . . . between the b. and the sellers. 145.13
Buying: Topic 28
    B. and selling is but winning and losing. 204.10
    which . . . must be persuaded into b. 6.31
buys: He that b. for credit 57.15
    He that b. land 64.19
    He that b. beef 64.19
    He that b. nuts 64.19
    He that b. good ale 64.19
bygones: In commerce b. are forever b. 41.23

cads: self-interest of c. 178.1
Caesar Augustus: went out a decree from C. 11

distaste for c. and industry 39.6
excessive wealth destroys the spirit of c. 213.24
Money is the measure of c. 124.8
money . . . instrument of c. 124.91
object of the law is to encourage c. 112.15
paper currency . . . is the life of c. 204.1
Piracy . . . C. without its folly-swaddles 139.1
commercial: C. credit 57.32
powerless to enforce . . . . c. morality 112.30
Committees: Topic 42
commodity: A taxed c. will not rise in proportion 196.59
If a foreign country can supply us with a c. 86.6
common: steals the goose from off the c. 39.1
commonsense: ingredients . . . c. and simplicity 193.18
communion: C. or community of labour 63.3
Communism: Topic 43
communist: can't run a business like a c. cell 117.25
Communists: theory of the C. 154.13
community: c. believes in the banker 15.7
c. of labour 63.3
Commuters: Topic 44
companies: Big c. are little c. that succeeded 193.23
c. like to look their best 1.12
unions and . . . c., like easter eggs 25.13
company: C. law is not static 112.35
c.'s research is another's development. 102.1
cannot buy a c. 194.2
fundamental principle of our c. law. 53.5
successful c. 119.4
compensation: C. for improvements 166.2
fails to give to the workman sufficient c. 150.23
Competence: Topic 45
competing: Costs merely register c. attractions. 56.7
Competition: Topic 46
immunity from c. 125.10
intolerable c. of a foreign rival 86.1
learned that free c. was wasteful 125.8
Planning and c. can be combined 141.2
substitution of c. for . . . mediaeval regulations 98.5
competitors: cutting out his c. 56.5
complain: That none may afterward c. 18.17
compliance: strict c. to the will of the people. 53.11
comprehension: no taxation without c. 196.34
Computers: Topic 47
concept: C. of Consumers' Sovereignty. 50.2
conception: c. of opportunity cost. 56.6
conciliator: Every lawyer should be a c. 113.27
conclusion: economists . . . would not reach a c. 66.15
conclusions: economics . . . does not furnish . . . c. 65.7
enjoy coming to c. 68.2
condition: effort of every man to better his c. 92.30
Conferences: Topic 48
confess: C. debt and beg days. 61.12
conflict: supposed c. of labour and capital 147.4
Congress: Topic 49
conscience: c. money 36.6
c. to be used in every trade 204.22
Debt is an evil c. 61.13
expect a corporation to have a c. 53.13
consents: My poverty but not my will c. 135.14
Conservative Party: C. has never believed 92.22
conspicuous: C. consumption of valuable goods 51.5
conspiracies: professions are c. against the laity. 149.15
conspiracy theory: c. of government 92.18
conspiracy: conversation ends in a c. against the public 33.4
constant: supply at a c. or diminished cost 56.5
constituencies: runs through more marginal c. 164.11
constraint: Laws describe c. 112.45
consultant: management c. 118.1
consume: income . . . maximum value which he can c. 96.6
Man produces in order to c. 148.1
Consumers: Topic 50
consumer: against the greed of his c. 195.2
c. is the person ultimately benefited 41.27

c. price index 100.11
C.'s delusions result in producer's blunders. 147.1
Concept of C.'s Sovereignty. 50.2
diffuse and inchoate c. interest 147.2
holdin' up th' c. 49.2
identify emerging c. needs 119.4
landlord . . . opposed to . . . the c. 166.5
person who saves . . . no less a c. 173.4
real conflict is between producers and c. 147.4
sacrifice of the c. to the producer 157.1
sovereignty of the . . . c. 120.21
taxes on production fall . . . on the c. 196.61
consumer: the c.s' ballot 30.13
Consumption: Topic 51
c. of the purse 20.12
contract: To c. new debts 61.35
Contracts: Topic 52
contrivance: some c. to raise prices 33.4
convenience: C. is the basis of mercantile law. 112.37
creating c. in the process of exchange. 124.23
conversation: c. ends in a conspiracy against the public 33.4
cook: 'Tis an ill c. 34.10
c. should be able to run the country. 34.6
The c. was a good c., as c.s go. 34.9
Cookery: C. is become an art 34.4
Coolidge: Calvin C. notwithstanding 180.3
coordinating: what the c. function creates. 46.3
corn: whoever could make two ears of c. 142.43
corporate: c. or joint-venture capitalism 117.13
corporation man: c. . . . emerges as much less heroic 176.6
corporation: easier than running a c. 117.7
Corporations: Topic 53
Correggio: correggiosity of C. 12.2
correspondence: in a universal c. 27.11
Corruption: Topic 54
corruptions: Politicks . . . nothing but c. 142.44
corset: The c. is, in economic theory 77.25
Cosmetics: Topic 55
cost accounting: if c. sets out 56.3
cost: Natural price is only another name for c. 145.8
Costs: Topic 56
government c. too much. 92.28
counsel: money is better than c. 124.95
count: Auditors . . . c. the dead and bayonet the wounded 13.1
If you an actually c. your money 213.14
counter: Money is the c. 124.88
counterfeiting: Inflation . . . legal c. 100.6
counteth: c. the cost 56.1
counting-house: c. of an accomplished merchant 3.11
counting houses: road that leads to publishers' c. 162.13
country: commerce knows no c. 41.22
good for the c. . . . good for General Motors 127.10
lying for one's c. 62.1
people who know how to run the c. 137.2
courageous: someone once made a c. decision 27.14
courtesy: Cultivate c. as a business asset 11.2
courts: Trade unionists and the c. 206.3
cow: front half of the c. 132.8
CPA: He was a C. 4.3
crafty: insidious and c. animal . . . a statesman 142.41
crank: C. until the idea succeeds. 105.17
crawl: c. up his bottom. 153.5
creates: Government c. scarcely anything 92.24
creative accountancy: With c. who needs cheating? 3.17
creative: c. reasons for changing the accounting system. 117.32
creativity: Levelling takes away all c. 184.1
credit card: c. is an anaesthetic 57.23
Credit: Topic 57
banker . . . if he has to prove he is worthy of c. 15.1
banking . . . depends so much on c. 16.6
no money . . . no . . . . c. 124.31
Creditors: Topic 58

cricket: C. is now a business 188.7
crime: bite of want drives men to c. 144.7
    Debt is the prolific mother of . . . c. 61.7
    If poverty is the mother of crime 144.19
    if you want to show that c. doesn't pay 128.1
crimes: worst of our c. is poverty 144.20
criminal: no distinctly native American c. class except 49.5
criminals: punishment of the poorer class of c. 144.7
crises: recurrence of economic c. and depressions 26.4
    these decennial c. 26.3
crisis: present c. for capitalism 30.10
critical: nothing better than c. saboteurs 68.29
crocodiles: c. as a tourist attraction. 203.1
cross: crucify man upon a c. of gold. 90.1
crown: this c. of thorns 90.1
crucify: c. man upon a cross of gold. 90.1
crusade: Popular capitalism is a c. 30.20
cul de sac: committee is a c. 42.7
culture: desperately need a training c. 68.43
    not a dependency c. 74.9
    respect in Australia for innovative c. 102.6
    we must have an enterprise c. 74.9
cunning: Two c. knaves need no broker 22.3
curiosity: public have an insatiable c. 158.5
currency: paper c. . . . is the life of commerce. 204.1
    When a c.'s only friends 124.22
curse: Work is the c. of the drinking classes. 64.37
custom: c. of the market 120.5
customer: c. is always right 59.1
Customers: Topic 59
    discipline which is exercised [by] c. 72.13
    don't want to push our ideas on to c. 82.1
    limit the number of its c. 99.8
Customs: Topic 60
cynic: What is a c? 145.15

dalliance: My business cannot brook this d. 25.68
damned: Publish and be d. 162.18
danger: d. from organised money 53.1
    Out of debt out of d. 61.28
dangerous: Innovations are d. 102.5
    most d. entrepreneur 76.1
Dante: As D. said 162.14
daring: most d. innovations 102.8
Das Kapital: If only Groucho had written D. 43.1
daughter: marry the boss's d. 153.5
day: all in the d.'s work 214.30
    not a minute on the d. 40.1
    put a man out of work for a d. 173.2
days: Confess debt and beg d. 61.12
dead: Auditors . . . count the d. and bayonet the wounded 13.1
    spending a year d. for tax reasons. 196.1
dead men: waite for dead men 153.3
dead men's shoes: He that waits for d. 153.2
deal: We demand that big business give . . . a square d. 25.62
dealer: d. must conduct his business 120.5
dear: If a man but knew what would be d. 186.1
death-bed: a d. is no place 1.5
death: d. and taxes. 196.33
death: tax, d. and more meetings. 42.14
    Tradesman . . . preparation for D. 1.4
Debt: Topic 61
    d. is accumulating like a snowball rolling 20.14
debtor: every man a d. to his profession. 149.2
    little debt makes a d. 61.10
    Not everyone is a d. 58.5
debtors: Creditors have no real affection for their d. 58.1
    Creditors have better memories than d. 58.4
    temptation to build up . . . d. 58.9
Debtors' Yard: In D. the stones are hard 61.36
debts: I am ashamed to owe d. I cannot pay 17.8
deceived: to avoid being d. by economists. 65.14
decennial: these d. crises 26.3

decentralization: question of centralization or d. 132.7
decentralize: question is not whether we shall d. 132.17
decision: harder to change a d. 24.1
    someone once made a courageous d. 27.14
    wish to avoid making a d. 42.9
decision-making: vast bulk of d. activity 132.16
decisions: d. to do something positive 107.5
    don't like coming to d. 68.2
    Executive . . . man who can make quick d. 117.16
defendant: Blind plaintiff, lame d. 115.8
defunct: slaves of some d. economist. 66.11
delusions: consumer's d. result in producer's blunders. 147.1
demand: d. a rent 166.7
    d. is greater or less in proportion 145.14
    d. just sufficient 211.5
    learn . . . two words 'supply' and 'd.' 66.1
    supply and d. . . . weary of all that 109.3
    The d. for money 124.68
democracies: distinguishes d. from dictatorships 192.7
democracy: Advertising . . . essence of d. 6.10
    Bureaucracy is not an obstacle to d. 24.7
    D. . . . government by popular ignorance. 142.23
    economic d. 30.13
    mixed economy essential to social d. 142.10
democratic: D. governments 92.15
dental: d. surgery is a hot-bed 122.7
dependency: not a d. culture. 74.9
depression: d. when you lose yours [job] 208.12
depressions: recurrence of economic crises and d. 26.4
designed: tax system . . . d. . . . on purpose. 196.71
despair: gospel of d. 109.3
despatch: On serious business, craving quick despatch 25.72
Detroit: It's a F.O.B., made in D. 127.5
development: company's research is another's d. 102.1
devil: Debt . . . d. in disguise 61.25
    takes a man to make a d. 58.2
devils: Creditors! – d. 58.8
dictatorships: distinguishes democracies from d. 192.7
die: Old economists never d. 66.9
dies: He that pays all debts. 61.34
diminished: supply at a constant or d. cost 56.5
diner: Fast train: One that has no d. 164.10
dinner: d. lubricates business. 75.3
    that we expect our d. 178.3
Diplomacy: Topic 62
direct tax: d. is one which is demanded 196.52
directors: d. . . . are always shareholders 92.25
discipline: real and effectual d. 72.13
Discontent: D. is the first step 152.5
disease: Monetarism is a worldwide d. 124.26
disgrace: poverty is a d. 144.11
dishonest: What is honest is not d. 94.1
dishonesty: Debt . . . fountain of d. 61.2
disinfectant: no d. like success. 193.22
Disneyland: He's at D. 66.2
disorganization: organization is always d. 132.6
distraction: mass production of d. 75.2
ditchers: gentlemen . . . d. 149.13
diversified: Money . . . made a d. civilisation possible. 124.93
Division of Labour: Topic 63
do: D. other men, for they would d. you 18.4
do-it-yourself: Edison . . . d. man. 105.3
doctor: absurd prescriptions of the d. 92.30
doctor: d. and patient . . . employer and employee. 122.25
    patient . . . given up by the d. 122.26
    specialist is a d. 122.2
doctrines: central d. of economics 65.9
    What makes all d. plain and clear? 54.4
dodges: other half d. taxes. 196.41
dog: haire of the d. 64.11
    when a man bites a d. 130.23
dole: happy man be his d., say I 25.70
dollar: almighty d. 124.51
    chief evil of an unstable d. 124.25

sort of rough e. 120.28
When women ask for e. 77.16
equall: E. imposition of taxes 196.40
equally: Taxation can never be so e. applied 196.60
equilibrium: monopolistic e. price 125.9
equitable: most e. tax 196.24
err: to e. is human. 138.1
errors: greatest e. of administration 92.30
    most serious e. in economic policy 92.21
esprit de corps: success of a business turns on its e. 193.8
essential: Always make yourself e. 193.2
ethic: Protestant E. and the Spirit of Capitalism 30.21
ethics: a point of business e. 25.19
    Some day the e. of business 25.28
    wise to understand e. 107.1
eunuchs: accountants were much like e. 4.9
Europe: A spectre is haunting E. 43.3
    glory of E. is extinguished 66.4
evasion: love, war and tax e. 196.69
    Tax E. as a Path to Damnation. 196.70
events: Income is a series of e. 96.5
everything: knows the price of e. 145.15
evil: chief e. of an unstable dollar 124.25
    Debt is an e. conscience 61.13
    love of money is the root of all e. 124.11
    poverty . . . evidently a great e. 144.13
evils: make out . . . can cure the e. of mankind. 92.3
exactions: Daily new e. are devis'd. 196.68
Exchange: Topic 78
    creating convenience in the process of e. 124.23
    fair e. is no robbery. 78.4
    value in e. 211.7
exchequer: King's e. was like the spleen. 160.1
excise: E. . . . hateful tax 196.44
executive: E. work is not that of the organization 132.2
    e.'s job involves not only making decisions 132.16
    E. . . . man who can make quick decisions 117.16
    E. . . . ulcer with authority 117.2
    vice-president is a form of e. fungus 117.1
executives: skill can not be painted on the outside of e. 117.12
exemptions: barnacled with e. 196.78
exercise: E. is bunk. 93.8
expands: Work e. so as to fill the time 214.34
expectation: e. of the poor 144.4
expectations: determined by its short-term e. 72.6
    politicians are dominated by . . . e. 92.17
expenditure: annual e. nineteen, nineteen and six 23.5
    e. twenty pounds ought and six, result misery 23.5
expenditure: general economy and particular e. 67.4
expense: everybody endeavours to live at the e. 92.5
    profits proportionable to . . . e. and hazard. 150.9
expense accounts: occupants all on e. 164.15
Expenses: Topic 79
experience: E. is the mother of custom. 60.1
    school o' e. 68.18
experts: e. . . . forget later what . . . they recommended 83.6
explain: If a scientist cannot e. 175.2
exploitation: Commerce is no longer e. 41.18
    Communism is the e. of the strong 43.5
    Property is the e. of the weak 43.5
exploited: misery of not being e. 30.14
exploits: Under capitalism man e. man, under socialism 184.2
exporting: E. higher education 68.32
Exports: Topic 80
    E. are becoming obsolete 119.1
    for other countries to tax our e. 195.1
extinguished: glory of Europe is e. 66.4
extravagance: e. of government 92.30
eye: With subtle art beguile the honest e. 172.4
eyes: buyer needs a hundred e. 28.4

faces: grind the f. of the poor 144.2
    There's business in these f. 25.69

Factories: Topic 81
    disease known as f. melancholia 81.2
    f. . . . a moral gymnasium 81.1
    In the f. we make cosmetics. 55.4
    Newspaper Office: A figment f. 130.40
facts: Comment is free, but f. are sacred. 130.60
    F. . . . are extremely dangerous. 161.3
    Practical politics consists in ignoring f. 142.1
fail: men will promise to do certain things and f. 83.3
failure: line between f. and success is so fine 193.5
    Success . . . thing that spoils many a good f. 193.10
failures: so-called market f. 146.1
fair: diplomacy of the peasant at the fair. 179.4
    f. exchange is no robbery. 78.4
falsehood: If you suspect my husbandry of f. 13.10
fantasies: some advertisements lead to f. 6.35
fantastical: nothing is more f. and nice than credit 57.6
farmers: f. are great blokes. 77.14
farmers: see also Agriculture: Topic 7
Fashion: Topic 82
    unreasoning laws of market and f. 10.1
fast food: aim of f. marketing 34.1
fat: Money is but the f. of the body politick 124.73
father: hold the credit of your f. 57.25
feather: To f. one's own nest. 178.2
fee: purge you without a f. 122.27
fees: dream of f. 113.51
feminist: can't be a f. and a capitalist 31.4
    f. pendulum 77.7
fetish worship: business is also f. 25.79
feudalism: prostrate themselves at the feet of f. 205.3
fiction: Government is the great f. 92.5
    newspaper . . . one form of continuous f. 130.14
fictitious: Money having . . . a f. value 124.50
fidelity: two qualifications: f. and zeal. 74.2
fiduciary: Gold . . . f. value par excellence. 90.3
fight: business is a f. 25.46
figment factory: Newpaper Office: A f. 130.40
figure: any f. that looks interesting is probably wrong. 189.1
figures: F. won't lie, but liars will figure. 189.4
    we still have these appalling f. 93.16
Finance: Topic 83
financial planning: Personal f. is of very little use 83.7
Financial Straits: dwelling beyond the F. 58.3
financial: hiding or misrepresenting f. information 3.6
    lot of a f. journalist 130.18
    to give f. advice 83.4
fired: I want him f. 168.3
firm: behaviour of each individual f. 72.6
first-rate: cannot be both fashionable and f. 82.12
first: educated to wish to be f. 46.6
fish and chip: newspapers are tomorrow's f. wrapping. 130.56
    f. shops 34.3
fish: Money . . . best bait to fish for men 124.35
    Treasury . . . could not run a f. and chip shop. 38.7
fit: All the News that's f. to print. 130.53
    most f. for business 25.65
fitters: some f. who could not fit 45.2
fittest: f. might survive 109.8
five shillings: Whenever you save f. 173.2
flat: money . . . is f. 124.18
Fleet Street: hard noses of F. 130.73
flesh: spare a pound of f. 58.7
    While there is f. there is money 124.13
fluctuations: momentary f. of affairs. 142.41
folly-swaddles: Piracy . . . Commerce without its f. 139.1
folly: can scarce be f. 86.6
    vice and f. of his trade 204.19
fool: f. all of the people all of the time 6.34
    f. and his money are soon parted. 124.27
    send a f. to market 120.14
    what any f. can do for a pound. 73.2
fools: Lawyer's houses are built on the heads of f. 113.23
Football: F. is business. 188.4

growth: claim that education will lead to more economic g. 68.23

guarantee: g. that he can pay. 165.1

guidelines: Moses would have come with the ten. g. 126.1

guilt: Life with industry is g. 99.14

gutter: Journalists belong in the g. 130.55

habit: prey to the drink h. 64.9

haire: h. of the dog 64.11

half: h. the money I spend on advertising is wasted 6.59

Hampden: ruined Mr H.'s fortune 196.17

hand: led by an invisible h. 120.29
    On the other h. 66.8

hands: maintaining unproductive h. 160.6
    many h. make light work. 214.18

hangover: h. is the wrath of grapes. 64.4
    If the h. came the night before 64.35

happiness: Employment is a source of h. 72.8
    expenditure nineteen, nineteen and six, result h. 23.5
    large income . . . best recipe for h. 96.1

hard work: H. never killed anybody 93.2
    no substitute for h. 214.15

hard: School of H. Knocks 68.40
    when times were not h. 155.1

Hardware: H. is the bit you can kick 47.4

Harvard Business School: One lesson a man learns in the H. 93.4

Harvard: if a man comes from Sing Sing or H. 72.3
    men who control H. 68.9

harvests: two seed-times and two h. 196.6

hath: to him that h. shall be lent 20.9

hazard: profits proportionable to . . . expense and h. 150.9

hazards: undertaker who h. his stock 150.24

head: if you can keep your h. 6.13

Health: Topic 93
    Lawyers Can Seriously Damage Your H. 113.33

health service: h. . . . the fundamental fallacy 93.12

healthy: Industry keeps the body h. 99.17

heavens: h. fill with commerce 41.36

hell: all buyers go to h. 28.7

hereditary: h. business of great magnitude 101.1

hero: h. must drink brandy. 64.15

higgling: h. and bargaining of the market 120.28

high: Pile it h. and sell it cheap. 179.1

hire: labourer is worthy of his h. 108.3
    labourer is worthy of his h. 212.1
    We h. a man not his history. 72.3

history: Accounting is . . . statistical h. 3.7
    case for a sense of h. 107.6
    H. suggests . . . capitalism is a necessary condition 30.5
    We hire a man not his h. 72.3

hole: h. . . . owned by a liar. 123.1

holes: First Law of H. 142.20

holiday: Being holiday 210.5

holidays: see also Vacation: Topic 210

home: charity begins at h. 36.5
    h. is his tax haven. 196.29
    never attempt to make at h. 86.6

honest eye: With subtle art beguile the h. 172.4

honest: An h. broker 22.2
    h. politician . . . will stay bought. 142.9

Honesty: Topic 94

honesty: Corruption wins not more than h. 54.7
    H. is the best policy. 94.6, 94.14, 94.15

hopeless: No situation is ever absolutely h. 30.10

horse: Do not trust the h., Trojans 89.4
    h. recognised as an agricultural animal 7.2

horsewhipping: h. my great-grandmother. 130.65

hospital: characteristics of an . . . industrial h. 99.11

hot-bed: Stock Market . . . h. of cold feet! 191.3

hours: committee . . . keeps minutes but wastes h. 42.2

House of Commons: Anybody who enjoys being in the H. 133.9
    H. is terribly outdated 133.12

House of Lords: H. is like Heaven 133.1
    H. . . . how to care for the elderly. 133.6

housekeeper: Marriage . . . bribe to make a h. 121.5

houses: Laws, like h. 112.12

housewife: radio . . . message of importance for every h. 163.5

human budget: Mr Bevin's phrase, a 'h.' 23.3

human relations: Industrial relations are like h. 97.4

human: Economics . . . studies h. behaviour 65.13
    to err is h. 138.1
    who says auditors are h? 13.3

humanity: H. is not an instrument of property. 154.24

hundred eyes: buyer needs a h. 28.4

hundred pounds: if you owe your bank a h. 16.8

hunting: half a million generations in the h. band 53.7

hurt: don't h. your credit 57.30

husband: marry a seven-dollar h. 25.48

husbandry: borrowing dulls the edge of h. 20.11
    If you suspect my h. of falsehood 13.10

husbands: English h. are so busy making money 121.3

hypocrite: He must be a perfect complete h. 27.12

idea: Crank until the i. succeeds. 105.17
    epoch-making i. is often not perceived 105.12

ideas: i. of economists 66.11

idiot: law is an ass – a i. 112.19

idle: condition of the i. 95.1
    Parliament . . . big meeting of . . . i. people. 133.3

ignorance: dark forces of time and i. 107.3
    Democracy . . . government by popular i. 142.23

ignorant: no stigma to be i. 68.36

ill: i. bargain, where no man wins. 18.13

immunity: i. from competition 125.10

impartial: market is totally i. 120.2

imports: take care of our i. 80.1

improvement: in the case of doubtful i. 102.4
    to help social i. 65.12

improvements: Compensation for i. 166.2

Incentives: Topic 95

incidence: laws of i. 196.30

Income: Topic 96
    Annual i. twenty pounds 23.5
    confusion between capital and i. 29.19
    future i. discounted . . . capitalised 29.3
    i. from property 154.18
    I. is a series of events. 96.5
    Net i . . . shaped . . . by the interaction of the blades 150.13
    One person's price is another person's i. 145.7
    Unequal distribution of i. 173.5

income tax: I. . . . is a tax on income. 196.48

income-value: link between i. and capital-value. 104.6

incompetence: rise to his level of i. 153.6

indecision: client's i. is final 6.7

Indian: The I. who sold Manhattan 104.11

individual: only i. men and women 185.5

individualism: any system other than i. 30.3
    principle of i. 78.3

individuals: Governments don't care, i. do. 92.33

Industrial Relations: Topic 97
    politics, government and i. 142.17

Industrial Revolution: Topic 98
    effects of the I. 46.21

industrial: salient characteristic of i. organization 132.18
    successful conduct of an i. enterprise 74.2
    Vulgarity of i. competition. 46.11

industrialize: takes more than industry to i. 99.13

industrious: An i. person is always a happy person 72.8
    Monopoly . . . taxation of the i. 125.7

Industry: Topic 99

industry: Consumption . . . the great end and object of i. 51.1
    disapproval . . . of commerce and i. 68.41
    distaste for commerce and i. 39.6
    efficiency of i. 95.2

male: advertising . . . agent of m. supremacy 6.44
  m. is by nature superior 77.4
man: crucify m. upon a cross of gold. 90.1
  m. without money 124.28
  No business remains greater than the m. who runs it 27.26
  No machine can do the work of one extraordinary m. 116.5
  put a m. out of work for a day. 173.2
  This book is about the organization m. 132.19
manage: Trade could not be managed by those who m. it 117.17
managed: Men are made to be m. 77.18
  public business is worse m. 159.2
Management: Topic 117
  Government m. 92.24
  I am not a m. type 105.14
  joint-stock m. 92.25
  M. and union . . . likened to a serpent 97.2
  m. can only be properly studied 53.8
  M. is personnel administration. 138.2
  Monopoly . . . enemy to good m. 125.13
  percentage of women in m. 77.17
  Scholarship is important to more effective m. 68.44
  what good m. knew 198.6
  Wise business m. . . . sagacious use of sabotage 25.83
Management Consultancy: Topic 118
manager: for the best advantage of the m. 83.1
  m. of a theatre is a man of business 10.17
  m. . . . person who sees the visitors 117.26
managerial: pollen of m. science 25.55
managers: women are born m. 77.18
Manchester School: The M. will tell you 99.4
Manhattan: The Indian who sold M. 104.11
manhood: Women have no need to prove their m. 77.15
mankind: Commerce links all m. 41.13
  Economics is the study of m. 65.8
  make out . . . can cure the evils of m. 92.3
manual: nobility of m. toil 214.19
manufacturer: Advertising is the m's shop window 6.48
  landlord . . . opposed to . . . m. 166.5
manufacturers: gain which is made by m. 63.1
manufacturing: fit for something besides m. 99.2
market: airlines have to m. something 14.3
  Price in a m. 145.6
  so-called m. failures. 146.1
  supply the entire m. 56.5
  to buy in the cheapest m. 86.2
  trouble about a free m. economy 109.1
market place: ballot, held daily in the m. 30.13
market-price: At m. have bought. 145.10
market research: actuaries are to m. 5.3
Marketing: Topic 119
  aim of fast food m. 34.1
  two basic functions – m. and innovation 25.24
Markets: Topic 120
  unreasoning laws of m. and fashion 10.1
Marks and Spencer: M. loves you 119.8
Marriage: Topic 121
  break-up of a m. 32.3
  No one asks a man how his m. survives 77.23
  Prostitutes believe in m. 156.6
marries: feller who m. for money 108.8
  man who m. it. 214.24
marry: I'll m. a landlord's daughter 64.22
  m. a seven-dollar husband 25.48
  m. the boss's daughter 153.5
  When you see what some girls m. 214.37
marrying: Millionaires are m. 176.11
mart: meet with you upon the m. 120.24
  venture madly on a desperate m. 41.33
martial: ever become valiant and m. 196.7
Marx: entrepreneur . . . sly rapacious moneybags of M. 181.3
Mason: M. may forget the word 130.47

mass production: m. of distraction. 75.2
  technology of m. 198.5
mass-consumption: age of high m. 98.3
masters: m. can hold out much longer 97.6
match: Every time I strike a m. 27.24
material: increase of m. comforts 126.4
mathematical: decent m. education 68.26
mathematician: He should have been a m. 4.14
matter: altering the position of m. 214.38
  Marketing is m. in motion. 119.2
May: Sell in M. 191.2
maze: law seems like a sort of m. 112.41
means: relationship between ends and scarce m. 65.13
measure: Money is the m. of commerce. 124.8
  money . . . m. of value. 124.91
mechanical: m. inventions of every age 105.12
media: Labour Party is paranoid about the m. 130.34
  when we get rid of the m. 163.2
mediaeval: substitution of competition for . . . m. regulations 98.5
Medicine: Topic 122
  M. is the only profession 149.6
medium of exchange: Money . . . m. 124.93
meet: People of the same trade seldom m. together 33.4
meeting: Parliament . . . big m. of . . . idle people. 133.3
meetings: tax, death and more m. 42.14
melancholia: disease known as factory m. 81.2
memorandum: law is only a m. 112.22
memories: Creditors have better m. 58.4
men: M. are but gilded loam 167.3
  M. are made to be managed 77.18
  M. have become the tools of their tools. 116.9
  M. keep their agreements 52.3
  m. make themselves machines also. 116.11
mercantile: Convenience is the basis of m. law. 112.37
mercer: fop of fashion is the m.'s friend 82.6
merchant: A true-bred m. is a universal scholar 27.11
  business of the wine m. and banker 64.32
  M. . . . engaged in a commercial pursuit. 41.8
  need be a m., but only one year. 186.1
  now I play a m.'s part 41.33
  The good m. 41.40
merchants: M. as such are not the first men among us 41.38
  Quick returns make rich m. 150.12
  when m. dispute about their own rules 112.11
  Ye tradefull m. 205.8
merit: m. will not serve you so much as money 124.53
merry: Tonight we will all m. be 64.8
message: radio . . . m. of importance for every housewife. 163.5
messengers: Commerce has made all winds her m. 41.12
methodological: m. bathwater 3.13
middle age: M. is when your age starts to show 93.13
millionaire: How can you be a m. and a socialist? 184.11
  I am a M. 213.25
  not difficult for a m. to make money 213.16
millionaires: M. are marrying 176.11
millions: Who made your m. for you? 213.26
mind: M. your own business 25.57
  triumph of m. over patter. 172.1
minds: governments' m. are unlikely to change 92.10
mine: take m. ease in m. inn 64.27
  What's m. is m. 128.4
miners: Vatican, the Treasury and the m. 123.2
Mining: Topic 123
minister: those who m. to poverty 144.21
minute: not a m. on the day. 40.1
minutes: committee . . . keeps m. but wastes hours. 42.2
misconduct: public prodigality and m. 160.6
miser: capitalist is a rational m. 31.3
  Rich honesty dwells like a m. 94.12
miserable: cannot bear successful people who are m. 193.11
Miserie: M. may be mother 144.10
miseries: equal sharing of m. 30.2

COLLINS CONCISE DICTIONARY OF QUOTATIONS

Donald Fraser

'*I might repeat to myself, slowly and soothingly, a list of quotations beautiful from minds profound; if I can remember any of the damn things.*' — Dorothy Parker.

Very much a book for the modern era, the coverage of the *Collins Concise Dictionary of Quotations* ranges from Thucydides to Thatcher, from William Shakespeare to Woody Allen, taking in all the classics as well as the colourful and witty sayings of the 20th century. The wit and wisdom, pithiness and poetry of over 1300 authors provide a total of over 8000 quotations, all arranged alphabetically by author. The extensive index, a vitally important part of any dictionary of quotations, comprises one third of the book, and features both keywords and the phrases in which they occur.

As a reference work the Dictionary can be used to verify half-remembered quotations, or to give the source of common phrases or sayings whose origin has been forgotten. It can also be used — with the aid of the index — to suggest apposite quotations on particular subjects or simply to provide hours of entertaining browsing.

Donald Fraser is a lecturer in English at the University of Strathclyde. He is also the co-author of *A Dictionary of Musical Quotations*.

'The dictionary is clear and comprehensive.' — *Sunday Times*.

ISBN 0 00 434376 X

COLLINS DICTIONARY OF LITERARY QUOTATIONS

Meic Stephens

There are three rules for writing the novel. Unfortunately, no one knows what they are — Somerset Maugham.

I never read any books except my own — Barbara Cartland.

The *Collins Dictionary of Literary Quotations* is a compilation of over 3000 fascinating quotations from the world of books, bringing together the wit and insight of novelists, poets, publishers, critics and readers on all aspects of creative writing and the writer's life, from rejection slips to royalties, the avant-garde to pulp fiction, free verse to censorship.

Whether in an appreciation of what the public wants ('Let blockheads read what blockheads write' — Lord Chesterfield) or a reflection on inspiration — ('Gin and water' — Byron) or on the pleasures of reading or the nature of good criticism, the Dictionary will provide a constant source of pleasure and illumination.

Ideal either for checking half-remembered witticisms or for hours of happy browsing, the *Collins Dictionary of Literary Quotations* is a welcome addition to the library of any book-lover.

Meic Stephens has written and compiled a number of books about language and literature, including the *Oxford Companion to the Literature of Wales*.

ISBN 0 00 434378 6

COLLINS DICTIONARY OF MEDICAL QUOTATIONS

Dr John Daintith and Amanda Isaacs

Your prayer must be for a sound mind in a sound body — Juvenal.

Who lives medically lives miserably — Anon.

The *Collins Dictionary of Medical Quotations* is a fascinating selection of witty, profound, touching and funny sayings on a topic of absorbing interest to us all — our bodies and the ailments which plague us. The choice of quotations ranges beyond the field of pure medical science to encompass such subjects as *snoring, fads* and *old age* ('I'll keep going till my face falls off' — Barbara Cartland), as well as including such familiar terrors as *dentists* and *hospitals* ('That should guarantee us at least 45 minutes of undisturbed privacy' — Dorothy Parker in hospital, having pressed the bell for the nurse). The Dictionary is fully up-to-date and includes quotations on contemporary health preoccupations such as *AIDS, smoking, healthy eating* and *biorhythms*.

The information within the main text is easily accessed through alphabetically arranged headings, from *addiction* to *X-rays*, by way of *allergies, death* and *sex*. An author index is included, and there is also a comprehensive index of key words and phrases.

The *Collins Dictionary of Medical Quotations* is an ideal companion for anyone involved in medicine and its related disciplines, and is also an entertaining and informative source of quotations for everyone interested in the mysteries of the human organism.

Dr John Daintith has compiled many reference works, including four major dictionaries of quotations. Amanda Isaacs is a freelance editor.

'Gives readers the weaponry to pierce the most inflated medical egos' — *Daily Telegraph*.

ISBN 0 00 459112 7

COLLINS DICTIONARY OF MILITARY QUOTATIONS

Trevor Royle

There's many a boy here today who looks on war as all glory; but boys, it is all hell — General Sherman.

Retreat, hell! We're just fighting in another direction — Major-General Smith.

The *Collins Dictionary of Military Quotations* is a compilation of over 3500 enthralling quotations on the world of war, from Biblical battles and skirmishes beneath the walls of Troy, to the modern era of long-distance weapons of destruction and the nuclear deterrent.

The quotations cover the whole field of war and its consequences, through the words not only of the great leaders and their campaigns — such as Alexander at the Issus, Wellington at Waterloo, Sitting Bull at the Little Big Horn and Montgomery at Alamein — but also of the common man in arms, whether on sick parade or watching the sky line in trepidation.

The book is divided into four main areas: *Captains and Kings, Battles and Wars, Armies and Soldiers* and *War and Peace*, with a final short section, *Last Post*, describing the tragic aftermath of conflict.

The author, Trevor Royle, is a well-known writer and broadcaster on military history. His other books include a highly praised biography of Lord Kitchener, *The Kitchener Enigma.*

ISBN 0 00 434377 8